MW01120477

This collection of provocative essays is the first attempt to expand the boundaries of restorative justice by tackling the myths that surround its definition and capabilities and by imaginatively addressing how its tenets can make transitional justice practice more relevant to those affected by direct and structural violence. By moving beyond the 'toolkit' of supposed restorative practices in transitional justice, these essays challenge the reader to reconceptualize the meanings of justice away from the perpetrator–victim dichotomy towards a transformational vision of societal change.

Professor Harvey Weinstein, *Senior Research Fellow, Human Rights Center; Clinical Professor (Ret.), School of Public Health; Co-Editor-in-Chief Emeritus,* International Journal of Transitional Justice, *Berkeley, USA*

This volume is simultaneously critical and inspirational. The authors reflect honestly on the deep structural challenges and the intense personal dimensions of addressing mass human rights violations while exploring options for navigating this complex terrain. The authors provide carefully considered and innovative suggestions for how restorative responses can be more effectively integrated into transitional justice approaches. These ideas present a timely challenge and stimulus for transitional justice scholars, practitioners and policy makers.

The key argument of this volume, that restorative justice can be used as a mechanism or lens through which local actors can claim a more significant stake in dealing with the past while building their future, is an important reminder of the transformative potential inherent in transitional contexts. This volume points to how this potential can be promoted through critical and creative scholarship.

Dr Hugo van der Merwe, *Head of Research, Centre for the Study of Violence and Reconciliation, South Africa*

Restorative Justice in Transitional Settings demonstrates how much needed and how fruitful it is to broadening, to deepening and to lengthening the concept of restorative justice. Through critical analysis of existing practices and opening up new perspectives, a well-selected group of international scholars explore the plural character of justice from different angles. This edited collection highly contributes to both our understanding and designing of innovative restorative justice approaches in a variety of societal and cultural contexts.

Professor Dr Ivo Aertsen, *Director KU Leuven Institute of Criminology (LINC), Belgium*

Many academics and activists have been 'pushing the envelope' for a number of years in terms of the promise of restorative justice in transitional settings. Kerry Clamp has put together a collection of some of the most important voices in the field and the results are impressive. What is needed is precisely such a cold-eyed, pragmatic yet ambitious assessment of the possibilities and pitfalls of restorative justice in such contexts. This book is a 'must-read' for anyone interested in the topic. Clamp and her contributors are to be warmly congratulated for putting it together.

Kieran McEvoy, *Professor of Law and Transitional Justice, Queens University Belfast*

A compilation of very good theoretical and empirical studies by leading scholars on a subject that is academically underdeveloped but of growing practical importance. You can agree or disagree with the conclusions of the authors but this book is a must read for all interested in the crucial subject on what is the best way for emerging democracies to deal with past atrocities.

Rodrigo Uprimny, *Professor of Law, National University of Colombia and Executive Director of the Center of Studies Dejusticia*

Restorative Justice in Transitional Settings

Restorative justice is increasingly being applied to settings characterised by large-scale violence and human rights abuses. While many embrace this development as an important step in attempts to transform protracted conflict, there are a number of conceptual challenges in transporting restorative justice from a democratic setting to one which has been affected by mass victimisation or civil war. These include responding to the seriousness and scale of harms that have been caused, the blurred boundaries between victims and offenders, and the difficulties associated with holding someone to account and compelling reparative activities. Despite reams of paper being devoted to defining restorative justice within democratic settings (where the concept first emerged), restorative scholars have been slow to comment on the integration of restorative justice into the transitional justice discourse.

Restorative Justice in Transitional Settings brings together a number of leading scholars from around the world to respond to this gap by developing and further articulating restorative justice for transitional settings. These scholars push the boundaries of restorative justice to seek more effective approaches to addressing the causes and consequences of conflict and oppression in these diverse contexts. Each chapter highlights a limitation with current conceptions of restorative justice in the transitional justice literature and then suggests a way in which the limitation might be overcome.

This book has strong interdisciplinary value and will be of interest to criminologists, legal scholars, and those engaged with international relations and peace treaties.

Kerry Clamp is a Senior Lecturer in Criminology in the Department of Social Sciences and Psychology at the University of Western Sydney. She received her Ph.D. from the University of Leeds in 2010 and also holds degrees from the University of Sheffield and the University of South Africa. Her research agenda focuses on the intersections of restorative justice and transitional justice, and of restorative justice and policing.

Routledge frontiers of criminal justice

Restorative Justice in Transitional Settings

Edited by Kerry Clamp

Routledge
Taylor & Francis Group

LONDON AND NEW YORK

First published 2016
by Routledge
2 Park Square, Milton Park, Abingdon, Oxon OX14 4RN

and by Routledge
711 Third Avenue, New York, NY 10017

Routledge is an imprint of the Taylor & Francis Group, an informa business

British Library Cataloguing-in-Publication Data
A catalogue record for this book is available from the British Library

Library of Congress Cataloging in Publication Data
A catalog record for this book has been requested

ISBN: 978-1-138-85193-1 (hbk)
ISBN: 978-1-315-72386-0 (ebk)

Typeset in Times New Roman
by Wearset Ltd, Boldon, Tyne and Wear

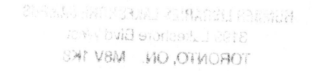

For Alexandra Ivy Wood, who makes my day, every day.

Contents

Contributors

John Braithwaite is a Distinguished Professor and founder of RegNet (the Regulatory Institutions Network) at the Australian National University. He is embarking on a 20-year comparative project called *Peacebuilding Compared*, with Hilary Charlesworth, Valerie Braithwaite and Kate Macfarlane. In the past he has worked on a variety of areas of business regulation and on the crime problem. His best known work is on the ideas of responsive regulation and restorative justice. He has been active in social movement politics around these and other ideas for 40 years in Australia and internationally. His most recent book is *Regulatory Capitalism: How it works, ideas for making it work better* (2008).

Isabella Bueno is an independent consultant in Cali, Colombia. She obtained a bachelor's degree in Law as well as a master's degree in International Law from the University of La Sorbonne in Paris and her PhD from K.U. Leuven in Belgium. Since 2008 she has been working as a researcher in the field of transitional justice and restorative justice in Colombia.

Hugh Campbell is Senior Lecturer on the restorative practices programme at the University of Ulster. Prior to this work, he was the course director for the Youth Work degree. He is engaged in the ALTERNATIVE research programme and research into judicial training in restorative justice.

Tim Chapman is Course Director of the Masters programme in restorative justice at Ulster University. He contributed to the development of restorative processes in both the voluntary and statutory sectors in Northern Ireland. He spent 25 years working in the Probation Service and played an active part in developing effective practice through the publication of *Evidence Based Practice* for the Home Office. His *Time to Grow* book has influenced youth justice practices, especially in Scotland. He is engaged in significant research into restorative justice in Northern Ireland including a major European (FP7) funded project into restorative justice and conflict in intercultural contexts. He published *A European Model for Restorative Justice with Children and Young People* and is a member of the Board of the European Forum for Restorative Justice.

Kerry Clamp is a Senior Lecturer in Criminology in the Department of Social Sciences and Psychology at the University of Western Sydney. She received her Ph.D. from the University of Leeds in 2010 and also holds degrees from the University of Sheffield and the University of South Africa. Her research agenda focuses on restorative justice and transitional justice and her work appears in a number of journals including the *British Journal of Community Justice* (2011, 2014), *Nottingham Law Journal* (2012), *International Criminal Law Review* (2012), *Northern Ireland Legal Quarterly* (2012), *Criminology and Criminal Justice* (2012) and *Policing: A Journal of Policy and Practice* (2014). She recently published a monograph *Restorative Justice in Transition* (Routledge, 2014) which explores how restorative justice is used and what the strengths and limitations of such an approach is in situations where the state has been either explicitly or implicitly involved in human rights abuses. She is also the chair of the editorial board for the European Forum for Restorative Justice, a role that she has held since January 2011. The editorial board produces four newsletters per annum which promote research, policy developments, and events on restorative justice across Europe.

Chris Cunneen is Professor of Criminology, Faculty of Arts and Social Sciences, University of New South Wales (UNSW), Sydney, Australia. He is also Conjoint Professor at the Cairns Institute, James Cook University. He has a national and international reputation as a leading criminologist specialising in Indigenous people and the law, juvenile justice, restorative justice, policing, prison issues and human rights. He taught criminology at Sydney Law School (1990–2005) where he was appointed as professor in 2004. He was also the director of the Institute of Criminology (1999–2005) at the University of Sydney. He has participated in a number of Australian Royal Commissions and Inquiries (including the Stolen Generations Inquiry, the Royal Commission into Aboriginal Deaths in Custody and the National Inquiry into Racist Violence), and in the federal Australian Human Rights Commission. He has wide research interests that cross the fields of criminology, social science and law. In particular his interests include Australian prisons and the growth in imprisonment, juvenile justice, restorative justice, and the relationship of Indigenous people to dominant legal systems both in Australia and internationally. His work also displays a strong interest in human rights and social justice.

Jonathan Doak is Professor of Criminal Justice at Nottingham Trent University. He is particularly interested in theoretical and socio-legal dimensions within the broad fields of criminal justice and transitional justice. In particular, his research focuses on victimology, restorative justice, modes of trial and the role of emotions within law. Currently he is conducting research into the various ways in which different legal orders have tended to conceptualise issues of redress and reconciliation. He is also completing a book on the relationship between criminal justice and restorative justice. Jonathan is a member of the editorial boards of the *British Journal of Community Justice*, the *Journal of Forensic Research and Crime Studies* and the *International Journal of Law, Crime and Justice.*

Mark Findlay is Professor of Law at the Singapore Management University and Professor of Criminal Justice and the deputy director of the Institute of Criminology, University of Sydney. Previously head of department of the Law School in 1998–99, and Pro Dean in 1999, he currently holds the fractional Chair in International Criminal Justice at the Law School, University of Leeds. He is also a senior associate research fellow at the Institute of Advanced Legal Studies, University of London. An experienced socio-legal researcher, he has worked as a research consultant for international agencies, governments and private consortia in many jurisdictions. He has recently undertaken consultancy work for AusAID, reviewing the law and justice sector in Papua New Guinea. He is the joint chair of the WUN International and Comparative Criminal Justice Network, which is helping shape the face of international criminal justice. His new books, *Governing through Globalised Crime, Beyond Punishment: Achieving international criminal justice,* and *Transforming International Criminal Justice* are contributing to the reconciliation of retributive and restorative justice paradigms internationally. He serves on a number of significant state and national policy committees, including, till recently, the Premier's Crime Prevention Council. He was appointed to the National Research Priorities Review Committee, Department of Education, Science and Training.

Ami Harbin is an Assistant Professor of Philosophy and Women and Gender Studies at Oakland University (OU) in the United States. Her research examines questions in moral psychology about how experiences motivate action. She has received doctoral and postdoctoral awards from the Social Sciences and Humanities Research Council of Canada, and was further supported in postdoctoral work by the Canadian Institutes of Health Research (CIHR) through a grant at Novel Tech Ethics Institute. In bioethics, her postdoctoral work focused on mental health ethics and health care for queer and transgender individuals. Her postdoctoral research in social philosophy focused on collective agency in working against North American colonialism. In 2012, she received a national grant from CIHR to organise a public symposium on the topic of mental illness and social isolation. She is currently serving on the executive boards of two international professional organisations: the International Network on Feminist Approaches to Bioethics; and the Society for Existential and Phenomenological Theory and Culture. She also co-edited a special journal issue of *PhaenEx* on phenomenology, affect and emotion, which was published in January 2013. Additionally, she was on a panel organised in January by the Oakland University William Beaumont School of Medicine about the 2007 film *The Diving Bell and the Butterfly* and is also participating in the executive committee of Women and Gender Studies at OU. She was selected to receive an OU University Research Committee Faculty Research Fellowship for the summer of 2013, to support research into experiences of disorientation and moral psychology.

Wendy Lambourne is a Senior Lecturer, Postgraduate Research Coordinator and Deputy Director at the Centre for Peace and Conflict Studies, University of Sydney. Her research on transitional justice, reconciliation and peacebuilding after genocide and other mass violence has a regional focus on sub-Saharan Africa and Asia-Pacific where she has conducted field research in a number of countries, including Rwanda, Burundi, Cambodia, Timor Leste and Sierra Leone. Recent publications include chapters in *Transitional Justice Theories* (Routledge, 2014), *Critical Perspectives in Transitional Justice* (Intersentia, 2012) and *The Development of Institutions of Human Rights* (Palgrave Macmillan, 2010), as well as articles in the *Journal of Peacebuilding and Development, International Journal of Transitional Justice, Genocide Studies and Prevention* and *African Security Review*. She has served as co-convenor of the Reconciliation and Transitional Justice Commission of the International Peace Research Association since 2006. In addition to her Ph.D. from the University of Sydney, she holds postgraduate degrees in International Relations and International Law from the Australian National University, and an Honours degree in Psychology from the University of Melbourne.

Jennifer Llewellyn is the Viscount Bennett Professor of Law at the Schulich School of Law, Dalhousie University. She has written and published extensively on the theory and practice of a restorative approach in both transitional contexts and established democracies. She was the director of the Nova Scotia Restorative Justice Community University Research Alliance, a collaborative research partnership between university and community partners focused on the institutionalisation of restorative justice, with particular attention to the example of the Nova Scotia Restorative Justice Program. Furthermore, she advises and supports a number of projects and programs using a restorative approach in Nova Scotia and internationally. For example, she has been an academic/policy advisor to the Nova Scotia Restorative Justice Program, the Provincial Restorative Approaches in Schools Project, the HASA Network developing a restorative approach to senior safety and the Nova Scotia Human Rights Commission. She is currently facilitating the design process for a restorative public inquiry into the Home for Colored Children and previously advised the Assembly of First Nations and Canadian Truth and Reconciliation Commission on the response to residential school abuse. She has also worked extensively in the field internationally, including with the South African Truth and Reconciliation Commission, the Jamaican government, the government of New Zealand and the United Nations. She recently co-edited two books in the area: *Being Relational: Reflections on relational theory and health law* (UBC Press, 2011) and *Restorative Justice, Reconciliation and Peacebuilding* (Oxford University Press, 2014).

Ray Nickson is a Lecturer, School of Behavioural, Cognitive and Social Sciences at the University of New England in Australia. He was awarded his Ph.D. in

Law at the Australian National University. His research examined the expectations held for transitional justice and how these expectations were frequently disappointed and proposed a normative theory for responding to expectations for justice in the wake of mass atrocity. His current research builds upon this study, exploring the potential of non-prosecutorial responses to mass violence in addressing the needs of victims, offenders and communities in societies in transition. He is also currently working on a collaborative project examining access to justice for victims of mass crimes in diaspora communities. He previously worked as a solicitor, specialising in criminal defence. He also has professional experience in the fields of international security and counter-terrorism.

Stephan Parmentier studied law, political science and sociology at the universities of Ghent and Leuven (Belgium) and sociology and conflict resolution at the Humphrey Institute for Public Affairs, University of Minnesota-Twin Cities (USA). He currently teaches sociology of crime, law and human rights at the Faculty of Law of the University of Leuven and is the former head of the Department of Criminal Law and Criminology (2005–09). He is in charge of international relations in criminology at Leuven University and in July 2010 was appointed Secretary-General of the International Society for Criminology. He also serves on the advisory board of the Oxford Centre of Criminology and the International Centre for Transitional Justice (New York).

Elmar Weitekamp is a Senior Research Associate at the Institute of Criminology, University of Tuebingen, Germany and his work focuses on victimology and restorative justice. He studied social work in Mönchengladbach (Germany) and criminology at the University of Pennsylvania (USA). He is a board member of the World Society of Victimology and has organised and co-directed the post-graduate course in Victimology, Victim Assistance and Criminal Justice in Dubrovnik, Croatia, for the past 17 years. He is also one of the co-founders of the African Victimology course.

Acknowledgements

I would like to thank each of my colleagues who agreed to write a chapter for this collection. Their knowledge, insight and experience of restorative justice and its place within transitional settings is inspirational and it is on this basis that they were approached to contribute to this book. As for many early career researchers, their previous work has informed my own thinking around the topic and I am grateful that they carved time out of their busy schedules to collaborate on this important area of study. It is hoped that the book will become a starting point for those new to the study of the intersection of restorative justice and transitional justice and a useful resource for those already working on the topic.

I would also like to thank my friends and colleagues who have supported and encouraged me to continue work in this area. A large debt is owed in particular to Professor Rob Stones, my mentor at the University of Western Sydney, who encouraged me to embark on this project. Last, but by no means least, thanks go to Tom Sutton, Heidi Lee and Hannah Catterall at Routledge for their support and encouragement and the broader editorial team for the work they put into preparing and finalising the collection.

Kerry Clamp
Sydney
June 2015

1 Restorative justice as a contested response to conflict and the challenge of the transitional context

An introduction

Kerry Clamp

Introduction

Restorative justice is a popular concept. Its use within neoliberal settings is capacious and has been applied to initiatives that seek to increase the role of victims and/or the community in responding to crime; to processes that deal with conflicts and complaints in schools and the workplace; and to outcomes that seek to 'restore' or 'repair' harm that has been caused. The promise that practitioners make about the power of restorative justice – that victims will have a sense of closure, that the underlying causes of offending will be addressed, that offenders will be held to account and that (implicitly) crime will be decreased – means that policymakers and governments have been clamouring to integrate such approaches within expensive institutional responses to crime. So prolific is restorative justice that it has featured in the story lines of popular daytime soap operas (such as *EastEnders*), popular chat shows (such as *Oprah*) and feature films (such as *Take* and *Face to Face*). Private consultancies and voluntary organisations have sprung up to train criminal justice practitioners in restorative practice and theory, to facilitate restorative processes where criminal justice agencies choose to refer cases out of the system, to conduct evaluations on the efficacy of schemes, and to generally spread the word about restorative justice.

In many respects, it is perhaps unsurprising that restorative justice rhetoric and practice as conceived in the West has made its way from institutions responding to crime in settled or industrialised democracies to those responding to mass conflict and/or oppression within emerging democracies or transitional states. For the most part, this is due to the centrality of restorative justice within the justice landscape, as outlined above, and the broad claims about what restorative justice can achieve. Elite networks and policy communities comprising international bureaucrats/civil servants, pressure groups, policy experts and supranational institutions (see Atkinson and Coleman 1992; Dolowitz and Marsh 1996), import their ideas and practices in the early days of a political transition. The receptiveness of emerging democracies to these international trends can be explained, in part, by their need to attract international capital, which 'compels governments (if they are to achieve status as modern states) to adopt similar economic, social and criminal justice policies' as are used elsewhere (Muncie 2005: 36).

Despite this trend, local context remains important as evidenced in the nuances of country-specific programmes. This means that emerging democracies do not merely adopt one model, but rather may decide to *copy* policy, legislation and techniques in their original form; *emulate* what another society has done by adopting the underlying premise of the policy or programme; *combine* a number of policies in order to achieve the 'best fit' for local conditions; or merely be *inspired* to develop a new policy or practice on the basis of what another nation has already done (Dolowitz and Marsh 2000). For example, even though the South African Truth and Reconciliation Commission architects drew upon experiences from Latin America and Eastern Europe (Boraine *et al.* 1997), the model presented something that had never before been attempted in transitional societies: amnesty was not blanketed as in Europe and Latin America and the Commission sought to address both 'victims' and 'perpetrators' simultaneously. Lauded as the model for addressing mass victimisation and oppression, the South African Truth and Reconciliation Commission represented, for many, a new 'restorative' way of dealing with mass victimisation (see Minow 1998; Tutu 1999).

The subsequent diffusion of restorative justice concepts and practices within emerging democracies is clear. Over the last 20 years, restorative justice has been linked with a wide variety of conflict-resolution settings and institutions, beyond the South African case, including a number of local indigenous-inspired responses: the *Gacaca* courts/hearings in Rwanda (see Waldorf 2006); the International Criminal Court in the Hague (see Baumgartner 2008); the Community Reconciliation Program in Timor-Leste (see Braithwaite *et al.* 2012); community-based alternatives to paramilitary punishment violence in Northern Ireland (McEvoy and Mika 2002); efforts to confront atrocities committed by paramilitary groups in Colombia (see Uprimny and Saffón 2007) and community-based approaches to deal with the violent conflict in Sierra Leone (see Park 2010), among others.

While many embrace the proliferation of restorative justice rhetoric and practice as an important step in attempts to transform protracted conflict and responses to it, there are a number of conceptual challenges in transporting restorative justice from a democratic setting to one which has been affected by mass victimisation and/or civil war (Clamp and Doak 2012). There is currently no consensus within the extensive literature about the conceptual meaning of restorative justice, the suitability of its application in response to serious forms of human rights abuses or what the objectives of restorative justice should be when addressing harm in different contexts (Clamp 2014). These contentious issues are said to reduce the ability of both proponents and critics to engage in meaningful conversation with each other, given that their conceptual understandings of and theoretical starting points for restorative justice may vary (Daly 2012). In many respects, this reality is evident in this book.

The purpose of the collection, however, is not to settle these debates. Much like Christie (1982), who refers to conflicts as a valuable commodity through which to learn and grow, the disagreements within the restorative justice literature create a rich environment for the development of more complex and normative understandings of how justice should be done for those most affected. In seeking to explicitly develop and further articulate restorative justice for transitional settings, the collection has been designed to encourage and challenge contributors to think more deeply about what restorative justice means with this context in mind. While the scope and focus of the content of each chapter was left intentionally broad, contributors were asked to first highlight a limitation of the application of restorative justice to transitional settings and then to suggest a way forward. It will perhaps be apparent to the reader that Nils Christie's (1977) charge that 'conflicts are stolen' from stakeholders still resonates within transitional settings. Rather than merely accounting for this reality, the contributors not only highlight a number of 'successful' projects that have returned conflicts to those most affected, but have also suggested ways in which this reality might be addressed. This collection is not a comprehensive overview of all of the issues that are raised when applying restorative justice to transitional settings, but rather should be viewed as an initial attempt to motivate debate on the topic.

The rationale for such an approach is based on the fact that current conceptions of restorative justice in transitional settings carry what Johnstone (2008) refers to as a limited 'agenda'. At the heart of the restorative justice movement is a desire 'not only to change our procedures for dealing with crime and other social problems, but also to bring about fundamental changes in the way that we construe these problems and in our conceptions of what constitutes a good solution' (Johnstone 2008: 60). While discussing the strengths and limitations of a restorative justice paradigm for dealing with the consequences of international crimes has become a regular feature within the transitional justice literature, this debate tends to revolve around a very narrow understanding of what restorative justice is and ultimately what the movement is trying to achieve (Johnstone 2008). In part, this is due to a limited knowledge of and engagement with restorative justice theory written in democratic settings. As such, this collection has sought to demonstrate the poverty of such a restricted focus by providing a discussion on the untapped potential of restorative justice for transitional settings.

Broadening the restorative justice 'lens'

To use Howard Zehr's (1990) metaphor of viewing restorative justice through a lens, this collection calls for a broadening of the lens through which we view restorative justice when applying it to transitional contexts. When responding to crime in democratic settings, restorative justice is employed to give a victim and an offender (and depending on the process, the community) a central role in responding to the harm that has been caused, as well as the underlying motivations for that harm. This is relatively straightforward when a restorative justice process is used to respond to a single incident that has occurred between identifiable individuals and when one of those individuals has admitted responsibility for the harm caused. However, international crimes (genocide, crimes against humanity and war crimes) are distinctive from those criminal incidents that take place in established democracies, because of their massive and systemic character and because groups of people (rather than individuals) are targeted based on their religious, cultural, ethnic or national characteristics (Drumbl 2000; Rohne *et al.* 2008). This makes the application of restorative justice, as it is used within democratic settings, problematic for a number of reasons.

First, individuals often do not fit into neat categories of victim and offender, as they can drift from one category to the other over the duration of the conflict. Furthermore, the sheer numbers of people involved can make identification difficult. Even in instances where it is possible to identify specific individuals, it is difficult to separate the act from the larger political environment in which it took place. As Zwi *et al.* (2002) explain, violent conflicts are underpinned by *unequal access* to political power (this may be based on where an individual lives, their social class, religion, race or ethnicity) and resources (such as health, employment and education). As such,

> the instrumental use of violence by people who identify themselves as members of a group – whether this group is transitory or has a more permanent identity – against another group or set of individuals, [occurs] in order to achieve political, economic or social objectives.
>
> (Zwi *et al.* 2002: 215)

This poses a problem, because current restorative justice practice in a criminal justice setting is not aligned to deal with such macro-political issues and has been criticised in this regard (see Cunneen 2010; Stubbs 1997). Rather, the common trend within the democratic literature on restorative justice tends to define crime in terms of its relational implications rather than in terms of its structural causes (Clamp 2014). David Dyck (2008: 527) relays the problem with such an approach as covering 'up deeply rooted dimensions of conflict in favour of "an ideology of harmony" which suggests that shared feelings create empowerment'. Chapman and Campbell (this volume, Chapter 7), Cuneeen (this volume, Chapter 11), and Harbin and Llewellyn (this volume, Chapter 8) thus argue that a significant limitation of current conceptions of restorative justice is the tendency for the causes and consequences of the conflict to be reduced to incidents that have occurred between individuals, rather than looking at the broader factors that allowed such acts to occur. If restorative justice is going to have a meaningful impact on intercommunal and intercultural conflict, then it has to address not only the collective responsibility of all parties, but also the broader structural causes which perpetuate conflict within these societies (see further Clamp, this volume, Chapter 12; Findlay, this volume, Chapter 9; Harbin and Llewellyn, this volume, Chapter 8).

Second, as Groenhuijsen and Pemberton note: 'The state participates in or at least condones the commission of these crimes and the direct or indirect involvement of government officials is conspicuous' (2011: 12). This situation is further complicated in that the 'state may also be regarded as a victim in the sense that its agents may have suffered direct harm as a result of the actions of non-state actors' (Doak, this volume, Chapter 5). A gap in the established restorative justice literature is that the role of the state has been under theorised, given that the primary pursuit of the restorative justice movement has been to 'deprofessionalise' justice. In transitional settings, however, there needs to be a place for the state in restorative justice processes given that, as Doak outlines, it has played an active role in the conflict.

Third, as proponents of outcome-based camps of restorative justice argue, it is not nearly enough to include all stakeholders – victims, offenders and communities – for a process to be considered restorative (see further Clamp 2014, this volume Chapter 2). Any process that claims to be restorative needs to be underpinned by particular values, and positive outcomes need to emanate from the process for all of those involved. Unfortunately, this does not always occur, and there is a tension within the established democratic literature on restorative justice that can be observed to result in a zero-sum game between victims and offenders. Either the victim wins at the expense of the offender or the victim loses so that particular outcomes for the offender might be secured (Hudson 2003). The problem for the transitional context is that we are transporting established modes and models of justice (retributive and restorative) and wondering why the outcomes (and failures!) of conventional criminal justice in the West are replicated. Weinstein highlights the consequence of such a restrictive approach:

> If these societies do not undergo a social transformation towards pro-social behaviours, then most victims may remain victims – consigned to second-class status and excluded from access to the rights and privileges of full citizenship. An emphasis on legalism and the litigation of human rights abuses may lead to the untoward consequence of neglecting the goals of social reconstruction rather than contributing to its achievement.
>
> (2014: 162)

The dominance of legalism or retributive thinking within the transitional justice landscape is highlighted by both Lambourne (this volume, Chapter 4) and Nickson (this volume, Chapter 6) as a contributing factor for the limited impact of so-called restorative justice initiatives. In order for the true potential of restorative justice to be realised for stakeholders – victims, offenders and communities – it is important that we move our conceptions of restorative justice beyond criminal justice (see Clamp, this volume, Chapter 2).

Fourth, reparation (material or symbolic) is a central feature of restorative justice in attempts to 'repair', 'redress' or 'restore' the consequences of crime and conflict. As Wemmers (2011: 148) explains, it plays an important role in 'attempts to restore equity by reducing the losses suffered by the victim or the community'. However, there are two principal issues with reparations conceptualised as restorative justice in response to protracted violence and/or oppression.

The first is that reparations are generally not sufficient to alter living conditions post-transition, largely due to the limited resources available to the state, and the narrow eligibility criteria that often accompany such programmes constrains the amount of people who actually benefit (see Cunneen, this volume, Chapter 11; Harbin and Llewellyn, this volume, Chapter 8). The second is that reparations create the perception that what harm has been caused now remains in the past, thus leaving the structural problems that continue to face affected groups intact (see Cunneen, this volume, Chapter 11; Mani 2002; Robins 2011). As such, a common theme running throughout the volume is that conceptions of restorative justice must become significantly more future oriented if it is to have any meaningful impact within transitional settings.

Fifth, restorative justice practice within established democracies is generally a one-off encounter. For the most part, given the types of offences that fall within its remit (not to belittle the amount of trauma that may be experienced by victims) and the amount of preparation that goes into that meeting with the facilitator beforehand, one meeting is often enough. However, in transitional settings (particularly within the case of truth and reconciliation commissions), there is a lack of rigorous groundwork in preparing victims to testify in public in front of their loved ones and complete strangers about their experience of often quite heinous incidents. Furthermore, once testimony is given, but certainly after the transitional justice mechanism has completed its mandate, victims receive no further help. Braithwaite (this volume, Chapter 10) suggests that the point at which transitional justice mechanisms are introduced and the length of time that they are available to deal with the past needs to be reconsidered. He notes that,

> Timing is the essence of justice that restores. This is not just a challenge of whether survivors are ready yet. It is also a problem of victims being ready right now and the justice institution not yet being in place now to hear them.

Given these realities, it is virtually impossible for the dominant conceptions of restorative justice as a *process* or as *outcomes* to make a meaningful contribution to resolving deep-seated conflict within transitional settings. Applying labels to particular individuals or groups as if clear binaries exist is not helpful, particularly given that each individual or group may see themselves as the victim and the other as the enemy or perpetrator. Our conceptions of restorative justice have to be much more *transformative* by seeking to deal with the broader structural violence that perpetuates conflict, given that this is what caused the conflict in the first place. In short, the strategies employed in responding to 'normal' crime guided by a restorative framework in established democracies need revising within societies emerging from periods of conflict and oppression, given the complexities involved in the motivations for and characteristics of the 'conflict'. Only limited analysis exists on this topic within the available literature written by restorative scholars, and this collection serves as an initial collaborative attempt to broaden discussion and debate on the issue.

Whither 'transitional' justice?

One's ideological standpoint is important in determining the key themes of importance in any reading of a particular topic. While the 'field' of transitional justice[1] has traditionally been firmly in the domain of legal and political scholars, criminology, although somewhat late to the party, is starting to make its presence felt. According to Chouliaras (2011: 35–36), those who approach the study of international crimes from a legal perspective often focus on the issue mainly as instances of individual deviance. It follows then that the issues of central importance in the study of transitional justice will necessarily be the pursuit of justice as it relates to 'individual criminal responsibility in the context of collective violence with systemic traits'. Criminologists, however, may approach the study of international crime as one of organisational deviance, with a focus on determining the accountability of a range of actors who have committed a range of human rights offences. Naturally, for criminologists, any response to such offences would include those that extend beyond the law. Three key issues can be identified within the transitional justice that have been highlighted by legal and political scholars, but arguably extended by the contributions of criminology in the form of restorative justice theorising and practice on the ground.

First, from a legal perspective, there remains a debate about the 'exceptionalism' of transitional justice in comparison to criminal justice in established democracies (Williams *et al.* 2012). Posner and Vermeule (2004) claim that it is incorrect to treat transitional justice as exceptional and distinct from other types of law and transitions that take place in more established democracies. In fact, they assert that 'legal and political transitions lie on a continuum, of which regime transitions are merely an end point' (2004: 763). They begin their argument by highlighting the oft-quoted jurisprudential, moral and institutional problems raised by legal scholars in pursuing transitional justice, namely that: prosecution and lustration will reduce the number of skilled workers in the new administration; returning confiscated property could unsettle property rights and harm the emerging economy; retroactive justice violates the rule of law; pursuing a policy of blanket prosecutions would overburden courts; transitional justice could taint the reputations of those needed to take the country forward; deciding who and what types of harm to compensate is arbitrary; and, finally, it is difficult to assign gradations of blame. They respond to these dilemmas of transitional justice by drawing parallels between law in emerging and established democracies and, in this respect, they are able to claim that transitional justice is 'ordinary' (also see Posner 2012).

However, while there are apparent structural similarities in the dilemmas faced by established and emerging democracies,[2] the purpose of law in each type of society is qualitatively different. In established democracies, law is used to ensure political stability and to punish those who transgress established norms. In transitional societies, law may also be used to renounce the political norms of the previous regime, secure political transformation and achieve a new legal order. These features, according to Teitel (2000: 30), 'are in tension with conventional understandings of the rule of law'. Furthermore, the consequences of adhering to the rule of law between these societies differ. In established democracies, citizens may protest against the 'injustice' of not holding perpetrators to account; in transitional societies, the risk of adhering to the rule of law by prosecuting previous human rights abusers may actually perpetuate political violence. The assertion that 'transitional justice is ordinary justice' may thus be challenged on the basis that accountability is not the primary aim of transitional justice and that the political needs of the transition require a redefinition of justice as it stands within established democracies (see Bell 2009).

Transitional justice is also more than legal or retributive justice. Although it remains the dominant conception within the transitional justice landscape, Diaz (2008) argues that the establishment of peace is often the key priority within transitional settings which requires the use of exceptional measures such as the suspension of ordinary criminal justice. This has included the development of a range of responses that have harnessed restorative features such as a:

> focus on reparation and healing of victims as opposed to retribution visited upon wrongdoers, [and] hearings which are directed towards truth finding rather than adversarial processes (which emphasise community involvement and ownership rather than exclusive 'professional' stewardship).
>
> (McEvoy and Newburn 2003: 4)

This collection demonstrates that notions of 'transitional justice as restorative justice' have become more attractive in recent years. Bell and O'Rourke (2007: 40) describe this conception of justice as having its 'theoretical roots in Habermasian traditions of "communicative ethics" and notions of justice as constructed through dialogue'. The use of restorative justice within transitional societies may also to some extent be considered 'exceptional' because, while the conditions for its adoption and the factors included in wider debates on the role of restorative justice in relation to resolving disputes may be the same, they are used in contrasting ways in transitional settings (see Clamp, Chapter 2).

Second, there is a further tension within the literature between those who view transitional justice as something temporary – focused on dealing with the specific period between the move from an undemocratic regime to a democratic one – (see, for example, Williams *et al.* 2012) and those who assert that the field has moved beyond perceiving it as a particular 'moment' in time (see, for example, Lundy and McGovern 2008). Williams and Nagy explain the rationale and importance of the time-limited character of transitional justice on the basis of both pragmatic and normative considerations:

> From a pragmatic point of view, transitional institutions should be time limited because they may place extraordinary demands on resources that are not sustainable over the long run. From an ethical perspective, transitions should be time limited because they impose moral obligations and sacrifices that are consistent with the demands of justice in ordinary times.... If justice

demands that all wrongdoers be punished or that all victims be compensated, the political constraints of a transitional context may require that justice be sacrificed for the sake of stable, relatively decent, political order – but it would be a moral mistake to 'normalise' such compromises.

(2012: 21)

There are a number of issues that can be raised about this position, however. First, as the contributions in this collection highlight, there are a number of creative ways that justice can be secured without the 'extraordinary demands on resources' required by a legal response. Realising these innovative methods means harnessing justice that is conceived differently from legal justice and empowering local actors to devise culturally appropriate responses for themselves. Second, to equate justice solely with punishment tends to 'marginalise issues, questions and approaches that … challenge the forms and norms of Western governance' and represents a narrow conception of justice that is limited to the legal sphere (Lundy and McGovern 2008: 102). Increasing discourse on both community-based responses to dealing with the legacy of the past (see McEvoy and McGregor 2008) and the role of restorative justice within the transitional justice landscape (this volume) are providing a challenge to the restrictive view of transitional justice as being time bound.

Third, Arthur (2009) draws attention to challenges made by a range of scholars about the utility of the transitional justice paradigm on the basis of a number of countries lapsing back into violence following the 'transition' (also see Braithwaite, this volume, Chapter 10; Doak, this volume, Chapter 5; Lundy and McGovern 2008). These critiques charge that 'the paradigm had raised false hopes, perhaps mostly among democracy promoters, of an easily identifiable, sequential path toward a new political regime' (Arthur 2009: 362). Furthermore, Mani (2014) argues that the continued presence of historical injustices experienced by certain segments of the population following transitional justice mechanisms suggest that they are not adequate in breaking the cycles of victimisation post-transition. The failure of transitional justice to establish long-term peace is perceived to be the result of solutions to the conflict being imposed without sufficient attention being paid to the reasons why that conflict exists in the first place. This collection argues that restorative justice can be used as a mechanism through which this can be addressed and whereby local actors can claim a much more significant stake in the approach to dealing with the past and charting a pathway for the future (see further Clamp, this volume, Chapter 12).

Given the range of problems associated with the transitional paradigm and the awkward way in which restorative justice is confined by other dominant models, perhaps it is time for a conceptual revolution. Perhaps we should not speak of restorative justice as a paradigm of transitional justice, but rather allow the word 'transitional' to wither away and more 'transformative' conceptions of restorative justice to come to the fore. As Clamp outlines in Chapter 2, this conception of restorative justice remains under theorised, but it does appear to have significant potential for transitional settings (also see Clamp 2014). This collection provides support for this proposal on two levels. First, Braithwaite (this volume, Chapter 10) calls for the 'lengthening' of transitional justice in order to allow victims to experience a sense of justice at a time and space that is appropriate for them. He acknowledges that transitional justice mechanisms cost money and that donors like to see that something is being done; however, he points to creative ways in which the legacy of the past might be harnessed to create capital for such long-term, future-oriented mechanisms. Second, to assume that human rights abuses cease once a political transition has taken place is to approach the issue in an overly simplistic manner. If the underlying causes are not addressed, then surely the system of inequality that perpetuates harm remains intact and 'victims' will continue to experience the same marginalisation under democracy. On this basis, Cunneen (this volume, Chapter 11) argues that transitional justice should be extended to deal with longer-term issues such as colonialism. Adopting a broader perspective of restorative justice and moving beyond the conventional 'single incident–single encounter' mode, means that much more creative ways of addressing societal conflict can emerge.

The collection

The first three substantive chapters of this collection highlight the contested nature of restorative justice and its limited character within transitional justice discourse. In Chapter 2, Clamp makes a case for more transformative conceptions of restorative justice. Drawing on established restorative justice conceptions in democratic settings, particularly those put forward by Johnstone and van Ness (2007), she demonstrates the poverty of emerging conceptions of restorative justice in transitional settings. Clamp argues that, if restorative justice is conceived in a much broader way, it can serve as a mechanism through which both the individual and the collective can achieve justice in a more meaningful way. In seeking to illustrate how existing institutions might be modified to more closely align to a transformative conception of restorative justice, she provides a number of proposals, whereby stakeholders might be empowered to assume responsibility for dealing with issues of central concern to them.

Similarly, Bueno *et al.* (Chapter 3) demonstrate the poverty of current responses in addressing harm following the transition. They embrace a maximalist conception of restorative justice to highlight the importance of the concept of 'restorative accountability' which involves addressing harm experienced by *all* stakeholders – victims, offenders and communities – and reintegrating offenders. Using Colombia as a case study, they make a case for the empowerment of offenders to repair the harm they have caused, for the creation of harm more generally to be acknowledged, and for offenders to be reintegrated into their communities. Approaching the issue from a slightly different angle, Lambourne (Chapter 4) suggests that restorative notions of justice have been insufficiently discussed and debated within the transitional justice literature and that the principles of restorative justice have not been sufficiently incorporated into the design and implementation of transitional justice mechanisms. She, therefore, seeks to 'develop an argument about how a more explicit understanding and incorporation of restorative justice as part of transitional justice can contribute to a more effective process of dealing with the past and building peace in societies recovering from mass violence'. In doing so, she makes a case for learning from and further supporting local indigenous justice practices.

The following four chapters focus on conceptualising the role of stakeholders within transitional justice settings. First, Doak (Chapter 5) explores the limited role of the state as a stakeholder in restorative justice. He begins by reviewing efforts by the state to deal with the past (i.e. providing reparations and issuing apologies) and questions whether these should be considered restorative at all. Instead, he provides a tentative attempt to articulate a role for the state in terms of its capacity as a lawmaker and potentially as a direct stakeholder within restorative justice processes. Such an approach, he argues, would challenge the power imbalance between the state and communities and thus 'create a space for deliberative democracy'. Second, Nickson (Chapter 6) evaluates victim participation within the International Criminal Court and the Extraordinary Chambers in the Courts of Cambodia. He argues that, because restorative justice essentially serves as an 'accessory to retributive justice', the involvement of victims is far more limited than what would be expected from a restorative justice perspective. He suggests that one way of overcoming the barriers to restorative justice within both institutions is by enabling greater process control (i.e. empowerment and engagement) through transitional boards. What is being proposed here, much as in Lambourne's chapter, is not a complete replacement of legal transitional justice mechanisms, but rather a complement to the process which would allow further participation and ownership by those most affected.

Third, Chapman and Campbell (Chapter 7) reflect on their findings as part of the ALTERNATIVE research project which sought to explore how community-based restorative justice might resolve the relational and cultural issues that political and institutional reforms have failed to resolve in Northern Ireland. Drawing on two different case studies, they demonstrate how community-based restorative justice can result in identity being conceived as multi-dimensional and open (rather than singular and closed), following a process through which people are able to communicate honestly with each other about issues that they find threatening. As such, they make a case for the empowerment of local communities to be able to devise solutions to conflict at a local level in lieu of state interference. Finally, Harbin and Llewellyn (Chapter 8) are concerned with the superficial engagement of the role of the 'community' within the transitional justice literature which they argue 'reveals the difficulty of moving beyond individualistic models in the implementation of restorative justice practices'. What is needed, they argue, is a move beyond the individual ascription of blame and liability for past harms to an understanding of the background structural factors and social injustices that propel conflict. In seeking to chart a way forward, the authors draw on the philosophical debates about collective responsibility and call for a relational approach to restorative justice in transitional contexts that revisits and revises notions of individual and collective responsibility.

In the remaining three chapters, restorative justice is explored in relation to transitional justice. Findlay (Chapter 9) points to a tendency to use dichotomies when we speak of retributive justice and restorative justice in relation to transitional justice. What emerges, he argues, is a failure to see the restorative qualities of the International Criminal Court under the *Rome Statute* which means that international criminal justice is thought of as retributive. He suggests that moving towards a more holistic vision of justice and an understanding of how retributive justice is being challenged at a formal level means that restorative qualities can more easily be recognised. Next, Braithwaite (Chapter 10) cautions against the frenzy of non-learning that is currently taking place within transitional settings and the potential of restorative justice to become swept up in this practice. Drawing on a range of international examples, he demonstrates not only that transitional justice is 'too transitional' (i.e. temporary) but also that it is too focused on mass atrocity and therefore neglectful of local and personal atrocity. As such, he proposes to scale up restorative justice and other forms of transitional justice, both in terms of the proportion of survivors benefitting from it and in terms of quality, and a broadening of the conception of justice to encompass participatory empowerment. In the final substantive chapter of the collection, Cunneen (Chapter 11) asserts that settled colonial states should be considered transitional settings given 'their need to confront and remedy past injustices arising from their own colonial histories'. However, he argues that restorative justice as it is currently conceived places offences in the past instead of realising that injustice can remain in the present. As such, he calls for a far more radical approach. The solution to this state of affairs, he suggests, is a transformation of restorative justice to be 'conceived as Indigenous justice; where Indigenous law, culture and politics define the values, processes and practices of restorative justice'.

In drawing together the overarching themes that are present within the collection, Clamp (Chapter 12) suggests that restorative justice in transitional settings needs to be characterised by three elements: (1) it should include all stakeholders, (2) it should be culturally relevant, and (3) it should be forward-looking. This demonstrates a desire to move beyond the status quo: to increase participatory opportunities for those who have been most directly affected by conflict and to overhaul the way in which we conceive justice. However, realising such a transformative vision of restorative justice will not be easy. Our current conceptions of justice are designed around a binary. There is one person or group who has been harmed and who needs to be vindicated and a different person or group who needs to be held accountable for such harms. Given this binary, our current approach to responding to violence and oppression (even where so-called 'innovative' mechanisms are used, particularly in the case of truth commissions), means that victims who have suffered the 'most' are placed at the centre and they become a 'symbol around which contested notions of past violence and suffering are constructed and reproduced' (McEvoy and McConnachie 2012: 532). This reality means that, rather than addressing the root causes of conflict or harm, once again the experiences and harm of one group is elevated above that of the other. It is perhaps unsurprising then that roughly 50 per cent of countries that emerge from war or conflict lapse back into violence within five years (Annan 2006; Lundy and McGovern 2008). This statistic undermines the often substantial financial investment that supports current approaches to respond to conflict. As Wilson (2001) argues, it is not only human rights abuses that affect individuals, but also interventions by international organisations and the state. We therefore arguably have a duty to push the boundaries of both retributive and restorative justice to achieve a more effective approach to dealing with the causes and consequences of conflict and oppression. This collection presents an initial attempt to do just that.[3]

Notes

1 See Bell (2009) for a good discussion on whether or not this actually exists.
2 Teitel (2000) states that they are merely more visible in transitional settings.
3 The author would like to thank Jonathan Doak for his valuable comments on an earlier draft of the chapter.

References

Annan, K. (2006) *In Larger Freedom*, New York: United Nations.
Arthur, P. (2009) 'How "Transitions" Reshaped Human Rights: A conceptual history of transitional justice', *Human Rights Quarterly*, 31(2): 321–367.
Atkinson, M. and Coleman, W. (1992) 'Policy Networks, Policy Communities and the Problems of Governance', *An International Journal of Policy and Administration*, 5(2): 154–180.
Baumgartner, E. (2008) 'Aspects of Victim Participation in the Proceedings of the International Criminal Court', *International Review of the Red Cross*, 90(870): 409–440.
Bell, C. (2009) 'Transitional Justice, Interdisciplinarity and the State of the "Field" or "Non-field"', *International Journal of Transitional Justice*, 3(1): 5–27.
Bell, C., and O'Rourke, C. (2007) 'Does Feminism Need a Theory of Transitional Justice? An introductory essay', *International Journal of Transitional Justice*, 1: 23–44.
Boraine, A., Levy, J. and Scheffer, R. (1997) *Dealing with the Past: Truth and reconciliation in South Africa*. Cape Town: IDASA.
Braithwaite, J., Charlesworth, H. and Adérito, S. (2012) *Networked Governance of Freedom and Tyranny: Peace in Timor-Leste*, Canberra: ANU Press.
Chouliaras, A. (2011) 'The victimological concern as the driving force in the quest for justice for state-sponsored international crimes', in R. Letschert, R. Haveman, A. de Brouwer and A. Pemberton (eds) *Victimological Approaches in International Crimes: Africa*, Cambridge: Intersentia.
Christie, N. (1977) 'Conflicts as Property', *British Journal of Criminology*, 17(1): 1–15.
Christie, N. (1982) *Limits to Pain*, Oxford: Martin Robertson.
Clamp, K. (2014) *Restorative Justice in Transition*, London: Routledge.
Clamp, K. and Doak, J. (2012) 'More than Words: Restorative justice concepts in transitional justice settings', *International Criminal Law Review*, 12(3): 339–360.
Cunneen, C. (2010) 'The limitations of restorative justice', in C. Cunneen and C. Hoyle (eds) *Debating Restorative Justice*, Oxford: Hart Publishing.

Daly, K. (2012) *Victimisation and Justice: Concepts, contexts, and assessment of justice mechanisms*, paper presented at the 14th International Symposium of the World Society of Victimology, The Hague, May.

Diaz, C. (2008) 'Challenging impunity from below: the contested ownership of transitional justice in Columbia', in K. McEvoy and L. McGregor (eds) *Transitional Justice from Below: Grassroots activism and the struggle for change*, Oxford: Hart Publishing.

Dolowitz, D. and Marsh, D. (1996) 'Who Learns What from Whom. A review of the policy transfer literature', *Political Studies*, 44(2): 343–357.

Dolowitz, D. and Marsh, D. (2000) 'Learning from Abroad: The role of policy transfer in contemporary policy-making', *Governance: An International Journal of Policy and Administration*, 13(1): 5–24.

Drumbl, M. (2000) 'Punishment Postgenocide: From guilt to shame to "Civis" in Rwanda', *New York University Law Review*, 75: 1221–1326.

Dyck, D. (2008) 'Reaching toward a structurally responsive training and practice of restorative justice', in D. Sullivan and L. Tifft (eds) *Handbook of Restorative Justice: A global perspective*, London: Routledge.

Groenhuijsen, M. and Pemberton, A. (2011) 'Genocide, crimes against humanity and war crimes: a victimological perspective on international criminal justice', in R. Letschert, R. Haveman, A. de Brouwer and A. Pemberton (eds) *Victimological Approaches in International Crimes: Africa*, Cambridge: Intersentia.

Hudson, B. (2003) *Justice in the Risk of Society*, London: Sage Publications.

Johnstone, G. (2008) 'The agendas of the restorative justice movement', in H. Millar (ed.) *Restorative Justice: From theory to practice*, Bingley, UK: Emerald Group.

Johnstone, G. and Van Ness, D. (2007) 'The meaning of restorative justice', in G. Johnstone and D. Van Ness (eds) *Handbook of Restorative Justice*, Collumpton, UK: Willan Publishing.

Lundy, P. and McGovern, M. (2008) 'The role of community in participatory transitional justice', in K. McEvoy and L. McGregor (eds) *Transitional Justice from Below: Grassroots activism and the struggle for change*, Oxford: Hart Publishing.

McEvoy, K. and McConnachie, K. (2012) 'Victimology in Transitional Justice: Victimhood, innocence and hierarchy', *European Journal of Criminology*, 9(5): 527–538.

McEvoy, K. and McGregor, L. (2008) *Transitional Justice from Below: Grassroots activism and the struggle for change*, Oxford: Hart Publishing.

McEvoy, K. and Mika, H. (2002) 'Restorative Justice and the Critique of Informalism in Northern Ireland', *British Journal of Criminology*, 42(3): 534–562.

McEvoy, K. and Newburn, T. (2003) *Criminology, Conflict Resolution and Restorative Justice*, London: Palgrave Macmillan.

Mani, R. (2002) *Beyond Retribution: Seeking justice in the shadows of war*, Oxford: Polity Press.

Mani, R. (2014) 'Integral justice for victims', in I. Vanfraechem, A. Pemberton and F. Ndahinda (eds) *Justice for Victims: Perspectives on rights, transition and reconciliation*, London: Routledge.

Minow, M. (1998) *Between Vengeance and Forgiveness: Facing history after genocide and mass violence*, Boston: Beacon Press.

Muncie, J. (2005) 'The Globalization of Crime Control – the Case of Youth and Juvenile Justice: Neo-liberalism, policy convergence and international conventions', *Theoretical Criminology*, 9(1): 35–64.

Park, A. (2010) 'Community-based Restorative Transitional Justice in Sierra Leone', *Contemporary Justice Review*, 13(1): 95–119.

Posner, E. (2012) 'Transitional Prudence: A comment on David Dyzenhaus, *"Leviathan as a Theory of Transitional Justice"*', in M. Williams, R. Nagy and J. Elster (eds) *Transitional Justice*, New York: New York University Press.

Posner, E. and Vermeule, A. (2004) 'Transitional Justice as Ordinary Justice', *Harvard Law Review*, 117(2): 761–825.

Robins, S. (2011) 'Towards Victim-centred Transitional Justice: Understanding the needs of families of the disappeared in postconflict Nepal', *International Journal of Transitional Justice*, 5(1): 75–98.

Rohne, H., Arsovska, J. and Aertson, I. (2008) 'Challenging restorative justice – state-based conflict, mass victimisation and the changing nature of warfare', in I. Aertson, J. Arsovska, H. Rohne, M. Valiñas and K. Vanspauwen (eds) *Restoring Justice after Large-scale Violent Conflicts*, Collumpton, UK: Willan Publishing.

Stubbs, J. (1997) 'Shame, defiance and violence against women', in S. Cook and J. Bessant (eds) *Women's Encounters with Violence: Australian experiences*, London: Sage.

Teitel, R. (2000) *Transitional Justice*, New York: Oxford University Press.

Tutu, D. (1999) *No Future without Forgiveness*, London: Rider Books.

Uprimny, R. and Saffón, M. (2007) *Uses and Abuses of Transitional Justice Discourse in Colombia*. Oslo: International Peace Institute.

Waldorf, L. (2006) 'Rwanda's failing experiment in restorative justice', in D. Sullivan and L. Tifft (eds) *Handbook of Restorative Justice*, London: Routledge.

Weinstein, H. (2014) 'Victims, transitional justice and reconstruction: Who is setting the agenda?', in I. Vanfraechem, A. Pemberton and F. Ndahinda (eds) *Justice for Victims: perspectives on rights, transition and reconciliation*, London: Routledge.

Wemmers, J. (2011) 'Victims' need for justice: individual versus collective justice', in R. Letschert, R. Haveman, A. de Brouwer and A. Pemberton (eds) *Victimological Approaches in International Crimes: Africa*, Cambridge: Intersentia.

Williams, M. and Nagy, R. (2012) 'Introduction', in M. Williams, R. Nagy and J. Elster (eds) *Transitional Justice*, New York: New York University Press.

Williams, M., Nagy, R. and Elster, J. (2012) *Transitional Justice*, New York: New York University Press.

Wilson, R. (2001) *The Politics of Truth and Reconciliation in South Africa*, Cambridge: Cambridge University Press.

Zehr, H. (1990) *Changing Lenses*, Scottdale, PA: Herald Press.

Zwi, A., Garfield, R. and Loretti, A. (2002) 'Collective violence', in E. Krug, L. Dahlberg, G. Mercy, A. Zwi and R. Lozano (eds) *World Report on Violence and Health*, Geneva: World Health Organisation.

2 Clearing the conceptual haze

Restorative justice concepts in transitional settings

Kerry Clamp

Introduction

Past and present atrocities and crimes against humanity have often roused international condemnation and calls for something to be done. Two concepts have been introduced into the international landscape as a result: one to describe the violence, oppression or persecution undertaken or allowed under law by the state (international crime) and one to encompass the variety of responses to that violence, oppression or persecution (transitional justice[1]). International crime is distinct from 'ordinary' offences (i.e. theft, burglary, shoplifting and sexual assault) in that the commission of these acts is primarily underpinned by political rather than acquisitory or deviant motivations. It is important to acknowledge, however, that there may be an overlap between these two crime types. For example, murder, sexual violence and other crimes may both amount to forms of ordinary crime (even when carried out with a political motive) and (if the legal elements are in place) also be considered war crimes. Thus, it has been acknowledged that established mechanisms to deal with offending behaviour (i.e. the conventional criminal justice process) need to be revised in order to respond to the contextually distinct factors that result in such offences being committed and the associated grey areas of law which may have actually allowed such acts to occur.

Given the complexities and sensitivities involved in bringing offenders to account in transitional settings where prosecutions run the threat of reigniting conflict, there tends to be limited local efforts to engage in retributive action against perpetrators. However, the dominance of a 'western centric' view of justice has meant that a number of institutions have emerged to increase opportunities to hold offenders to account by the international community. At an international level, three institutions can be traced back to Nuremberg/Tokyo that have been devised to combat the climate of impunity for those who have committed serious international crimes: the temporary ad hoc criminal tribunals for the former Yugoslavia (ICTY) and Rwanda (ICTR) and the International Criminal Court. While the ICTY and the ICTR were developed to deal with international crimes committed in Yugoslavia and Rwanda respectively, the International Criminal Court, which came into force in 2002, is a permanent international body with a global mandate (Waddell and Clark 2008). At a

national level, hybrid courts have been devised to investigate and prosecute indi-
viduals responsible for international crimes, in which international and national
judges preside over cases together. Examples include: the War Crimes Chamber
of the Court of Bosnia and Herzegovina; the Special Court for Sierra Leone; the
Special Panels for Serious Crimes in Timor-Leste; the Special Tribunal for
Lebanon (Weirda *et al.* 2007) and the Extraordinary Chambers in the Courts of
Cambodia (see broadly Ivanišević 2008; Perriello and Wierda 2006a, 2006b;
Reiger 2006; Scheffer 2008). These developments have been accompanied by
institutions that drive transitional justice at a national level to support the necessary objective of nation-building and include truth (and reconciliation) commissions, reparations bodies and criminal justice reform to secure a fairer and more
efficient delivery of justice (see Aukerman 2002; Leebaw 2001; McEvoy 2008).

Within this complex justice terrain is the concept 'restorative justice'. At
times, restorative justice has been linked to some of the institutions outlined
above (see Braithwaite, this volume, Chapter 10; Nickson, this volume,
Chapter 6; Findlay, this volume, Chapter 9) and articulated as justice that is
distinct from prosecutions and a framework through which more local (as
opposed to Western) justice traditions can be embraced (see Cunneen, this
volume, Chapter 11; Lambourne, this volume, Chapter 4). Bronwyn Leebaw
(2003: 32) suggests that restorative justice came to the fore 'where formalism
and legalism had been identified as obstacles to radical [political] transformation' and 'as a basis for compromise and depoliticisation of debates on past
crimes'. This has resulted in, at times, quite heated debates about the role and
utility of restorative justice, with some arguing that restorative approaches
within transitional settings encourage impunity. To some extent, this was the
case in Guatemala, Haiti and Uganda where only low-level operatives were
held accountable for past abuses, despite no legal restriction on the truth and
reconciliation commission's ability to hold highly placed individuals accountable for past human rights (see Hayner 2000).

Nevertheless, others have defended the political convenience and ethical
superiority of using the restorative justice model as the dominant paradigm of
transitional justice (see Minow 1998; Tutu 1999). Llewellyn (2007), for
example, suggests that truth and reconciliation commissions might serve as an
example of what justice means and how just institutions might function in the
future. Dimitrijevic (2006) argues that a truth and reconciliation commission
tells the story of the conflict in a comprehensive way; investigates the motives
and produces a broad account of what happened; and helps to heal ethnic divisions better than a response that is focused on assigning responsibility to particular individuals for particular acts. In this way, restorative justice is said to
legitimise transitional justice and, more importantly, keep it focused on human
rights (Uprimny and Saffón 2006).

Before we can engage in a meaningful debate about the utility of restorative
justice within transitional settings, it is important to have a discussion about
what restorative justice means in transitional settings and to understand the different ways in which it is used. Despite reams of paper being devoted to defining

restorative justice within democratic settings (where the concept first emerged), there is a dearth of analysis on this topic within the transitional justice literature with only a handful of notable exceptions (see Aertsen *et al.* 2008; Clamp 2014; Clamp and Doak 2012; Daly and Proietti-Scifoni 2011; Leebaw 2001; Lewellyn 2007). Some would argue that such an exercise has been futile within democratic settings, as no consensus on the issue has been reached. Nevertheless, understanding what restorative justice is and being able to assess the 'restorativeness' of an initiative is important for a number of reasons, as Declan Roche explains:

> To practitioners it may help critically inform the work they do. It may give practitioners ideas about how they can improve what they are doing. And even where practitioners' actions already conform to restorative justice principles, practitioners may benefit by becoming more self-conscious and deliberate about what they do.
>
> (2001: 342)

Restorative justice has been applied to situations of mass violence and/or oppression without sufficient conceptual and theoretical development of the term for that context. This reality arguably limits the amount of deliberate restorative justice action that can be taken by practitioners. This chapter sheds further conceptual clarity on 'restorative justice' by exploring and problematising the use of the concept within transitional settings. The discussion begins by reviewing the established restorative justice literature within democratic settings to plot the key themes of the concept, as a basis from which to evaluate its use within transitional settings. In the next section, two distinct conceptions of the term used within transitional settings are outlined and attention is drawn to how this might be similar to or deviate from established conceptions in democratic settings. In the final substantive section, suggestions are made as to how restorative justice conceptions and practice might be strengthened within transitional settings.

Established conceptions of restorative justice

Restorative justice is a messy concept. Most will suggest that the first person to use the term was Robert Eglash (1977)[2] and that the emergence of restorative justice *practice* occurred at around the same time as the 'aetiological crisis' which drew attention to the inherent failings of criminal justice in the 1970s (see Young 1988). It is at this point where consensus diminishes dramatically. Disagreements range from the origins of restorative justice (some view it as a modern invention, whereas others see it as something that has been revived from 'ancient traditions'), to the type of behaviour restorative justice is an appropriate measure for (some view it as something that should be restricted to minor offending committed by juveniles, whereas others view it as more suitable for serious offending by adults), and even to its conceptual meaning (some hold a restrictive view of restorative justice as a process; others a more expansive view as they interpret particular outcomes as being restorative; and a maximalist conception even exists whereby particular values are said to be restorative). In an acknowledgement of the capaciousness of the term, McCold (2000: 358) rightly observes that 'restorative justice has come to mean all things to all people'.

Despite these points of contention, a number of key features may be discerned when traversing the broad literature on the topic (see generally Dignan 2005; Zehr 2002). First, there is a general focus on putting right the harm caused. This may be in the form of either material gestures (such as money or the replacement of damaged items) or symbolic gestures (such as apologies or undertaking work to compensate for any losses) by the individual responsible for any emotional or physical loss or damage. Second, there is a need for a balanced concern for the parties involved. While the victim has a right to some form of reparative redress, and this will form a significant part of the discussion and subsequent agreement that emerges, there also needs to be a focus on the offender's accountability, well-being and the underlying motivations for offending. Finally, it is thought that meeting these features should occur within an inclusive, non-coercive decision-making process in which those most directly involved and affected by the offence should have the opportunity to participate fully in the response should they wish. Unsurprisingly then, in most discussions on restorative justice, there is generally one person who has been 'harmed' and therefore needs some level of restoration, and another individual who has caused the 'harm' and thus needs to take steps to 'repair' the damage that has been caused.

While restorative practice has emerged primarily within the criminal justice setting, other applications can also be observed within schools, the workplace, the community and even as a mechanism through which to deal with complaints. Within all contexts, the problem-solving nature of restorative justice is harnessed by allowing all participants to contribute to both the discussions and the out-comes in a meaningful way. Specifically within a criminal justice setting, this process is thought to be better facilitated by allowing supporters of both the harmed and the wrongdoer (generally friends and/or family) and the wider 'community' to participate, for two reasons. The first is underpinned by Jonathan Braithwaite's (1989) notion of reintegrative shaming, which highlights the fact that disapproval by one's community (i.e. peers or family) is more likely to foster remorse and provide the most support in terms of dealing with the under-lying causes of the offending behaviour (Braithwaite and Mugford 1994; Johnstone 2002). The second is that, by allowing the broader 'community' to be involved in the resolution of offences that have taken place within the local area, it will result in an increased understanding of the triggers for offending so that further offending may be prevented more generally (Christie 1977; Crawford and Clear 2003; Kurki 2000).

However, the mainstreaming or popularisation of restorative justice has led commentators to point to a 'misappropriation', 'institutionalisation' or what Umbreit (1999: 213) refers to as the 'McDonaldization' of restorative justice whereby it has been expanded to mean almost anything that departs from traditional sentencing. This has included community-based schemes (such as community justice panels in Australia, Canada, England and the United States), diversionary schemes (such as reparation boards in the United States and referral orders in England and Wales), sentencing schemes (such as peace-making circles in Canada or forum sentencing in Australia) and even crime prevention schemes (such as conferencing initiatives undertaken with persistent and prolific offenders prior to release from prison in England). It should be noted that accusations of co-option do not arise because the criminal justice system has embraced restorative justice; the accusations occur because it is used as a mechanism through which criminal justice practitioners might achieve the goals of criminal justice rather than as a tool for doing justice better as envisaged by restorative justice proponents. Within the criminal justice variants of restorative justice, although the right language is used, at times practice can depart from what many restorative proponents would consider to be restorative. For example, the devolution of power down to stakeholders (i.e. victims, offenders, communities) sometimes does not occur, but rather professionals continue to dominate proceedings; restorative processes and principles can be used to 'responsibilise' the offender (i.e. to get him or her to acknowledge responsibility) rather than to deal with the underlying causes of behaviour; victims can be used in the service of severity to run the consequences of offending home to offenders rather than to have their own needs met; and supporters can be used to drive home to the offender that the restorative process is a 'lucky escape' and that changes should be made if further and more severe consequences are to be averted.

A popular trend has also recently emerged whereby restorative justice has been equated with anything that is victim focused. Victims are often viewed as the 'forgotten actor' within criminal justice, and restorative justice is viewed as a means through which this imbalance can be rectified. While victims are certainly central to the restorative justice process, it cannot be said that they are more important than offenders or the community. All three stakeholders have to have a central and equal role to play in order to meaningfully respond to the consequences of the offending behaviour and to create a response that will ensure that future harm is not caused. These tensions within the literature have resulted in restorative scholars putting forward a model whereby the 'restorativeness' of programmes can be assessed according to the extent to which stakeholders are able to participate in them (see McCold 2000; McCold and Wachtel 2003; Van Ness and Strong 2002). It has been suggested that, where all stakeholders are able to participate, this would be *fully* restorative (for example, conferencing initiatives and peace-making circles), where only two out of the three stakeholders participate, this would be considered *mostly* restorative (for example, victim–offender mediation, victimless conferences and victim support services), and, where only one out of the three stakeholders are the focus of the scheme, it could at best be considered *partially* restorative (for example, reparative boards, victim services and offender family services).

Johnstone and Van Ness (2007) have added to the broad literature on what restorative justice is by capturing the range of contributions as three distinct but overlapping conceptions which focus respectively on encounter, reparation and transformation. In relation to the first conception, restorative justice is equated with a *process* that allows stakeholders to engage with each other with the 'soft' assistance of professionals who facilitate rather than direct. Thus, restorative justice within this conception would fall within the *fully* and *mostly* restorative processes outlined above. To further distinguish restorative justice encounters from other processes which bring stakeholders together, but that can hardly be considered restorative, scholars have outlined a number of values which need to be present. Two principal contributions may be singled out. The first is put forward by Jonathan Braithwaite (2002), who helpfully groups values together in terms of those that should guide the process, those that should be encouraged during the process and those that *may* emerge as a result of the process. The second is a chapter written by Kay Pranis (2007), who reviews the literature on restorative values and provides not only a summary of procedural and individual values but also the contribution of values to restorative justice more generally.

Those who hold a reparative conception, on the other hand, tend to stress that an act which harms another individual does not necessarily need to be resolved through punishment. Rather, what is more important is that the incident is resolved in a manner that *addresses the harm* that has been caused, not only to the victim but to the offender as well. In this respect, while restorative justice proponents in this camp would prefer an encounter to arrive at ways in which harm can be addressed, they are also supportive of any action which seeks to repair. This increases the boundaries of what might be considered restorative to include those *partially* restorative approaches outlined above and to a more inclusive transformative project of justice processes more generally. Both Braithwaite (1999) and Dignan (2002), for example, have put forward models of how the conventional criminal justice system can be made more restorative by increasing both reparative opportunities for victims and sanctions that will hold some meaningful value for the offender.

Finally, proponents of the transformative conception of restorative justice suggest that restorative justice should be harnessed to change the way in which 'we understand ourselves and relate to others in our everyday lives' (Johnstone and Van Ness 2007: 15). This conception of restorative justice is the least articulated of all of the conceptions outlined. Some proponents of this conception see restorative justice as a means through which we can transform the way in which we view crime and the responses to it (see Braithwaite 2003) and as a means through which the social distance between individuals can be reduced (Christie 2004). Nils Christie (2004), for example, has for a long time questioned what crime is, drawn attention to the uneven application of the concept to some behaviours committed by certain groups over others and called for crime to be deprofessionalised. Walklate (2005) and Young (2002) have also suggested that current conceptions of restorative justice tend to endorse similar stereotypical notions of victimhood that are found within conventional criminal justice. This is primarily because restorative justice is perceived as an alternative to formal justice that relies on established legal definitions of victims and victimisation (Pavlich 2005). This conception of restorative justice thus seeks to resolve these issues by transcending the criminal justice lens that frames the other conceptions outlined above. As such, Johnstone (2008) describes restorative justice as 'a social movement – a collective endeavour that seeks to transform numerous aspects of contemporary society' that 'seeks to bring about a set of far-reaching changes in ourselves and in existing social relations'. This perspective of restorative justice, although not as popular as the two conceptions outlined above, has important consequences for transitional settings whereby the motivations for offending may be a little murky and the actors may not be clearly defined. This assertion will be further unpacked following a discussion of conceptions of restorative justice in transitional settings, to which we now turn.

Emerging conceptions of restorative justice: something old and something new

Two conceptions are discussed within this section. The first is a micro-political usage of restorative justice, which is focused on the instrumental dimensions of law in that it is wholly concerned with the regulation and resolution of disputes between individuals. In this way, restorative justice conceptions conform to established notions of victim and offender and coalesce around a specific incident that needs to be resolved. The second is the role of restorative justice at the macro-level, which is primarily concerned with introducing new values and concepts into society, particularly in terms of those which relate to justice institutions. This is perhaps the most conceptually distinct in that restorative justice has been used to describe efforts to overcome the past that rely primarily on *symbolism* whereby accountability is secured in creative ways.

The micro-political usage of restorative justice in transitional settings

The first conceptualisation of restorative justice, in many respects, can be seen to complement practice in established democracies whereby restorative processes and values are used to underpin responses to offending behaviour within criminal and community-based justice. At both levels, the impetus towards alternative justice strategies is propelled by attempts to respond to a legitimacy deficit. Due to the central role of state agencies and criminal justice institutions in human rights abuses or perpetuating injustice under undemocratic regimes, criminal justice reform is naturally of central concern to successor governments. Establishing the rule of law is an important *symbol* that distinguishes the new regime from the old and suggests that steps have been taken to prevent atrocities from being committed in the future.

Given the prevalence of restorative justice rhetoric within the Western world, it is perhaps unsurprising that the restorative justice project has emerged during periods of criminal justice reform within transitional settings. As in democratic criminal justice systems, both 'fully' (i.e. conferencing) and 'partially' (i.e. victim–offender mediation) restorative justice programmes are run by the state and communities to deal with criminal offences. The most notable restorative criminal justice systems in transitional settings include the Czech Probation and Mediation

Service (see Clamp 2012); the Northern Ireland youth conferencing system (see O'Mahony *et al.* 2012); and the South African child justice system (see Clamp 2008). In all of these jurisdictions, restorative processes (mediation in the Czech Republic and conferencing in Northern Ireland and South Africa) and values (such as repairing the harm, reintegration and reparation) have been used to underpin adult and/or youth justice systems during periods of reform. In each of these systems, restorative processes are available to victims, offenders and (to a lesser extent) communities before sentence, to determine sentencing and following sentence (see Clamp 2010). The consequences of such 'top-down' applications of restorative justice are said to contribute to securing the broader values of transitional justice. Reflecting on the Northern Ireland youth conferencing system, O'Mahony (2012) explains that the reforms are securing:

> a fairer and more effective system of justice, which has the potential to inspire confidence in the criminal justice system in the community as a whole. This is particularly relevant ... given the significant legitimacy deficit suffered by the institutions of criminal justice over the duration of the conflict.

Restorative justice has also been applied to schemes developed and run by communities in response to a *justice gap* experienced prior to or in the early days of the transition. This has occurred in Northern Ireland (see, for example, Alternatives and Community Restorative Justice Ireland) and South Africa (see, for example, Community Peace Programmes/the Zwelethemba Model) whereby initiatives akin to conferencing have been developed to deal with problems blighting communities at the local level in lieu of state intervention. The development of restorative processes within the community allows justice that is needs focused to take root, which may also respond to the consequences of the conflict such as challenging 'cultures of violence'. The debates around dispute resolution or legal culture within the new democratic dispensation may therefore be 'thickened' from below by the norms and values of non-elites (for an example of this in action, see Chapman and Campbell, this volume, Chapter 7).

Transitional societies are typically characterised by strong communities and weak state structures, which is in contrast to many established democracies (Eriksson 2009). It is this dynamic that leaves space for restorative justice to flourish, as it provides a mechanism through which to highlight (and reject) the illegitimacy of unreformed institutions and a means through which to deal with conflict that is respectful of human rights. Indeed, Braithwaite argues that:

> A legitimacy ideal that has been articulated for restorative justice is that it would assist the justice of the law to filter down into the justice of the people and the justice of the people to bubble up into the justice of the law.
>
> (2007: 149)

However, while the presence of innovative uses of restorative justice from 'above' and 'below' may be discerned within the transitional justice landscape, there is often limited mutually beneficial interaction between state and community structures. In part, this is due to the fact that until recently professionalised justice has 'monopolised the language of legitimacy' (Cain 1988: 66) and, as a result, community programmes have been viewed as a source of contention by the state (Cain 1988; Cohen 1994; McEvoy and Eriksson 2008). Nevertheless, Woolford and Ratner (2010) suggest that any competitiveness between the state and communities is inevitably stymied by the need for referrals, support and funding from the state. The development of standards or protocols through which community programmes are 'legitimated' from the top down means that the potential that Braithwaite outlines above is often unrealised (see Chapman and Campbell, this volume, Chapter 7, for a good example of this in Northern Ireland). In this sense, the debates and issues that arise in relation to the micro-political use of restorative justice mimic those that are found in the established literature on restorative justice within democratic settings whereby state justice often trumps community justice.

The macro-political usage of restorative justice in transitional settings

Ruti Teitel (2003) associates restorative justice with her Phase II paradigm of transitional justice. She outlines that, following the Nuremburg trials (Phase I), responses evolved away from international transitional justice towards alternative strategies that would create 'an alternative history of past abuses' through truth and reconciliation commissions. Since the 1970s there have been roughly 46 truth commissions around the world (see Hayner 2011), the popularity of which is said to be based on such institutions providing an overarching narrative for the conflict rather than sentences being handed down to individual perpetrators for isolated incidents (Teitel 2003). Teitel suggests that the importance of this evolution was that it 'transcended the single-minded focus on individual accountability in favour of a more communitarian conception', that it provided 'a vehicle for victims to reconcile and recover from past harms' and 'a move away from ... universalising judgment to a focus on rebuilding political identity through rule of law' (2003: 90).

The first truth commission was established in Uganda in 1974, but it did not become a staple institution within the transitional justice landscape until the mid-1980s when it emerged in Latin America. Truth in these contexts was something that victims called for in a bid to find out what happened to those who had been 'disappeared' during the previous regime (i.e. 'truth-seeking'). It was not until the South African Truth and Reconciliation Commission, however, that truth was packaged as a form of justice in and of itself and tied to the concept of restorative justice through the act of 'truth-telling'. The Truth and Reconciliation Commission Report states that it represented:

> another kind of justice – a restorative justice which is concerned not so much with punishment as with correcting imbalances, restoring broken

relationships – with healing, harmony and reconciliation. Such justice focuses on the experience of victims; hence the importance of reparation.

(TRC 1998, Vol. 1, Ch. 1, Para. 36)

As one of the most researched institutions in the world (McEvoy and McGregor 2008), it is perhaps not surprising that the particular conception of restorative justice held by Archbishop Desmond Tutu, the Chair of the SATRC, has been perpetuated throughout the transitional justice literature. Restorative justice has thus been equated (primarily) with truth commissions that claim to create an environment through which reconciliation, forgiveness, healing and something that is more victim focused might be achieved (see Tutu 1999).

However, this macro-level conception of restorative justice is distinct from how restorative justice is conceived within the established democratic literature on a number of fronts. First, truth commissions seek to establish a community that has never before existed through the language of restorative justice, whereas restorative justice relies on established and functioning communities to bring about change within an offender. Second, truth commissions seek to develop national narratives of conflicts, whereas restorative justice seeks to deal with a single incident (even where this involves multiple actors and more protracted and nuanced conflicts). Third, offenders are not held directly to account to their victims within truth commissions in the form of repairing the harm caused and the state tends to assume responsibility for reparations, whereas in restorative processes offenders are encouraged to make amends directly to their victims or symbolically to the community (see Clamp and Doak 2012 for more on this point). Finally, the public participate through public engagement activities or through witnessing testimony, whereas in restorative justice processes victims, offenders and the community are able to directly engage with one another. The reasons for the distinctions in restorative justice praxis between democratic and transitional states is a result of the unavoidable political compromises that have to take place, as well as the long historical view that needs to be taken into account when discussing experiences under an undemocratic regime. Nevertheless, current conceptions within the transitional justice literature seem to fall short of what restorative justice proponents would expect from a *process* that claims to be restorative.

Although the language of restorative justice is used and justice is said to be done in the name of victims and affected communities, in reality the principle objective of national transitional justice mechanisms (such as truth and reconciliation commissions) is to draw a line under the past. Transitions, much like the criminal justice process, are firmly in the domain of elites and conflict is defined in a limited way, thus resulting in a failure to adequately engage with the true causes of the conflict, to address unequal social relations and to remedy socio-economic conditions in any meaningful way. Indeed, during national transitional justice mechanisms, such as a truth commission, discourse is often framed around societal notions of 'forgiveness', 'reconciliation' and 'nation-building', and therefore the opportunity for individual empowerment and active participation is reduced. As van der Merwe explains:

Individual cases are addressed in order to create national awareness of the consequences for perpetrators (national scale deterrence) and to build national consensus around values. If the victim and the perpetrator are not directly affected by the intervention, but an effective message was sent regarding consequences of certain behaviour or affirmation of certain rules, the intervention would be seen as successful...

(1999: 102–103)

Thus, transitional justice is very much a public affair constrained by its over-riding aims of 'reconciliation' and 'nation-building'. What typically occurs is a linear dialogue by one stakeholder, who is asked a series of questions by a representative of the transitional justice mechanism. The objective here is to develop a shared narrative for the healing of society, not to create an opportunity for the victim and the offender to understand, qualify and question their victimisation with each other (Clamp and Doak 2012). Furthermore, within an institution like a truth commission it is very difficult to harness the type of shame discussed by Braithwaite (1989) that is so necessary for the successful reintegration of offenders; rather, he would argue that the confrontational shaming that occurs ultimately minimises the acknowledgement of responsibility and causes individuals to react defensively. As Wilson (2001) explains within the context of the South African Truth and Reconciliation Report, the findings are to be understood as a chronicle of acts embedded within a moral framework of denunciation. In this sense, transitional justice is qualitatively different from restorative justice in that its aims are communal. What emerges from this process is a compromising 'justice' – justice that is possible within the confines of the political settlement rather than that which is seen as legitimate by the stakeholders of a single event. This is an entirely new conception of restorative justice, one that challenges the established boundaries of what is considered to fall within the parameters of restorative justice.

Reconceptualising restorative justice conceptions for transitional settings

The lack of a single conception of restorative justice means that it has been moulded to suit a number of political, practical and instrumental agendas simultaneously. This is viewed as both a positive and a negative for restorative justice. It is positive in the sense that it can be adapted to suit local conditions (in terms of cultural constraints and/or requirements) and the type of conflict (individual, communal, societal) that needs to be resolved. However, it is negative in the sense that it may be used to achieve more disingenuous aims, such as legitimating (at a superficial level at least) inhumane acts of informal social control by groups within communities, right through to the introduction of policies by the state that appear to increase democratic participation while 'widening the net', increasing professionalised justice and raising unrealistic and unachievable expectations amongst those most affected by conflict.

As such, it is important that adequate space is given over to efforts to address the gap that exists within transitional settings in respect of the claims that are made about what restorative justice will achieve and what is experienced by stakeholders in reality. One approach to such an exercise is to cast our gaze back to the democratic restorative justice literature for some potential solutions in order to further enrich the use of restorative justice within transitional settings. In doing so, a number of opportunities arise whereby existing conceptions and processes can be modified to increase restorative outcomes not only for victims, but also for offenders and communities. These will be discussed in relation to the encounter, reparative and transformative conceptions outlined previously.

Strengthening encounter conceptions

In selecting cases that will qualify to give testimony, Freeman (2006) explains that commissions tend to adopt broad criteria which ensure a mix of people who reflect the country's regional, ethnic, racial and religious diversity; that less well-known cases may be given precedence over those that are familiar to the public; and that the readiness of a case for inclusion is assessed according to the stage of investigations that have taken place. It is natural to assume that there will be a number of enabling and constraining variables within the scope of a truth commission's remit; however, a lack of understanding about the reasons why particular issues are more important than others can be bewildering for stakeholders. In reflecting upon the South African TRC, for example, Leebaw (2001) highlights that victims were 'confused' and 'suspicious' about case selection as the cases chosen were often not of significant importance to the local community. Being transparent in decision-making and honest about the political context in which decisions are made may assist in making sure that victims and communities are better informed about what transitional mechanisms can achieve.

The way in which truth commissions are currently designed means that there is relatively little opportunity for stakeholders to engage directly with one another. However, it is possible to envisage how existing features might be adapted to promote more meaningful engagement between stakeholders. For example, it could be possible to engage in a normative dialogue with an offender (as opposed to just seeking to obtain the facts from him/her about previous transgressions) that may follow a similar structure to that found in conferencing processes (see Braithwaite 1999). This might be done by encouraging commissioners and other criminal justice practitioners to involve people that the offender cares about and also victims (where appropriate) in discussions about the offence and the circumstance that gave rise to it (Dignan 2002). It is interesting that, although there is relatively frequent reference to the need to reintegrate offenders, little attention is paid to how this might be done in transitional settings.

In addition, commissioners might be trained in conferencing techniques, which would allow them to develop the necessary skills required to facilitate discussion. Where this happens, it would be theoretically possible for larger numbers of people to talk about particular events from a number of different perspectives. Holding conferencing sessions within communities on issues that the community sees as being of importance would arguably lend greater legitimacy to the new administration than current nation-building attempts through remote truth and reconciliation commissions (see, for example, Millar 2011). Currently, within these transitional justice mechanisms, testimony from a single person is extrapolated to the broader community in terms of either the suffering endured under the previous regime or the values needed to transition to a peaceful future. Drawing on experiences more generally and categorising the broad themes that emerged from the discussions may not only be more important to local communities, but may also offer a deeper appreciation of what it is that communities need in order to move forward in a peaceful way. A good example of such an approach in action is provided by Coates *et al.* (2006) in which 150 people participated in a community conference dealing with hate crimes and racial tensions in the United States.

Some criticisms levelled at truth commissions are that it reduces the previous conflict to a series of single incidents between individuals and that those who participate are not given adequate support to deal with the trauma that they have experienced. A more radical suggestion could be to transform the place of stakeholders within national transitional justice mechanisms altogether. In order to meet the objective of nation-building, truth commissions might be reserved to deal with the broader themes of the conflict, including the role of institutions in committing or perpetuating human rights abuses. In seeking to deal with issues of inter- and intra-personal importance, local justice mechanisms could be harnessed. Roche (2005), for example, has suggested that referrals could be made to existing local justice institutions, which would be able to report findings and make recommendations to national commissions on the basis of their own experiences, thus reducing the gulf between these institutions and local communities. Where community-based justice initiatives have ownership over processes, work carried out by perpetrators to assist in meeting not only their victims needs but also the community's needs could form a condition under which amnesty would be granted. Mallinder (2009: 158) suggests that by including a more integrative approach to justice it can 'contribute to breaking the cycles of power and oppression which frequently exist in transitional societies' and potentially result in a better chance of perpetrators becoming fully reintegrated into their communities.

In many ways, these alterations would serve to deprofessionalise transitional justice mechanisms to allow a more effective response to the needs and concerns of stakeholders on the ground. It has been suggested elsewhere that, where face-to-face meetings are not possible between stakeholders, it may still be possible for discussions to occur through a facilitator who acts as a messenger for the parties to communicate with one another (see Clamp 2014). This would circumvent some of the issues raised whereby relations are very fragile or where location (i.e. distance between stakeholders) and/or incapacitation might be an issue.

Strengthening reparative conceptions

At present, the way in which reparation is approached in transitional settings is far from ideal from a restorative perspective. Not all victims receive reparation, nor are all reparative activities representative of the amount of harm experienced by victims and, much as in democratic settings, victims often have to wait a considerable amount of time for any compensation to be paid (frequently in small sums) and on terms set by the state. Furthermore, the victim and offender are not only passive in the process, but could be described as missing altogether in deciding what reparations would be suitable and how they could be realised. As such, the kind of reparation that is ultimately received is often inferior in many respects to the kind of reparation that might be expected to emanate from a restorative justice process. For example, Dignan suggests that state-funded reparation:

> is far less flexible, is less likely to address the particular needs and sensitivities of the parties, and lacks the empowering potential that may ensue when victims and offenders are given the opportunity to participate actively in the offence resolution process.

(2002: 183)

One way to overcome these limitations is to draw on the experience of conventional criminal justice whereby offenders (this could be individuals, communities or institutions) are fined or directed to engage in a form of reparation through community service. Although, in the democratic restorative justice literature, direct reparation (whether material or symbolic) would always be preferable whereby a known offender repairs a specific harm directly to a known victim, this, for obvious reasons, is not always achievable in transitional settings. As such, a symbolic gesture of remorse for any wrongdoing could be made in terms of a financial donation to a 'Victim's Fund', which would enable victims to receive reparation from a meaningful source. Unlike the Victim's Fund of the ICC which accepts voluntary contributions from indivdiuals, corporations, governments and others more generally, what is being proposed here is that contributions are from local actors who have been directly involved in the conflict themselves, either as perpetrators or beneficiaries. Victims could then be offered reparations directly from the funds available in the pot or the state could offer the funding upfront and be reimbursed as the pot grew. Naturally, individuals are often far less able to offer large sums of money and policymakers could look to drafting enabling legislation that would seek suitable funds from corporations who benefitted from the policies of the previous regime in the form of fines.

An alternative approach would be to adapt other mechanisms, such as community justice programmes that may have been developed during the conflict to respond to the legitimacy deficit, to ensure that they are capable of producing more reparative outcomes. Where offenders were unable to provide financial recompense for their harmful actions, they could undertake voluntary work on behalf of the victim (this could involve assisting in repairing damaged property or cultivating land on which to grow food or undertaking chores where a victim has been incapacitated) or for the community more broadly (this could involve a range of regeneration projects) that would draw on their skills and/or interests. In many respects, this would not only be more restorative than handing over money as outlined above, but it may also contribute to responding to the lack of reintegration initiatives evident in transitional justice settings. For the most part, this is due to the fact that such activities would not only have some meaning for the offender, but may also contribute to their self-worth in knowing that they have provided something of tangible value to the community. Harnessing these untapped resources within transitional settings may have two further consequences. The first is that additional resources would be secured not only in terms of funds, but also in terms of valuable labour that would help to improve day-to-day living in a meaningful way. The second is that further criminal behaviour may be avoided if ex-political prisoners and mercenaries can find positive, and perhaps more importantly, legitimate ways of contributing to community life post-transition (Dwyer 2015; Ozerdem 2012). This strengths-based approach to rehabilitation is gaining ground within democratic settings and could have significant and important consequences if applied to transitional justice settings.

Strengthening transformative conceptions

Calls to move away from established definitions and responses to crime such as those that fall under the transformative conception of restorative justice clearly have some resonance for transitional settings where the boundaries between victims and offenders are often blurred. In order for restorative justice to be successful, all stakeholders are required to perceive each other with humility, to accept differences and to compromise (Marshall 2007). However, this creates something of a dilemma for restorative justice in situations where group identity is emphasised over individual identity (Clamp 2014). Requiring one party to make amends for atrocities that have occurred may only serve to further embed the perception of 'us' versus 'them' and a feeling that a further injustice has occurred. In many respects, this conception of restorative justice calls for a radical transformation of the concept itself, whereby it would need to be defined beyond criminal justice.

Perhaps embracing a social harm definition of crime such as that outlined by Henry and Milovanovic (1994, 1996) would be of more value to transitional settings. The authors suggest that crimes can be categorised as 'harms of reduction' and 'harms of repression'. The former involves actions in which individuals experience some form of material loss and the latter involves an experience of future losses (i.e. aspirations and development). Refocusing crimes as harms means that the consequences of any behaviour, policy or action is propelled to a higher status than determining who was responsible for the harm and what needs to happen to them in order to restore the moral balance. In many respects, this could be realised by harnessing the community conferencing approach outlined earlier, whereby individuals are able to contribute to a discussion about a particular incident from a number of different positions, thus reducing the social distance between them. As Christie (2004) notes, it is easier for punitive or retributive justice to be applied to cases where the individuals concerned are not likely to inhabit the same communities. In transitional settings, however, victims and offenders often have to live in the same neighbourhoods as each other. Approaching the past without creating criminals can result in better understanding and a more stable basis from which to chart a peaceful future.

One challenge to this suggestion, as Braithwaite outlines in his chapter in this volume (Chapter 10), is that the structure and priorities of transitional justice mechanisms such as truth commissions can often be influenced or even set by individuals and organisations that do not have any local knowledge. Emerging democracies often rely on external funding, given that local resources may be substantially diminished following a protracted period of conflict and/or oppression. Nevertheless, there are creative solutions to this constraining variable in relation to restorative justice if we cast our attention to praxis in established democracies. In these settings, many restorative schemes are outsourced to non-governmental organisations or conducted in-house by various criminal justice agencies (such as REMEDI in the UK, Suggnomè in Belgium or the Restorative Justice Centre in South Africa). Restorative justice in emerging democracies could, arguably, be conducted in a similar way, with referrals being given to service providers (newly established or existing) who have sufficiently trained staff and who are fully supportive of restorative justice values. This would allow both victims and perpetrators to feel that they could explore both the causes and consequences of offending at a more personal level, thus generating an insight into each other's circumstances, away from the political justifications that emerge from societal platforms such as truth commissions and tribunals. In this way, it would allow what Halpern and Weinstein (2004) term an 'empathic connection' to emerge, which would allow adversaries to move beyond a position of co-existence and cohabitation to one of lasting peace.

Conclusion

This chapter has demonstrated that established conceptions of restorative justice can be a useful framework through which to evaluate the current conceptions of restorative justice that abound in transitional settings. Two particular conceptions were outlined, those that are concerned with the *interaction* between stakeholders (micro-level usage) and those that are more concerned with *symbolism* (macro-level usage). It has been argued that the former resonates with practice in democratic settings, although practice tends to be much bolder with both processes and values (encounter and reparative conceptions) underpinning responses to crime. In respect of the latter, it has been suggested that macro-political conceptions or uses of restorative justice tend to stretch the boundaries of restorative justice, given the prioritisation of symbolism at this level. For the most part, this is due to the fact that the macro-level usage of restorative justice often seeks to plug a justice gap (rather than to secure justice) and to secure hegemony over justice practices (rather than to find a means to return conflicts to the stakeholders).

While conceptual models of restorative justice are useful in examining programmes that claim to be restorative, there continue to be wide gaps between proponents in terms of what they conceive restorative justice to be. Indeed it has been suggested that some assert their particular conception with such zeal that they take on 'the tone of a weird inter-faith squabble in an obscure religious sect' (Bazemore and Schiff 2004: 51, cited in Johnstone and Van Ness 2007). However, restricting our conceptions of what restorative justice is to one model, given the complexities associated with justice, conflict and stakeholders in transitional settings, is perhaps not the most useful. As such, the chapter has sought to suggest ways in which the political uses of restorative justice might be strengthened to hold more positive outcomes for stakeholders by using the conceptual framework put forward by Johnstone and Van Ness (2007) and drawing on proposals put forward by scholars writing about democratic settings.

As Clamp and Doak (2012) have outlined, given the problematic nature of thinking about restorative justice within democratic settings, it follows that a much greater degree of caution needs to be exercised in how the 'restorative' label is employed in relation to transitional societies. It has been suggested that a more radical transformation of our conception of restorative justice is needed; transforming from a response that is concerned with responding to criminal acts to one that is focused on social harm more generally would yield more meaningful results for stakeholders. Muncie (2000: 223) articulates this approach as one that is 'less concerned with controlling, preventing and punishing and more with enabling, empowering and restoration'. He suggests that such a strategy is essential because, if we continue to ground our discussions 'within the established discourses of crime and criminal justice', it will only serve to 'close the door to any imaginative thinking' (Muncie 2000: 6). Undoubtedly, more theoretical and conceptual work is required to develop restorative justice that is suitable for the complex circumstances that underpin harm within transitional settings. It is hoped that this chapter and more broadly the contributions to this collection will provide a starting point for a much richer debate on how we might realise such an objective.[3]

Notes

1 It should be noted that this is a summary version of what transitional justice is. Various scholars have put forward definitions (see for example: Bell 2000, 2009; Bell *et al.* 2004; Benomar 1995; Posner and Vermeule 2004; Roht-Arriaza 2006; Teitel 2000) which have been critiqued and expanded by others (see for example: Boraine 2004; Nagy 2007; Otto 2006).
2 Although see Skelton (2005) who provides a challenge to this as the first use of the concept.
3 The author would like to thank Jonathan Doak for his valuable comments on an earlier draft of the chapter.

References

Aertsen, I., Arsovska, J., Rohne, H., Valiñas, M. and Vanspauwen, K. (2008) *Restoring Justice after Large-scale Violent Conflicts: Kosovo, DR Congo and the Israeli–Palestinian case*, Collumpton, UK: Willan Publishing.

Aukerman, M. (2002) 'Extraordinary Evil, Ordinary Crime: A framework for understanding transitional justice', *Harvard Human Rights Journal*, 15 (Spring): 39–97.

Bell, C. (2000) *Peace Agreements and Human Rights*, Oxford: Oxford University Press.

Bell, C. (2009) 'Transitional Justice, Interdisciplinarity and the State of the "Field" or "Non-field"', *International Journal of Transitional Justice*, 3(1): 5–27.

Bell, C., Campbell, C. and Ni Aolain, F. (2004) 'Justice Discourses in Transition', *Social and Legal Studies*, 13(3): 305–328.

Benomar, J. (1995) 'Justice after transitions', in N. Kritz (ed.) *Transitional Justice*, Washington, DC: United States Institute of Peace Press.

Boraine, A. (2004) *Transitional Justice as Emerging Field*, paper presented at the Repairing the Past: Reparations and Transitions to Democracy Symposium, Ottawa, Canada, 11 March.

Braithwaite, J. (1989) *Crime, Shame and Reintegration*, Cambridge, UK: Cambridge University Press.

Braithwaite, J. (1999) 'Restorative Justice: Assessing optimistic and pessimistic accounts', *Crime and Justice*, 25: 1–127.

Braithwaite, J. (2002) 'Setting Standards for Restorative Justice', *British Journal of Criminology*, 42: 563–577.

Braithwaite, J. (2003) 'Principles of restorative justice', in A. von Hirsch, J. Roberts, A. Bottoms, K. Roach and M. Schiff (eds) *Restorative Justice and Criminal Justice: Competing or reconcilable paradigms?* Oxford: Hart.

Braithwaite, J. (2007) 'Building legitimacy through restorative justice', in T. Tyler (ed.) *Legitimacy and Criminal Justice: International perspectives*, New York: Russell Sage.

Braithwaite, J. and Mugford, S. (1994) 'Conditions of Successful Reintegration Ceremonies: Dealing with young offenders', *British Journal of Criminology*, 34: 139–171.

Cain, M. (1988) 'Beyond informal justice', in R. Matthews (ed.) *Informal Justice?* London: Sage Publications.

Christie, N. (2004) *A Suitable Amount of Crime*, New York: Routledge.

Clamp, K. (2008) 'Assessing alternative forms of localised justice in post-conflict societies – youth justice in Northern Ireland and South Africa', in D. Frenkel and C. Gerner-Beuerle (eds) *Selected Essays on Current Legal Issues*, Athens: ATINER.

Clamp, K. (2010) 'The receptiveness of countries in transition to restorative justice: a comparative analysis of the role of restorative justice in transitional processes and criminal justice reform', unpublished thesis, University of Leeds.

Clamp, K. (2012) 'The Influence of Legal Culture, Local History and Context on Restorative Justice Adoption and Integration: The Czech experience', *Nottingham Law Journal*, 21: 107–120.

Clamp, K. (2014) *Restorative Justice in Transition*, London/New York: Routledge.

Clamp, K. and Doak, J. (2012) 'More than Words: Restorative justice concepts in transitional justice settings', *International Criminal Law Review*, 12(3): 339–360.

Coates, R., Umbreit, M. and Vos, B. (2006) 'Responding to Hate Crimes through Restorative Justice Dialogue', *Contemporary Justice Review: Issues in Criminal, Social, and Restorative Justice*, 9(1): 7–21.

Cohen, S. (1994) 'Social control and the politics of reconstruction', in D. Nelken (ed.) *The Futures of Criminology*, London: Sage Publications.

Crawford, A. and Clear, T. (2003) 'Community restorative justice: transforming communities through restorative justice?', in E. McLaughlin, R. Fergusson, G. Hughes and L. Westmarland (eds) *Restorative Justice: Critical issues*, London: Sage Publications.

Christie, N. (1977) 'Conflicts as Property', *British Journal of Criminology*, 17(1): 1–15.

Daly, K. and Proietti-Scifoni, G. (2011) 'Reparation and restoration', in M. Tonry (ed.) *The Oxford Handbook of Crime and Criminal Justice*, Oxford: Oxford University Press.

Dignan, J. (2002) 'Restorative justice and the law: the case for an integrated, systemic approach', in L. Walgrave (ed.) *Restorative Justice and the Law*, Collumpton, UK: Willan Publishing.

Dignan, J. (2005) *Understanding Victim and Restorative Justice*, Maidenhead: Open University Press.

Dwyer, C. (2015) 'Prisoner reintegration in a transitional society: The Northern Ireland experience', in A. McAlinden and C. Dwyer (eds) *Criminal Justice in Transition: The Northern Ireland Context*, Oxford: Oxford University Press.

Eglash, A. (1977) 'Beyond restitution: creative restitution', in J. Hudson and B. Galaway (eds) *Restitution in Criminal Justice*, Lexington, MA: DC Heath and Company.

Eriksson, A. (2009) *Justice in Transition: Community restorative justice in Northern Ireland*, Collumpton, UK: Willan Publishing.

Freeman, M. (2006) *Truth Commissions and Procedural Fairness*, Cambridge: Cambridge University Press.

Halpern, J. and Weinstein, H. (2004) 'Rehumanising the Other: Empathy and reconciliation', *Human Rights Quarterly*, 26(3): 561–583.

Hayner, P. (2000) *Unspeakable Truths: Confronting state terror and atrocity*, New York: Routledge.

Hayner, P. (2011) *Unspeakable Truths*, London: Routledge.

Henry, S. and Milovanovic, D. (1994) 'The constitution of constitutive criminology: A postmodern approach to criminological theory', in D. Nelken (ed.) *The Futures of Criminology*, London: Sage.

Henry, S. and Milovanovic, D. (1996) *Constitutive Criminology: Beyond postmodernism*, London: Sage.

Ivanišević, B. (2008) *The War Crimes Chamber in Bosnia and Herzegovina: From hybrid to domestic court*. New York: International Centre for Transitional Justice.

Johnstone, G. (2002) *Restorative Justice: Ideas, values and debates*, Collumpton, UK: Willan Publishing.

Johnstone, G. (2008) 'The agendas of the restorative justice movement', in H. Millar (ed.) *Restorative Justice: From theory to practice*, Bingley, UK: Emerald Group.

Johnstone, G. and Van Ness, D. (2007) 'The meaning of restorative justice', in G. Johnstone and D. Van Ness (eds) *Handbook of Restorative Justice*, Collumpton, UK: Willan Publishing.

Kurki, L. (2000) 'Restorative Justice and Community Justice in the United States', *Crime and Justice*, 27: 235–303.

Leebaw, B. (2001) 'Restorative Justice for Political Transitions: Lessons from the South African Truth and Reconciliaton Commission', *Contemporary Justice Review*, 4(3–4): 267–289.

Leebaw, B. (2003) 'Legitimation or Judgment: South Africa's restorative approach to transitional justice', *Polity*, 36(1): 23–51.

Llewellyn, J. (2007) 'Truth Commissions and restorative justice', in G. Johnstone and D. Van Ness (eds) *Handbook of Restorative Justice*, Collumpton, UK: Willan Publishing.

McCold, P. (2000) 'Toward a Holistic Vision of Restorative Juvenile Justice: A reply to the maximalist model', *Contemporary Justice Review*, 3(4): 357–372.

McCold, P. and Wachtel, B. (2003) *In Pursuit of Paradigm: A theory of restorative justice*. Paper presented at the XIII World Congress of Criminology, Rio de Janeiro, Brazil. www.realjustice.org/library/paradigm.html

McEvoy, K. (2008) 'Letting go of legalism: Developing a "thicker" version of transitional justice', in K. McEvoy and L. McGregor (eds) *Transitional Justice From Below: Grassroots activism and the struggle for change*, Oxford: Hart Publishing.

McEvoy, K. and Eriksson, A. (2008) 'Restorative justice in transition: Ownership, leadership and "bottom-up" human rights', in D. Sullivan and L. Tifft (eds) *Handbook of Restorative Justice: A global perspective*, London: Routledge.

McEvoy, K. and McGregor, L. (2008) *Transitional Justice from Below: Grassroots activism and the struggle for change*, Oxford: Hart Publishing.

Mallinder, L (2009) 'Exploring the practice of states in introducing amnesties', in K. Ambos, J. Large and M. Wierda (eds) *Building a Future on Peace and Justice: Studies on transitional justice, peace and development*, Berlin: Springer-Verlag.

Marshall, C. (2007) 'Terrorism, religious violence and restorative justice', in G. Johnstone, and D. Van Ness (eds) *Handbook of Restorative Justice*, Collumpton, UK: Willan Publishing.

Millar, G. (2011) 'Local Evaluations of Justice through Truth Telling in Sierra Leone: Postwar needs and transitional justice', *Human Rights Review*, 12: 515–535.

Minow, M. (1998) *Between Vengeance and Forgiveness: Facing history after genocide and mass violence*, Boston: Beacon Press.

Muncie, J. (2000) 'Decriminalising criminology', in G. Lewis, S. Gewirtz and J. Clark (eds) *Rethinking Social Policy*, London: Sage.

Nagy, R. (2007) *Transitional Justice as Global Project: Critical reflections*. Available from: www.cpsa-acsp.ca/papers-2007/Nagy.pdf

O'Mahony, D. (2012) 'Criminal Justice Reform in a Transitional Context: Restorative youth conferencing in Northern Ireland', *International Criminal Law Review*, 12(3): 549–571.

O'Mahony, D., Doak, J. and Clamp, K. (2012) 'Restorative Justice and Transitional Justice in Post-conflict Societies: Youth justice reforms in Northern Ireland and South Africa', *Northern Ireland Legal Quarterly*, 63(2): 267–288.

Otto, M. (2006) 'Transitional justice in the former Yugoslavia: the desirability and feasibility of an international TRC', unpublished thesis, University of Amsterdam.

Ozerdem, A. (2012) 'A Re-conceptualisation of Ex-combatant Reintegration: "Social Reintegration Approach"', *Conflict, Security and Development*, 12(1): 51–73.

Pavlich, G. (2005) *Governing Paradoxes of Restorative Justice*, London: Glasshouse Press.

Perriello, T. and Wierda, M. (2006a) *Lessons from the Deployment of International Judges and Prosecutors in Kosovo*. New York: International Centre for Transitional Justice.

Perriello, T. and Wierda, M. (2006b) *The Special Court for Sierra Leone under Scrutiny*. New York: International Centre for Transitional Justice.

Posner, E. and Vermeule, A. (2004) 'Transitional Justice as Ordinary Justice', *Harvard Law Review*, 117(2): 761–825.

Pranis, K. (2007) 'Restorative values', in G. Johnstone and D. Van Ness (eds) *Handbook of Restorative Justice*, Collumpton, UK: Willan Publishing.

Reiger, C. (2006) 'Hybrid attempts at accountability for serious crimes in Timor Leste', in N. Roht-Arriaza and J. Mariezcurrena (eds) *Transitional Justice in the Twenty-First Century*, Cambridge: Cambridge University Press.

Roche, D. (2001) 'The Evolving Definition of Restorative Justice', *Contemporary Justice Review*, 4(3–4): 341–353.

Roche, D. (2005) 'Truth Commission Amnesties and the International Court', *British Journal of Criminology* 45(4): 565–581.

Roht-Arriaza, N. (2006) 'The new landscape of transitional justice', in N. Roht-Arriaza and J. Mariezcurrena (eds) *Transitional Justice in the Twenty-First Century*, Cambridge: Cambridge University Press.

Scheffer, D. (2008) 'The extraordinary chambers in the courts of Cambodia', in M. C. Bassiouni (ed.) *International Criminal Law*, The Hague: Martinus Nijhoff Publishers.

Skelton, A. (2005) 'The influence of the theory and practice of restorative justice in South Africa with special reference to child justice', unpublished LLD Thesis, University of Pretoria, South Africa.

Teitel, R. (2000) *Transitional Justice*, New York: Oxford University Press.

Teitel, R. (2003) 'Transitional Justice in a New Era', *Fordham International Law Journal*, 26(4): 893–906.

TRC (1998) *Final Report*, Cape Town: Juta & Company.

Tutu, D. (1999) *No Future without Forgiveness*, London: Rider Books.

Umbreit, M. (1999) 'Avoiding the marginalization and "McDonaldization" of victim–offender mediation', in G. Bazemore and L. Walgrave (eds) *Restorative Juvenile Justice: Repairing the harm of youth crime*, New York: Criminal Justice Press.

Uprimny, R. and Saffón, M. (2006) 'Transitional Justice, Restorative Justice and Reconciliation. Some insights from the Columbian case', paper presented at 'Coming to Terms with Reconciliation: Critical Perspectives on the Practices, Politics and Ethics of Reconciliation' at the University of Wisconsin, November. Available at http://global. wisc.edu/reconciliation/library/papers_open/saffon.html

Van der Merwe, H. (1999) 'The Truth and Reconciliation Commission and community reconciliation: an analysis of competing strategies and conceptualizations', unpublished dissertation, George Mason University.

Van Ness, D. and Strong, K. (2002) *Restoring Justice: An introduction to restorative justice*, Cincinnati, OH: Anderson.

Waddell, N. and Clark, P. (2008) *Courting Conflict? Justice, peace and the ICC in Africa*, London: Royal African Society.

Walklate, S. (2005) 'Victimhood as a Source of Oppression', *Social Justice*, 32(1): 88–99.

Weirda, M., Nassar, H. and Maalouf, L. (2007) 'Early Reflections on Local Perceptions, Legitimacy and Legacy of the Special Tribunal for Lebanon', *Journal of International Criminal Justice*, 5(5): 1065–1081.

Wilson, R. (2001) *The Politics of Truth and Reconciliation in South Africa*, Cambridge: Cambridge University Press.

Woolford, A. and Ratner, R. (2010) 'Disrupting the Informal-formal Justice Complex: On the transformative potential of civil mediation, restorative justice and reparations politics', *Contemporary Justice Review*, 13(1): 5–17.

Young, J. (1988) 'Radical Criminology in Britain: The emergence of a competing paradigm', *British Journal of Criminology*, 28(2), 159–183.

Young, R. (2002) 'Testing the limits of restorative justice: the case of corporate victims', in C. Hoyle and R. Young (eds) *New Visions of Crime Victims*, Portland, OR: Hart Publishing.

Zehr, H. (2002) *The Little Book of Restorative Justice*, Intercourse, PA: Good Books.

3 Exploring restorative justice in situations of political violence

The case of Colombia

Isabella Bueno, Stephan Parmentier and Elmar Weitekamp

Introduction

When Canadian criminologist Howard Zehr published the book *Changing Lenses* in 1990, he could hardly have anticipated the enormous impact of this publication for many scholars and practitioners around the world. Not only has his work over the past quarter century proven to be highly seminal in changing the ways that many look at crime and conflicts, it has served to change the way to address them too. His unwavering plea for restorative justice is nowadays also taken as a point of departure to explore new areas of crime, including international crimes and serious human rights violations, which are commonly grouped together under the heading of 'transitional justice'. This is the main focus of the present volume.

This chapter also takes the field of international crimes and serious human rights violations as its object. Its central focus is to understand what a restorative justice 'lens' to such crimes and violations might look like and to what extent a 'restorative transitional justice' approach can be developed. As a way to connect theory and practice, this chapter focuses on the situation of ongoing violent conflict in Colombia, in which many human rights violations and international crimes have been and continue to be committed. By reporting on personal interviews with victims of and offenders in the violent conflict, it aims to highlight their understanding of a restorative approach in situations of transitional justice.

Our contribution takes the following structure: first, we briefly highlight some major characteristics of the restorative approach to justice and then explore their applicability to the field of transitional justice. Second, we sketch the main components of the Colombian violent conflict and report on some empirical data obtained from victims and offenders and relating to restorative justice. Our ultimate goal is to contribute to a richer understanding of restorative justice in situations of violent conflict and transitions to post-conflict situations.

'Changing lenses' to restorative justice for dealing with crime

Picca (2009) has argued that since the 1960s two phenomena in relation to crime and justice have caught the attention of the public: the rapid increase of grave criminality on the one hand, as well as the failure of criminal law and criminal justice to deal with it on the other hand. The latter was seriously criticised as an old-fashioned system that was and is operating according to 'the abstract philosophical and metaphysical notions of the Age of Enlightenment' (Fattah 2002: 309), a system susceptible to intensifying conflicts instead of promoting peace (Zehr 2002). As the idea of considering other ways of doing justice became a pressing necessity, it is no coincidence that restorative justice emerged in the late 1970s as an effort to address some of the needs and limitations of the conventional criminal justice system (Bueno 2014).

The limitations of the conventional criminal justice system are well known and documented by many. Criminal trials are considered too long, too expensive, too alienating, too exclusive, too complex and, above all, unable to meet the needs of victims, offenders and the communities. In the words of restorative justice scholars, criminal trials have taken the conflict away from the people involved in it (Christie 1977) and have failed 'to engage and empower those most directly affected by crime' (Sawin and Zehr 2007). Such criticisms stem from criminal justice systems that have been particularly conceived to inflict punishment on offenders and have downplayed, if not neglected, the reparation of the traumatic harm to victims and the reintegration of offenders (Bueno 2014).

In our view, the rapid development of restorative justice in the last decades can be seen to display three main characteristics (Bueno 2014): first, its general goal is to radically transform the vision and response to crime and the role of the justice system in contemporary societies (Johnstone and Van Ness 2007); second, its scope of application has gradually evolved from an initial focus on minor common crimes related to property offences to encompass more serious crimes of a physical nature (Umbreit *et al.* 2007); and third, in terms of its definition, debates are still ongoing between the 'process-oriented approach' (the purist or minimalist approach) aimed at bringing together all stakeholders in a conflict (McCold 2000), and the 'outcome-oriented approach' (the maximalist approach) intended to actually repair the harm that was caused by the offence (Bazemore and Walgrave 1999; Walgrave 2008). Looking at these extensive debates, Bueno (2014) has argued that three elements seem 'necessary' to define restorative justice: (a) the intention to repair the harm inflicted, (b) a non-vengeful active accountability aiming at repair of the harm and eventual reintegration of offenders, and (c) the intention to establish a respectful, participatory and flexible process of justice.

Within the maximalist view of restorative justice, and following Walgrave (2008), in this chapter we pay particular attention to the issue of 'active accountability', through which offenders thoroughly reflect on their acts and are willing to assume responsibility for them. While active accountability can play a role in various models of justice, including retributive justice, in our view it takes a special form in the context of restorative justice, as it is crucial in the process of repairing the harm inflicted upon victims as well as upon offenders themselves (Bueno 2014). We henceforth will use the notion 'restorative accountability' to imply accountability aiming at the repair of the harm inflicted on victims, offenders and communities on the one hand, and the eventual reintegration of offenders on the other hand. We will briefly discuss these two aspects of restorative accountability below.

Connecting accountability to repair of harm

What does accountability mean from a restorative justice perspective? According to Zehr (2002: 16), 'real accountability involves facing up to what one has done: it means encouraging the offenders to understand the impact of their behavior – the harms they have done – and to take steps to put things right as much as possible'. Following this logic, restorative accountability implies that offenders are encouraged to comprehend in depth the implications of their behaviour and take actions to put things right to the maximum possible extent. Some actions are focused on their own person, such as expressing remorse or regret, which in the words of Van Ness and Strong (2002) may have a great influence in stopping re-offending. Other actions are geared towards repairing the harm done to their victims and the community. Even in cases where the harm cannot (easily) be repaired, the acknowledgement of responsibility and symbolic measures of reparation could contribute to the repair of the harm to victims, communities and the offenders themselves (Braithwaite 2002; Zehr 2002). In our view and that of many others, the mere punishment of offenders does not constructively contribute to a repair of harm and cannot therefore be seen as an accountability measure in a restorative justice sense.

Connecting accountability to reintegration

Restorative justice in a maximalist view also establishes a close connection between accountability and reintegration. Although some offenders may need temporary restraint, nearly all of them are offered an opportunity to reintegrate into 'normal' society again, of course after having acknowledged their wrongdoings and taking positive steps to put things right. In Braithwaite's view shame may play a key role in the regulation of social behaviour by preventing or increasing reoffending. 'Reintegrative shame' focuses on the offenders' behaviour rather than on their person, and intends to bring them back into society as law-abiding citizens (Braithwaite 1989). Shame in this sense is not understood as an attack or aggression, but instead as the shame in admitting guilt in the face of family members, friends, and significant relations for whom the person feels respect and admiration. Other authors believe that empathy, more than shame, may trigger remorse and therefore consider that restorative justice should further implement processes that focus on repairing the harm and on the consequences of offending for others, families, communities and victims, instead of implementing shaming (disapproval) processes (Maxwell and Morris 2002). The bottom line of restorative justice is to judge the act and not the offender, based on the belief that those committing bad actions are not bad people in themselves (Stovel 2003).

'Broadening lenses' to transitional justice in the case of international crimes

What does the foregoing mean in the case of serious human rights violations, some of which amount to international crimes, such as systematic torture and/or rape, widespread disappearances, ethnic cleansing, the destruction of villages, massive killings, and genocide targeted at specific groups during violent conflicts? Is it thinkable to apply restorative justice, or some of its principles, to situations of mass violence and mechanisms of transitional justice? Is there, alongside theoretical schemes, any empirical evidence to support these ideas?

Discussions about how to deal with the dark legacy of the past tend to come up after authoritarian regimes have been replaced, by force or by negotiations, by more democratic forms of government. In such contexts of political transition the newly formed or newly elected elites face the difficult question of how to address the crimes and violations committed during and often by the former regime (Huyse 1996). In the early literature of the 1990s, transitional justice was defined as 'the study of the choices made and the quality of justice rendered when states are replacing authoritarian regimes by democratic state institutions' (Siegel 1998: 431). More recently, the United Nations has accepted a definition that is somewhat broader and more specific at the same time: transitional justice is seen as 'the full range of processes and mechanisms associated with a society's attempts to come to terms with a legacy of large-scale past abuses, in order to ensure accountability, serve justice and achieve reconciliation' (United Nations 2004: 4). Particularly the latter definition involves a number of elements, such as truth seeking, accountability, reparation and reconciliation, which scholars have considered relevant when analysing transitions (Parmentier and Weitekamp 2007; Teitel 2000). Moreover, it also broadens transitional justice to situations that do not include regime changes but relate to human rights abuses in established democracies and even during ongoing conflict (which is the case in Colombia, as explained below). Transitional justice mechanisms are many, but are usually considered to include the following four or five major pillars (ICTJ 2015; Teitel 2003): (1) criminal prosecutions, (2) truth commissions, (3) victim reparations, (4) memorialisation, and (5) institutional reforms. In our view, transitional justice does not constitute another approach to justice but rather a field of justice relating to extraordinary contexts.

It should be emphasised from the very outset that international crimes or serious human rights violations differ substantially from common or classical crimes in at least three major respects (Parmentier and Weitekamp 2007): first, the extremely violent character of the crimes, that frequently goes back to deeply rooted conflicts in the society concerned and generates a 'culture of violence'; second, the massive numbers of victims, which in the view of Fattah (1991) not only include individuals but also entire groups; and third, the political nature of the crimes, to the extent that they are committed for political reasons (defending power or defying power), directed against political objects (buildings, persons, etc.), and take place within a political context of (violent) conflict.

While the restorative justice model has increasingly gained attention in trans-itional contexts (Villa-Vicencio 2008), it may be seen as surprising that leading advocates of restorative justice have thus far remained quite modest in develop-ing a theoretical framework about the linkages between the two concepts. It seems that influential theories on restorative justice have primarily focused on common or classical crimes in times of normality and remain largely silent in respect of transitional justice contexts, including the role of restorative justice in addressing mass atrocities resulting from violent conflicts and repressive regimes (Llewellyn 2007; Weitekamp *et al.* 2006). The question of the applicability of restorative justice in cases of systematic political violence has been raised mostly as a result of concrete practices such as the renowned South African Truth and Reconciliation Commission (Llewellyn and Howse 1999; Parmentier 2001), the Rwandan *gacaca* courts (Clark 2011) and the Commission for Reception, Truth and Reconciliation in East Timor (Kent 2012), or in relation to specific forms of crime, such as state crime (Weitekamp and Parmentier 2014). Clamp (2014: 1) argues convincingly that:

> Whereas sophisticated work explores the use of reparation to respond to the past, the functioning of truth commissions and some community-based schemes, and the role of truth and amnesty in relation to reconciliation and political transition, only a limited analysis exists on what may be achieved by adopting a restorative framework in situations of mass violence and oppression.

Indeed, the scarce literature on the linkages between restorative justice and trans-itional justice refers to some existing mechanisms of transitional justice, but has not gone further to build a solid framework of their linkages (Aertsen *et al.* 2013).

As noted earlier, the main objective of our contribution is to understand the implications of restorative justice, not in the case of property and physical crimes of a common nature committed by individuals and organisations, but rather in situations of international crimes and serious human rights violations in which many individuals, groups and even state agencies play an active role. While we accept the major differences between common or classical crimes on the one hand, and international or political crimes on the other hand, we nevertheless wish to explore whether there is any value in applying restorative justice prin-ciples in the context of the latter category of crimes. Approaching transitional justice from a restorative perspective thus implies 'broadening lenses' to encom-pass other forms of crime, as well as other political and social contexts. For this purpose, we take the maximalist view of restorative justice as our point of depar-ture and hence focus on developments and mechanisms of transitional justice that aim at repairing the harm caused to victims, offenders and communities, as well as reintegrating offenders.

As highlighted above, the issue of accountability has generated many debates within restorative justice. With Villa-Vicencio (2008), we contend that restorative justice, because of its focus on restoration of the common good, can significantly contribute to transitional justice processes and mechanisms. Moreover, in our view 'restorative accountability' in transitional justice contexts can take place in exactly the same way as in the context of common crimes, i.e. by making the connection with the repairing of harm to victims, offenders and communities and the reintegration of offenders.

Connecting restorative accountability to repair of harm in transitional contexts

While the issue of accountability seems fairly straightforward in respect of common or classical crimes, it poses very different challenges in the case of international crimes, which may engage a multitude of individuals, groups and even state agents. Who can and should be held accountable in the case of mass atrocities, and how can and should this take place? The practice of national and international tribunals and courts over the last two decades clearly demonstrates that only a very selective number of guilty perpetrators are brought to criminal justice, leaving behind many individuals and groups who have significantly contributed to the violence and the victimisation but have succeeded in not being caught. Moreover, criminal justice pays no attention whatsoever to the category of bystanders, who – often literally – stood there and watched as the crimes were committed without taking any action, and sometimes even benefitted tangibly from the actions. As Fletcher and Weinstein (2002) have noted, 'trials do not address the complicity of those who stood by or cheered a vicious leader or who elected a war criminal to represent them'. Another aspect relates to the objectives of criminal justice for international crimes. Over the years, it is becoming more questionable whether retributive approaches to international crimes, whether through domestic or international tribunals, have clear and coherent purposes. Drumbl (2007) argues that even judges still doubt and frequently remain divided about the purpose of the punishment they inflict.

Truth commissions in particular, more than criminal prosecutions, have paid attention to repairing the harm inflicted upon the victims. The South African Truth and Reconciliation Commission, for example, has focused heavily on digging up various levels of truth about the many crimes committed during the Apartheid years for victims, communities, and even the offenders. In its view, 'a truth that would contribute to the reparation of the damage inflicted in the past and to the prevention of the recurrence of serious abuses in the future' can be called restorative truth (TRC 1998: 114). This type of truth can serve as a means to repair and acknowledge the victims' suffering, as well as liberate the heavy emotional burden of both victims and perpetrators through a process of storytelling and memory building. Furthermore and perhaps importantly, since international crimes tend to involve many perpetrators, forms of group dialogue and truth-telling processes can take place to generate a solid and deep reflection on the attitudes and structures that lie behind the atrocities and that need to be changed in the future. Another mechanism to discuss the suffering of those affected and provide some kind of truth consists of traditional forms of conflict settlement and justice, such as Mato Oput in Uganda, that can be used and reactivated in post-conflict settings (Salter and Huyse 2008).

Connecting restorative accountability to reintegration in transitional contexts

Stovel (2003: 1) has argued that approaching transitional justice from a restorative perspective would be obviously beneficial since

> [i]t is the form of justice most directly concerned with reconciliation. It addresses the reintegrative needs of both victims and most perpetrators. In poor countries with weak judicial systems, it offers an alternative to lengthy and expensive trials. And in much of Africa, it draws on pre-existing restorative justice traditions and institutions.

She continues that 'for the purposes of national peace building, there is no convincing reason why the victim needs to reconcile with, or even forgive, the perpetrator' (Stovel 2003: 11). In our view, repairing the harm, and not reconciliation between victims and offenders, constitutes the main goal of restorative justice, because reconciliation within oneself or with another person is an ideal emotional internal process and goal that cannot be imposed by any judicial process. This, however, does not in any way downplay the importance of the reintegration of offenders into society.

Towards 'restorative transitional justice'

In the preceding paragraphs, we have tried to explore some linkages between a restorative justice approach and the field of transitional justice. In the long run, both concepts could further integrate into a new model of what can be called 'restorative transitional justice', consisting of two major elements: on the one hand, offenders will have the opportunity to individually and collectively repair the direct and/or indirect harm to individual victims, the social harm to society, and even the harm to themselves; on the other hand, offenders who have repaired the harm will be given the possibility of reintegrating into society and avoiding similar violent behaviour in the future. For the moment, however, the question of 'restorative transitional justice', which refers to 'the variety of processes and mechanisms established to restore, to the extent possible, the individual and social harm caused by mass abuses' (Bueno 2013: 99), is hardly developed and suffers from a huge knowledge gap on the part of scholars, policy makers and practitioners.

One way of addressing this gap is by looking at the restorative elements of existing mechanisms of transitional justice, such as truth commissions or community-based forms of conflict resolution, and using them as illuminations for the further development of solid restorative mechanisms. In our opinion, transitional justice mechanisms that are restorative-oriented are likely to strongly contribute to the global restorativeness of a transitional justice society. The degree of 'restorativeness' in the words of McCold lies in the potential of restorative justice mechanisms to combine the interests of victims, offenders and community (McCold 2000). To the extent that transitional justice mechanisms, such as truth commissions or the like, are able to bring these three dimensions together, they can contribute to a higher level of restorativeness. For this to happen, various disciplines such as criminology, psychology, law, theology, and anthropology, among others, will need to study with creativity and openness the various pathways to the repair of the individual and social harm of victims and the reintegration of offenders.

All in all, we subscribe to the argument voiced by Arsovska *et al.* (2008: 453) that transitional justice requires

> a broad understanding of accountability which goes beyond mere individual responsibility. 'Accounting' for a violent past will include not only a recognition of what happened and the responsibilities associated with it, but also a commitment to make up for those wrongs and to prevent them in the future.

In fact, in the same ways in which crowds can massively harm and destroy, collective actions may have a greater impact in trying to restore what has been broken.

The arguments developed above have led Bueno (2014) to construct the following model (see Figure 3.1), which attempts to visualise the main features of a restorative justice approach in relation to mass atrocities and international crimes. Its primary goal is to repair the harm of all concerned and reintegrate the offenders along the lines highlighted above. The model encompasses the main components of a restorative approach when applied to the field of transitional justice: the various actors (victims, offenders and communities), the goals (repairing the harm and reintegration), the various forms of accountability (active, collective, direct/ indirect), and the principles and values of restorative justice. Following McCold's model, we argue that restorative justice mechanisms in transitional contexts that focus on one actor (offenders, victims, community) or two actors (victims–offenders, offenders–community, victims–community), are likely to contribute to restorativeness in a partial way. If they involve all three actors (as did the truth commissions with direct encounters between victims and offenders, followed by repairing of the harm and the reintegration of offenders) they are likely to reach the highest level of restorativeness. Such mechanisms are safe, respectful, non-vengeful, flexible and participatory. Finally, it should be noted that restorative transitional justice in this model is part of a larger context that also includes the promotion of human rights and the rule of law in the longer run.

The case of Colombia

How do these concepts relate to the ongoing violent conflict in Colombia? In this section, we provide a brief overview of the Colombian conflict and illustrate

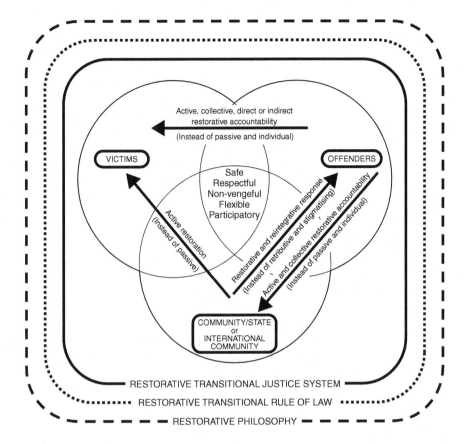

Figure 3.1 Primary goal of restorative justice is to repair the harm to victims and reintegrate the offenders.

the above concepts by means of some empirical findings. The following paragraphs draw heavily on the personal interviews with victims and perpetrators of the political violence conducted by Bueno (2014) in Colombia.

A brief sketch of transitional justice in Colombia

For more than half a century, Colombian society has lived through a very complex violent conflict that has generated millions of largely civilian victims of systematic and widespread crimes, including kidnappings, forced disappearances, sexual violence, under-age recruitment of minors, torture, extrajudicial executions, and massacres (Bueno and Diaz Rozas 2013). In particular, two left-wing oriented groups, the FARC (*Fuerzas Armadas Revolucionarias de Colombia*) and the ELN (*Ejército de Liberación Nacional*), and one right-wing group, the AUC (*Autodefensas Unidas de Colombia*, also known as the paramilitaries) have been behind these crimes. In the course of time, very lucrative revenues from illegal activities, such as drug trafficking, drug taxation, expropriation and kidnapping, have allegedly ended up controlling these groups' agendas to the point of distorting their original ideological motivations (Bueno and Diaz Rozas 2013).

In the last decade, several state-organised measures have been taken to establish a complex transitional justice process in Colombia (Bueno 2014; Gomez 2008; Uprimny and Saffón 2009). The starting point came on 25 July 2005, when Law 975 – better known as the Justice and Peace Law (JPL) – was enacted by presidential decree to 'ease the peace negotiations with the armed groups and the individual and collective reincorporation of the members into civil life, guaranteeing that the victims will have the right to truth, justice and reparation' (Article 1 – our translation). This law established a legal framework to offer reduced sentences with a maximum of eight years' imprisonment to members of paramilitary and guerrilla groups responsible for serious violations of human rights and not eligible for amnesty. According to Lyons (2010), the JPL established a criminal justice model based on confessions and offering the participants a significant reduction of sentences (five to eight years in prison) in exchange for the fulfilment of several conditions, including the cessation of criminal activities, full confessions of past crimes, and submission of all personal assets for victim reparation. In 2006, over 35,000 combatants – mostly paramilitary – demobilised and handed in more than 18,000 weapons (www. altocomisionadoparalapaz.gov.co), and, by 2013, more than 50,000 guerillas and paramilitaries together had demobilised (www.reintegracion.gov.co). In 2010, Congress enacted Law 1424, which established a non-judicial truth-seeking mechanism to unearth the patterns of serious human rights violations, and provided legal benefits to members of illegal organised armed groups in exchange for information about the conflict (ICTJ 2015). A year later came Law 1448 – the Victims' Law – with a comprehensive reparations programme and land restitution procedures for the many victims of the armed conflict (ICTJ 2015). In September 2012, the government and the FARC confirmed their intentions to start peace talks, which have been going on ever since, sometimes with unexpected interruptions and the temporary resuming of hostilities. As long as the political negotiations are ongoing, the violent conflict formally speaking also continues.

From a restorative justice perspective, it is noteworthy that Colombia has also introduced over the last 20 years several measures of restorative justice to address common crimes in an alternative manner, both in the Constitution of 1991 and in the Code of Criminal Procedure of 2004 (Pearson 2004). It could be seen to illustrate a growing interest in Colombian legal circles in dealing with crimes in a different and novel manner, which could be inspiring for the transitional justice mechanisms in the country. In the following paragraphs, we will briefly sketch how the fieldwork in Colombia was done, as well as describing some salient findings from the personal interviews with victims and ex-combatants of the violent conflict.

Victim and ex-combatant voices from the field

As part of her doctoral research on mass victimisation and restorative justice in Colombia, Bueno (2014) carried out extensive empirical work in various parts of the country and at different times within the period 2009–12. She conducted nearly 60 in-depth face-to-face interviews – nearly all in Spanish – both with victims and perpetrators of the violent conflict, ex-paramilitaries as well as ex-guerillas. Both samples were first constituted on the basis of objective criteria (types of victimisation for victims and ideological and group affiliation in the case of ex-combatants), and later completed on the basis of snowballing techniques. The interviews were audiotaped (unless the respondents opposed this), fully transcribed in the original language and analysed with the use of NVivo software. The preliminary results of the face-to-face interviews were later contextualised through three focus group meetings, with victims, indigenous communities and ex-guerillas respectively. The most relevant passages and quotes were translated into English. Throughout the empirical research process, the researcher used a semi-structured questionnaire with the aim of learning more about four key issues of transitional justice, i.e. truth-seeking about past facts, accountability for the acts committed, victim reparations and reconciliation between former enemies (based on the original TARR model developed by Parmentier 2003). She paid particular attention to the attitudes and opinions of her respondents in relation to a restorative justice approach to the violent conflict in Colombia.

Here, we briefly report on just three specific aspects that relate to restorative justice, namely the way in which victims and offenders looked at the harm inflicted upon them during the violent conflict, their perceptions about how to heal this harm, and their views on accountability for the crimes committed. The names of the respondents in the quotes have been changed to allow their anonymity and security.

Victims of the violent conflict were interviewed with the objective of understanding their experiences of victimisation and their attitudes towards healing. Although each individual had experienced the violent conflict in a different way, some common threads could be identified, mostly based on the type of victimisation they had encountered. Victims of kidnappings, for example, mostly talked about the feeling of 'being dead alive' and also expressed a deep rage about the human cruelty experienced during the period of abduction. Other victims were obliged to abandon their homes and talked about the trauma of losing everything and having to start life all over again 'from scratch'. Some also felt ashamed for having been displaced and not being able to do anything about this. Those victims who lost a loved one, often suddenly and in violent circumstances, expressed their deep trauma caused by the violence and later the permanent sense of loss. Some also talked about their desire for revenge, as well as the frustration of not knowing the truth about the facts that had occurred. Finally, members of indigenous communities mentioned the long-standing harm, over many centuries, as a result of the dominance of Western mentality and their necessary subjugation to it. They also expressed the pain of having to resist out-right extermination as a group and losing their spiritual guides during the violent conflict. Given these many different experiences of harm, it is not surprising that victims expressed diverse needs for healing and ideas about overcoming their state of victimisation. During the interviews, the most frequently mentioned options related to the importance of love and assistance from loved ones, the power or spirituality and values, the importance of professional psychological assistance and sharing with other victims, and the desire to participate in peri-odic healing programmes. Also particular forms of institutional assistance were often invoked, with a view to seeking for truth and obtaining reparation from the state of from the perpetrator directly. Some victims even expressed an interest in meeting the ex-combatant whom they considered responsible for the acts com-mitted. Bueno (2014: 170) concluded that 'victims live victimisation in different ways' and that their horrendous experiences and traumatisations had drastically altered the lives of most. Some had allegedly overcome these experiences, while for others it remained very difficult to recover from them.

Bueno (2014) also deliberately invested considerable time and energy in con-ducting interviews with ex-combatants, both ex-paramilitaries and ex-guerillas, which was far from obvious and, at times, far from secure. The strongest added value of these interviews definitely lay in gaining access to the viewpoint of per-petrators and understanding that they have also incurred harm and have been marked for life by the violent conflict. Being victimised, or considering them-selves victims, of the Colombian situation seemed one of the major causes of joining one of the illegal armed groups. Homero was a victim before he joined the left-wing guerilla group of the ELN-ERG:

> Right now we're [seen as] the accused, but, above this reality, we're also victims [of] this conflict, because the Colombian conflict has origins and it is in these roots that we found the motivation to take our arms and fight.
>
> (Bueno 2013: 170)

Also Alexandre explained how his initial displacement influenced his path towards paramilitarism (AUC):

> I started by being displaced and ended up being part of a subversive armed group ... I don't totally agree with the term 'offender'; people tell me I'm an 'offender', but you must not forget that I was first a victim, we, a family of 20, were forced to leave our hometown Amalfi...
>
> (Bueno 2013: 170)

More generally, ex-combatants talked about the trauma of having to live violent lives during the conflict, without much love from their families or peers, or freedom, and always facing the risk of being betrayed by other fighters. While they themselves were fighting, their families were often at risk and could also incur harm by other parties in the conflict. After demobilisation, ex-combatants expressed the heavy burden of being stigmatised and the difficulties of having to start their lives all over again. In terms of options for healing, they echoed the victims' wishes for love, spiritual guidance and professional assistance. Even more so, some expressed a deep interest in telling their stories and listening to those of others, and some also expressed a commitment to being held accountable and trying to repair the harm to their victims.

In addition to the findings reported above, it should be noted that one of the most controversial issues arising from Bueno's empirical research on transitional justice in Colombia relates to accountability for the crimes committed (Bueno 2014). Victims and offenders of the violent conflict across the board were thinking that mass atrocities would not have taken place without the collaboration and support of thousands of human beings working directly or indirectly, and for various different reasons, towards the development of the conflict. They concurred in their considerations that the Colombian conflict was not limited to the illegal armed groups, but also covered a vast range of variables and indirect offenders, without whom the conflict would never have reached such dimensions. Bueno's research clearly highlights that several victims and offenders of the violent conflict considered the Colombian state responsible because of its institutional absence and inability to offer economic and social opportunities to the poor. It had also been unable to fight against the corrupt politicians who had not ceased to steal the nation's public funds, and who had collaborated and financed the phenomenon of paramilitarism, together with generals, policemen and businessmen. One important respondent – paramilitary chief Alexandre, known as *El Aleman* – said that the Colombian state should assume its responsibility for having participated hand in hand with the paramilitaries during the conflict:

> For 46 years the politicians of this country have not been able to find a solution to a conflict that pushed me to take weapons and break the law and the constitution, and be here today assuming a responsibility that I must assume. But today, that institution that has been unable to find a solution to the problem pretends to prove to the world and to the Colombian society that we are responsible for everything.
>
> (Bueno 2013: 252)

Moreover, the interviews underscore the finding that many Colombians have strong opinions against the role of some non-governmental organisations (NGOs), which have financed and defended the actions of the guerrillas, as well as the international community, particularly some developed countries, which has financed the Colombian drug business. Along these lines, a victim of kidnapping by the guerrilla movement ELN argues that:

> The drug consumers, mainly the social ones, the NGOs defending these guerrilla groups, the weapon producers who gain so much money and cause so much prejudice, are equally responsible; they are active actors that

consciously cause harm because they want to cause it. And there are passive guilty ones, like the local authorities that allow this to happen and corruption to take place; corrupted authorities are guilty by omission, the other ones are guilty by action. I am amazed by the tolerance towards the consumption of drugs, it's amazing, amazing, you see it everywhere, it's amazing; each person that consumes drugs is killing someone, is killing someone physically!

(Bueno 2013: 257–258)

It could be argued that the international dimension of the conflict has frustrated many Colombians: not only do they consider developed countries guilty for the damages occurring on Colombian territory, but this international dimension also leads to pessimism with regards to an eventual solution to the conflict (Bueno 2014).

Finally, it should also be mentioned that some members of the indigenous communities considered that the roots of the violent conflict could be traced back to a disrespectful Western mentality. This is illustrated, for example, by Eliecer, a member of the Arhuacan indigenous community, who explained in his own words the way his community has been brutalised for many centuries:

For more than 500 years we have been victimised physically and mentally by various actors, call them Catholic missionaries, colonizers, settlers, peasants, guerrillas, paramilitaries and delinquents, all of them inflamed by their needs, in one way or another ended with the peace in our territory, amputating our rights as a community.

(Bueno 2013: 167)

Given the limited number of interviews and the specific type of questions, it is clear that these findings cannot be extrapolated to the whole of the Colombian population. But we argue that they are instructive nevertheless for two reasons: first, they provide more insight into the concrete ways that people have experienced various types of harm during the violent conflict – material, physical and emotional harm, that can also be linked to the types of victimisation experienced; second, the findings illustrate that not only have victims and communities at large incurred harm, but also perpetrators have been experiencing various types of harm in their capacity as members of paramilitary or guerilla organisations and even more so, some perpetrators can also be regarded, in some way, as victims of the conflict. These insights are of crucial importance in trying to link our empirical findings from Colombia back to the theoretical framework about restorative justice, and particularly the issue of restorative accountability.

Towards a restorative approach to the violent conflict in Colombia?

Given the complexity of the violent conflict in Colombia and the multitude of actors involved – individuals, organisations, the state, as well as international actors – it can be argued that a traditional criminal justice approach is not likely to generate fruitful ways to address some specific features of the violent conflict. First of all, criminal trials still largely operate on the basis of individual account-ability for massive collective crimes. In the words of Fletcher and Weinstein (2002): 'because the criminal justice system addresses only individual account-ability for criminalised acts, the evidence from social psychologists forces us to rethink the question of collective responsibility'. Although this expression is largely based on the operation of domestic criminal law and justice systems, it is mostly also applicable in the case of international criminal law and justice. Fur-thermore, it seems unlikely that the criminal prosecution of individuals will prevent future crimes or human rights violations from being committed. The argument of prevention is often formulated in defence of national and inter-national criminal prosecutions, but in our view lacks any hard evidence to back it up. As Aukerman (2002) notes, 'it is virtually impossible to assess whether or not the threat of prosecution has ever prevented genocide and war crimes'. Like-wise, the presence of national and/or international criminal trials has not pre-vented suicide bombers from committing atrocities, or actual guerrilla members in Colombia from continuing their illegal activities. Even in cases of eventual deterrence, we join Aukerman's (2002) point of view according to which 'it is unlikely that post-atrocity prosecution is the most effective way to prevent future atrocities'. Bueno's (2014) research highlights that there could even be a counter-effect, namely that some guerrillas have not demobilised and continue to fight because of fear of being locked up in prisons with poor living conditions and high levels of violence, to the extent of the possibility of being killed during detention. Thirdly, Bueno's empirical research has clearly demonstrated that some victims and offenders of the Colombian violent conflict believe that mass atrocities will continue to occur as long as they do not find a solution to the causes of the conflict – particularly corruption, the lack of social and economic opportunities for all citizens, and, above all, the drug business.

For these reasons, we suggest that it can be fruitful to explore a restorative justice approach to the violent conflict in Colombia, without implying that this is an easy or a certain road to travel. In line with the theory of restorative account-ability, such a road in our view comprises two aspects. The first is to connect accountability to restoration, and allow offenders to repair the harm that they have inflicted upon the victims, the communities and themselves. We know from the interviews that the harm is very extensive after five decades of conflict, that it encompasses various types (material, physical, emotional) and that it reaches deep into the daily lives and the psychological state of mind of the victims. But the interviews also highlight that the ex-combatants, who are normally seen as perpetrators of the crimes, have incurred harm. In our view, the recognition that all parties to the conflict have suffered and/or are suffering from the con-sequences thereof would be a major step forward in breaking through the binary black–white logic of dividing a society into two opposing categories, (innocent) victims on the one hand and (guilty) perpetrators on the other hand. The next step could be the mutual recognition by all parties involved of each other's harm, and, possibly, the acceptance of accountability on behalf of those who have caused harm. This, in turn, is essential in view of the repair of harm in its various types and levels, in the short and the long term. As mentioned before, the second aspect of restorative accountability lies in the reintegration of offenders in society. The interviews are instructive in suggesting that, without the restoration of the harm to victims, the successful integration of perpetrators in society is virtually impossible, because victims will continue to be frustrated otherwise. But if the repair of harm seems crucial, it will not be sufficient in itself to guarantee that the reintegration runs in a smooth manner. Other mechanisms and processes will be needed to allow offenders to become part of Colombian society again, if only because they can contribute in their own way to the fundamental transformation of society.

In our view, no transitional justice institution in Colombia seems to provide the space to allow for these processes of restoration and reintegration to take place on a large scale: the traditional criminal justice system suffers from the classical weaknesses in relation to accountability and reparation, while the recent truth commission and the victim reparations programmes seem – at first sight – too fragmented to encompass all aspects under one heading. As a result, much more imagination will be needed to even start thinking along the lines of a restorative justice approach. This assessment, however, does not make any efforts in such a direction redundant or useless, particularly in view of the vast needs in Colombian society to put an end to the violence and move towards a better future. Maybe the growing attention on restorative justice mechanisms to deal with common crimes, as now entrenched in Colombian codes, could provide an interesting source of inspiration and mutual enrichment.

Note to conclude

Although it is difficult to come up with hard conclusions at the end of this chapter, it is worthwhile recalling the major tenets of our intellectual journey. As our point of departure, we argued that restorative justice has developed in and largely remained constrained to the field of common or classical crimes and has remained quite silent in the face of the rapidly developing field of transitional justice that deals with international crimes and serious human rights violations. Hence the central focus of our contribution, namely to understand how the restorative justice 'lens' could be 'broadened' to include transitional justice developments and mechanisms. In doing so, we have focused on restorative accountability for the crimes committed, and identified two crucial aspects: the repairing of the harm to victims, communities and offenders, and the reintegration of offenders into society. These two aspects are equally important in the case of common crimes as in the situation of international crimes.

Through the angle of the violent conflict in Colombia, we have tried to generate some empirical findings in relation to these theoretical concepts. The interviews with victims and ex-combatants have highlighted many interesting ideas about the two aspects – the repairing of the harm and the reintegration into society. It is now clear that all parties to the violent conflict have suffered and continue to suffer from many different types of harm, and we think that the mutual recognition of each other's harm is essential to assume accountability and try to effectively restore the harm. This is very important, and possibly even a prerequisite, for the successful reintegration of offenders into society. The findings also support the idea that the current transitional justice mechanisms in Colombia seem unlikely to generate any of the above effects, because they are insufficiently equipped to address the many challenges posed by a long and violent conflict with the involvement of many parties, individual and collective, and deeply rooted in social and economic problems. For this reason alone, it is worthwhile to explore innovative options – in research and practice – to address the past and construct a better future, both for Colombia and other conflict areas in today's world.

References

Aertsen, I., Parmentier, S., Vanfraechem, I., Walgrave, L. and Zinsstag, E. (2013) 'An Adventure is Taking Off. Why *Restorative Justice: An International Journal?*', *Restorative Justice: An International Journal* 1(1): 1–14.

Arsovska, J., Valinas, M. and Vanspauwen, K. (2008) 'From micro to macro, from individual to state: restorative justice and multi-level diplomacy in divided societies', in I. Aertsen, J. Arsovska, H. Rohne, M. Valiñas and K. Vanspauwen (eds) *Restoring Justice after Larger-Scale Conflicts: Kosovo, DR Congo and the Israeli–Palestinian case*, Collumpton, UK: Willan Publishing.

Aukerman, M. (2002) 'Extraordinary Evil, Ordinary Crime: A framework for understanding transitional justice', *Harvard Human Rights Journal*, 15 (Spring): 39–97.

Bazemore, G. and Walgrave, L. (1999) 'Restorative justice: in search of fundamentals', in G. Bazemore and L. Walgrave (eds) *Restorative Juvenile Justice: Repairing the harm of youth crime*, Monsey, NY: Criminal Justice Press.

Braithwaite, J. (1989) *Crime, Shame and Reintegration*, Cambridge: Cambridge University Press.

Braithwaite, J. (2002) *Restorative Justice and Responsive Regulation*, Oxford: Oxford University Press.

Bueno, I. (2013) *Mass Victimization and Restorative Justice in Colombia. Pathways towards peace and reconciliation?*, Doctoral dissertation, Leuven: Faculty of Law, KU Leuven.

Bueno, I. (2014) *Mass Victimization and Restorative Justice in Colombia*, Saarbrücken: Scholars' Press.

Bueno, I. and Diaz Rozas, A. (2013) 'Which Approach to Justice in Colombia under the Era of the ICC', *International Criminal Law Review*, 13(1): 211–247.

Christie, N. (1977) 'Conflicts as Property', *British Journal of Criminology*, 17(1): 1–15.

Clamp, K. (2014) *Restorative Justice in Transition*, London: Routledge.

Clark, J. (2011) 'Transitional Justice, Truth and Reconciliation: An under-explored relationship', *International Criminal Law Review*, 11(2): 241–261.

Drumbl, M. (2007) *Atrocity, Punishment, and International Law*, Cambridge: Cambridge University Press.

Fattah, E. (1991) *Understanding Criminal Victimization*, Scarborough CA: Prentice Hall Inc.

Fattah, E. (2002) 'From philosophical abstraction to restorative action, from senseless retribution to meaningful restitution: just deserts and restorative justice revisited', in E. Weitekamp and H. Kerner (eds) *Restorative Justice: Theoretical foundations*, Collumpton, UK: Willan Publishing.

Fletcher, L. and Weinstein, H. (2002) 'Violence and Social Repair: Rethinking the contribution of justice to reconciliation', *Human Rights Quarterly*, 24: 573–639.

Gómez, F. (2008) 'Verdad, justicia y reparación en el proceso de desmovilización paramilitar en Colombia', in F. Gómez (ed.), *Colombia en su laberinto. Una mirada al conflicto*, Madrid: Los Libros de la Catarata.

Huyse, L. (1996) 'Justice after transition: on the choices successor elites, make in dealing with the past', in A. Jongman (ed.) *Contemporary Genocides*, Leiden: PIOOM.

International Centre for Transitional Justice (2015) *What is Transitional Justice?* Available at: www.ictj.org.

Johnstone, G. and Van Ness, D. (2007) 'The meaning of restorative justice', in G. Johnstone and D. Van Ness (eds) *Handbook of Restorative Justice*, Collumpton, UK: Willan Publishing.

Kent, L. (2012) *The Dynamics of Transitional Justice. International models and local realities in East Timor*, London: Routledge.

Llewellyn, J. (2007) 'Truth Commissions and restorative justice', in G. Johnstone and D. Van Ness (eds) *Handbook of Restorative Justice*, Collumpton, UK: Willan Publishing.

Llewellyn, J. and Howse, R. (1999) 'Institutions for Restorative Justice: The South African Truth and Reconciliation Commission', *University of Toronto Law Journal*, 49(3): 355–388.

Lyons, A. (2010) 'For a just transition in Colombia', in M. Reed and A. Lyons (eds) *Contested Transitions: Dilemmas of transitional justice in Colombia and comparative experience*, Bogota: International Centre for Transitional Justice.

McCold, P. (2000) 'Toward a Holistic Vision of Restorative Juvenile Justice: A reply to the maximalist model', *Contemporary Justice Review*, 3(4): 357–372.

Maxwell, G. and Morris, A. (2002) 'The role of shame, guilt and remorse in restorative justice processes for young people', in E. Weitekamp and H.-J. Kerner (eds) *Restorative Justice: Theoretical foundations*, Collumpton, UK: Willan Publishing.

Parmentier, S. (2001) 'The South African Truth and Reconciliation Commission: towards restorative justice in the field of human rights', in E. Fattah and S. Parmentier (eds) *Victim Policies and Criminal Justice on the Road to Restorative Justice. Essays in Honour of Tony Peters*, Leuven: Leuven University Press.

Parmentier, S. (2003) 'Global Justice in the Aftermath of Mass Violence: The role of the International Criminal Court in dealing with political crimes', *International Annals of Criminology*, 4(1–2): 203–224.

Parmentier, S. and Weitekamp, E. (2007) 'Political crimes and serious violations of human rights: towards a criminology of international crimes', in S. Parmentier and E. Weitekamp (eds) *Sociology of Crime, Law and Deviance: Vol. 9, Crime and Human Rights*, Oxford: Elsevier Press.

Pearson, A. (2004) *Can Colombian Community Justice Houses Help the New Criminal Justice System Achieve Restorative Results?* Paper presented at 'New Frontiers in Restorative Justice: Advancing Theory and Practice', Centre for Justice and Peace Development, Massey University at Albany, New Zealand, 2–5 December.

Picca, G. (2009) *La Criminologie*, Paris: PUF.

Salter, M. and Huyse, L. (2008) *Traditional Justice and Reconciliation after Violent Conflict: Learning from African experiences*, Stockholm: IDEA.

Sawin, J. and Zher, H. (2007) 'The ideas of engagement and empowerment', in G. Johnstone and D. Van Ness (eds) *Handbook of Restorative Justice*, Collumpton, UK: Willan Publishing.

Siegel, R. (1998) 'Transitional Justice: A decade of debate and experience', *Human Rights Quarterly*, 20: 431–454.

Stovel, L. (2003) *When the Enemy Comes Home: Restoring justice after mass atrocity.* Vancouver: Restorative Justice Conference. Retrieved from www.sfu.ca/cfrj/fulltext/stovel.pdf.

Teitel, R. (2000) *Transitional Justice*, New York: Oxford University Press.

Teitel, R. (2003) 'Transitional Justice Genealogy', *Harvard Human Rights Journal*, 16(Spring): 69–94.

Truth and Reconciliation Commission of South Africa (TRC) (1998) *Final Report*, Cape Town: Juta & Company.

Umbreit, M., Vos, B. Coates, R. and Brown, K. (2007) 'Victim-offender dialogue in violent cases: a multi-site study in the United States', in E. Van der Spuy, S. Parmentier and A. Dissel (eds) *Restorative Justice: Politics, policies and prospects*, Cape Town: Juta Publishers.

United Nations, Security Council (2004) *The Rule of Law and Transitional Justice in Conflict and Post-conflict Societies*, Report of the Secretary-General to the Security Council, 23 August 2004, S/2004/616.

Uprimny, R. and Saffón, M. (2009) 'Uses and abuses of transitional justice in Colombia', in M. Bergsmo and P. Kalmanovitz (eds) *Law in Peace Negotiations*, Oslo: International Peace Research Institute.

Van Ness, D. and Strong, K. (2002) *Restoring Justice*, Cincinnati, OH: Anderson Publishing.

Villa-Vicencio, C. (2008) 'Transitional justice, restoration, and prosecution', in D. Sullivan and L. Tifft (eds) *Handbook of Restorative Justice: A global perspective*, London: Routledge.

Walgrave, L. (2008) 'Restorative justice: an alternative for responding to crime?', in G. Shlomo Shoham, O. Beck and M. Kett (eds), *International Handbook of Penology and Criminal Justice*, Oxford: Taylor & Francis, CRC Press.

Weitekamp, E. and Parmentier, S. (2014) 'Restorative justice and state crime', in D. Weisburd and G. Bruinsma (eds) *Encyclopedia of Criminology and Criminal Justice*, New York: Springer Verlag.

Weitekamp, E., Vanspauwen, K., Parmentier, S., Valiñas, M. and Gerits, R. (2006) 'How to deal with mass victimization and gross human rights violations: a restorative justice approach', in U. Ewald and K. Turkovic (eds) *Large-Scale Victimisation as a Potential Source of Terrorist Activities – Importance of Regaining Security in Post-Conflict Societies*, Amsterdam: IOS Press.

Zehr, H. (1990) *Changing Lenses*, Scottdale, PA: Herald Press.

Zehr, H. (2002) *The Little Book of Restorative Justice*, Intercourse, PA: Good Books.

4 Restorative justice and reconciliation

The missing link in transitional justice

Wendy Lambourne

Introduction

The literature on restorative justice is rich and complex, with various definitions and understandings of how to practise restorative justice in a domestic criminal justice and other settings and, more generally, as a value or principle for living. It is perhaps no wonder then that the understanding of restorative justice reflected in the transitional justice literature is neither clear nor comprehensive (Clamp and Doak 2012). Transitional justice comprises both judicial and non-judicial mechanisms designed to deal with past human rights violations with a view to achieving accountability and building democracy, rule of law, peace and reconciliation (United Nations 2004). Overall, however, the field of transitional justice has failed to grapple sufficiently with the concept of justice and the multiple ways in which it can be interpreted and achieved. This is especially so in light of the 'justice cascade' (Sikkink 2011) and the 'duty to prosecute' (Orentlicher 1991) which are reflected in the Joinet principles and the key pillars of transitional justice as espoused by the United Nations (2010).

The existing literature on justice more broadly, and restorative justice in particular, has not been sufficiently discussed or debated within the transitional justice field which sees itself as defining justice in relatively narrow legal, judicial, criminal and prosecutorial terms. Retributive justice is assumed and promoted actively as a goal, often without regard for the value of other forms of justice, most notably restorative justice and socioeconomic or distributive justice – the forward looking arm of reparations or restitution – and how these various forms of justice interact, contradict or complement each other in theory or in practice.[1] In some cases, truth commissions have been seen as providing a restorative justice alternative or complement to prosecutions for societies in transition, in much the same way as various restorative practices have done in the domestic criminal justice context, but how the process works in the transitional justice setting has not been studied in anywhere near as much depth as in the restorative justice literature.

This chapter will unpack the concept of restorative justice as debated in domestic criminal justice settings and its application in the context of transitional justice, and how the key pillars of transitional justice interconnect with restorative justice as a means, a mechanism and a goal. As part of this analysis, I consider the relationship between restorative justice and reconciliation, which I argue is pivotal to understanding how to produce restorative outcomes in transitional justice settings. I suggest that, by excluding reconciliation as a pillar of transitional justice; regarding it as an overarching goal; and privileging retributive justice in the form of prosecutions, transitional justice is failing to achieve its potential as a restorative or transformative process. By contrast, the combination of restorative and retributive elements in many traditional informal justice approaches provides a model of transitional justice that is more comprehensive and, I argue, more likely to support peacebuilding. The main focus of this chapter is thus to develop an argument about how a more explicit understanding and incorporation of restorative justice as part of transitional justice can contribute to a more effective process of dealing with the past and building peace in societies recovering from mass violence.

Restorative justice

Restorative justice in the domestic criminal context has been defined in various ways – in terms of process, participants, values and goals or outcomes (Johnstone 2011). A prescriptive approach to restorative justice conceptualises the process as creating an obligation to put things right or repair the harms caused by the crime or act – physical, material and emotional harms primarily, but also potentially moral and spiritual harms. In this model the goal is to address underlying causes and meet the needs not only of victims, but also of offenders and the community, and thus to produce restorative outcomes (Zehr 2005). The process is thus an inclusive one, and envisages an encounter between the victim and offender and the key stakeholders or community members, such as the friends, family or colleagues of each party. This is seen as contrasting with the dominant Western criminal justice focus on retributive justice for a crime that is a violation of the law of a state, where the perpetrator's crime is the centre of the process and the goal is to determine guilt and an appropriate punishment (Zehr 2002).

In this normative perspective, restorative justice is seen as requiring a transformation in how crime is viewed and responded to in society (Braithwaite 1989; Zehr 2005). However, in more pragmatic approaches to restorative justice, some of these key distinguishing features may be missing or conceived differently. One major approach defines restorative justice in terms of a process – i.e. how the offender, victim and key stakeholders interact – while others focus instead on values that produce a restorative outcome – i.e. healing rather than hurting (Braithwaite and Strang 2001). A restorative process may therefore result in a non-restorative outcome, while a non-restorative process may produce a restorative outcome. These approaches are essentially descriptive, in that they report on what happens rather than seeking to engineer social change. Without taking a normative approach, restorative justice is unlikely to achieve social transformation.

Braithwaite's concept of reintegrative shaming as forming a key part of the restorative justice process is a normative and value-based approach that aims to reconnect punishment with shaming in a way that does not stigmatise, but rather enables the reintegration of the offender into society (Braithwaite 1989; Johnstone 2007: 97–101). This is reminiscent of many traditional, indigenous non-Western justice processes where the offender acknowledges what he or she has done and the harm that it has caused, and as a result may undergo some form of punishment determined by a community elder, and yet the final outcome of the process is seen as a restoration of the relationship between the offender and the community (Lambourne 2010a; Walgrave 2008). In both cases, there is an experience of shame rather than guilt that enables the offender to voluntarily take on obligations to repair the harm, rather than being forced to do so by the state or a court of law (Braithwaite 1989). Zehr (2005: 209) also suggests that some aspects of restorative justice such as paying restitution may be experienced as painful or as punishment, so we can conclude that retributive justice may be experienced as complementary or even part of the same justice process (Lambourne 2010b).

To further illustrate the underlying psychological processes at work in restorative justice, Stauffer (2007) provides an account of a normative and value-based approach that aims to capture the 'spirit' of restorative justice through three primary images. He suggests that restorative justice can be represented, first by an anchor of safety and security; second, as a reservoir of relational networks and community building; and, finally, as a beacon for harmony, well-being and life-purpose. The first two images of Stauffer's model directly relate to the three steps of trauma recovery identified by Herman (1992): safety, acknowledgement and reconnection. Stauffer explains his second image in terms of the need of those caught up in 'the chasms of social and criminal breaches' to find a sense of community, and to regain hope and pursue healing through acknowledgement and identity transformation, which he contrasts with the isolation and humiliation of the dominant narrative of retributive justice. His process-oriented approach to restorative justice thus draws on psychosocial theory as well as spiritual inspiration, especially in his third image of the healing power of the survivor and the potential for rehabilitation of the offender.

The principle of mutual participation in an encounter and in determining harms and obligations that is associated with various restorative justice models is consistent with the principle espoused by scholars and practitioners of conflict resolution or conflict transformation – which depends on mutual participation and ownership of the process and outcome (Lederach 1995). Conflict or dispute settlement, by contrast, is seen as less sustainable because the process is controlled by an outside body such as a court, and the outcome is determined by an outside arbiter such as a judge (Sanson and Bretherton 2001). The goal of conflict resolution is to meet the underlying needs of all participants in the conflict, not just one aggrieved party, while the goal of conflict transformation is to transform the relationships and structures that produce and enable destructive and violent outcomes (Burton 1990; Lederach 1995). Restorative justice as a practice in Western societies is thus intimately bound up with the principles of conflict resolution and conflict transformation, which envisage win–win outcomes, rather than with the traditional Western court system, which produces winners and losers (Zehr 2002).

However, the principle of mutual participation in determining the outcome differs from some non-Western traditions in which the victim may still play a key role in the process, but it is a trusted elder who determines the appropriate punishment or reparation to be made by the offender to the community. The entire community is seen as the party that has been harmed, including the offender, so the fundamental aim of a traditional non-Western justice or conflict resolution processes is to restore community. It is therefore not the individual victim or party to the conflict who negotiates the outcome with the offender or other party, but rather a representative of the community who decides. Now this process is starting to sound very familiar – the community/state is the harmed party, and the arbiter is a representative of the community/state (a judge).

So what is the distinguishing feature of restorative justice practice compared with the type of justice produced by the traditional Western court system? I argue that it is the conversion of means into ends that has undermined the efficacy of the Western court system as a restorative justice system in both domestic and international criminal justice settings. Punishment and incarceration have become the end goals rather than being seen as means to an end: the restoration of the legal and moral order in society. From this perspective, retributive justice thus becomes effective only when it is implemented in the context of a restorative justice aim. This is the basis of my critique of the transitional justice field: it has failed to successfully grapple with the need to restore community as a fundamental goal and has instead focused on the right to justice in prosecutorial and retributive terms. This is, of course, similar to the arguments for the introduction of restorative practices in the domestic criminal justice context.

One of the challenges in the application of restorative justice in both the domestic criminal justice system and transitional justice context is the perception of victims that restorative justice is an alternative to retribution. As I have argued elsewhere, the human need for justice includes the need to see 'just desserts' for the perpetrator of a harm or crime (Lambourne 2009) and this is often the first response to suffering caused by another human being or group of human beings: to see them also suffer. This is consistent with Judith Herman's first step in the process of recovery from trauma: the need for safety (Herman 1992). Safety is produced by stopping the perpetrator from reoffending – and what better way than to punish them, to put them in jail and banish them from society, if not apply the death penalty? However, from a longer term perspective, this does not solve the problem. New perpetrators will take their place, societies will be weakened and victims will not be able to heal from their trauma. It may temporarily restore the moral and legal order, but it does not restore community or build peace in the positive sense.

These distinctions become particularly important when considering the challenges of transitional justice after mass violence when the context is seen as peacebuilding, or restoration of community, rather than simply punishment of those guilty of perpetrating mass violations of human rights. In situations where there are large numbers of victims, survivors, perpetrators and others in the community who must live together in close proximity after mass violence, such as in Rwanda after the 1994 genocide against the Tutsis, the goal of restoring community, if not restoring relationships, becomes critical. The restoration of legal and moral order is also important to prevent a recurrence of such violence, so retributive justice also has its place as a means of reinforcing the rule of law and ending a culture of impunity.[2] But the traditional punishment of banishment for serious crimes committed by individuals, whether or not it involves incarceration, becomes untenable and undesirable in the context of mass crimes.

A clear example of this can be found in Rwanda following the genocide of 1994, in which close to one million people were killed. Initially, both the international community and the Rwandan Government emphasised prosecutorial retributive justice: the United Nations established the International Criminal Tribunal for Rwanda (ICTR) in Arusha, Tanzania and the Rwandan Government passed the Organic Law of 30 August 1996, which enabled the prosecution in domestic courts of those accused of perpetrating the genocide. The leaders of the genocide tried by the ICTR and found guilty were sentenced to periods of imprisonment from 12 years to life (Kamatali 2003). Even though the ICTR's mandate specified that its goals were to produce justice and reconciliation for Rwandans, little thought was put into how to achieve reconciliation defined as restoration of the relationship between the two main ethnic groups, the Hutus and Tutsis, who were respectively the main perpetrators and victims of the genocide. In other words, the ICTR was created without considering the need for a restorative process in order to produce such a restorative outcome, so it was unlikely to be achieved from the adversarial, prosecutorial, purely retributive court proceedings (Kamatali 2003). In Cambodia, by contrast, the Extraordinary Chambers in the Courts of Cambodia (ECCC) established ten years later was purposively designed to produce restorative outcomes appropriate for such mass crimes through at least partly restorative processes – the participation of civil parties in the court proceedings (Holmes and Ramji-Nogales 2011; also see Nickson, this volume).

Meanwhile, in Rwanda almost 130,000 suspects were held in overcrowded jails without charge or due process, and it was estimated that it would take more than 100 years to try all those accused. Faced with this impossible task, the Rwandan government decided on a unique experiment in transitional justice: to revive the traditional community justice system of *gacaca* in a modern form adapted to deal with the crimes of the genocide with the aim of promoting both justice and reconciliation. Both the traditional and modernised *gacaca* process combined elements of retributive and restorative justice, and reflected the Rwandan government's commitment to building peace in the country through national unity and reconciliation. As a result, the government abandoned the death penalty, encouraged confessions and provided a community service option instead of longer periods of imprisonment so that the perpetrators of the genocide could be reintegrated into the community. The *gacaca* process itself contained a number of restorative elements, most significantly the potential for an encounter between the victim, perpetrator and the local community, but the outcomes were not always restorative because of the connection with the classical court system and the continuing threat of incarceration for those accused of serious crimes (Lambourne 2010b).

This apparent tension between retributive and restorative justice is a key topic of debate in transitional justice (Lambourne 2010b), and will be explored further in the following section which outlines the four key pillars of transitional justice as defined by the United Nations and their relationship to restorative justice.

The key pillars of transitional justice

The key pillars of transitional justice according to the United Nations are prosecutions, truth-telling, reparations and institutional reform (United Nations 2010). These four key pillars have been derived from the Joinet principles of the right to justice, the right to know, the right to reparation and the right to non-recurrence (swisspeace 2012). The United Nations also includes a fifth pillar of national consultations which is important for a more restorative process that is inclusive of key stakeholders – the members of the local affected population (United Nations 2010).[3]

The interpretation of the right to justice as meaning an end to a culture of impunity through prosecutions seems to marginalise, if not completely undermine, restorative justice as a transitional justice process supported by the United Nations (UN). As I have argued elsewhere, interpreting the right to justice as a right to prosecution is too narrow, fails to take into account other types of justice and undermines the potential for a transformative justice consistent with a sustainable peace (Lambourne 2009). In other words, this narrow definition ignores the need for restoration of community that is also necessary for prevention or fulfilling the right to non-recurrence. In order to be effective, these four pillars thus need to be seen as interdependent and creating a holistic, comprehensive model of how to pursue transitional justice. The achievement of non-recurrence requires more than institutional reform and a focus on prosecutorial or retributive justice. Non-recurrence is defined by the UN in terms of structures and institutions that need to be built or rebuilt, such as the rule of law and courts. However, this fails to consider the restoration of the relationships of trust and understanding that need to underpin these structures and institutions in order for them to be effective tools of prevention and peacebuilding. Again we see the confusion of means and ends and a lack of appreciation of interdependence between the four pillars as defined by the UN.

Similarly, the right to know requires more than a court of law, which is limited in its ability to elicit the full truth of what occurred when the focus is on proving the guilt of the accused (who therefore has an incentive to hide or distort the truth in order to evade punishment). Furthermore, by focusing on the perpetrator's relationship with the state, prosecutorial justice in the Western court system does not normally allow the individual victim, group or community to express the truth of what happened and how it has affected them.[4] Thus, while a court may establish some aspects of the factual or forensic truth, it is limited by the guilty/not guilty or win/lose context and associated procedures that mitigate against personal narrative truths being shared by either the perpetrator or the victim (Boraine 2006). For transitional justice to be restorative, I argue, mechanisms need to be designed in order to encourage rather than inhibit the expression of personal, narrative truths. The existence of the court and the prosecution of the accused provide some acknowledgement for the victim of the crime that was committed against them, but discourages the perpetrator from admitting guilt and thus providing a sense of personal acknowledgement of responsibility (Lambourne 2009). This can interfere with the second stage of trauma recovery identified by Herman (1992) – acknowledgement – and with the ability to rebuild relationships in the community as the perpetrators continue to deny their accountability. The ability to produce a shared social or historical truth is thus undermined, along with the potential for a healing or restorative truth (Boraine 2006).[5]

The right to reparation is seen as a means of restitution for past harm that has been caused and may include rehabilitation, memorialisation, and symbolic as well as material or financial restitution. The provision of reparations by the state may provide an important symbolic gesture of acknowledgement, especially where state actors may be responsible for the crimes committed. However, again, by not involving the individual perpetrators in the provision of reparations, the overarching goal of reconciliation or peace may be undermined. The potential for restorative justice through reparations may be further compromised if they are promised but not implemented. For example, the South African TRC failed to deliver sufficiently in terms of financial reparations, but they did provide symbolic and moral reparations in the form of medical treatment, counselling and the naming of parks and schools (Minow 1998: 92–93). In Cambodia more recently, the ECCC provided symbolic and moral reparations including memorials, psychosocial support and education programmes.

In the above analysis of the UN or Joinet principles of transitional justice, I have applied concepts of justice, truth and reparations that have been developed by scholars and practitioners of transitional justice in response to their theoretical and philosophical reflections and/or practical experiences. For example, the four types of truth cited above were developed in the course of the South African Truth and Reconciliation Commission (Boraine 2006), while the various types of justice have been defined and proposed by transitional justice scholars including Mani (2002) and Lambourne (2004). The South African TRC was also instrumental in defining and expanding the notion of reparations, as have been the ECCC and the International Criminal Court in more recent years. These attempts to define and expand notions of justice, truth and reparations in the transitional justice context reveal the complexity and contested nature of these concepts as also discussed in the restorative justice literature pertaining to domestic criminal justice settings (Clamp 2014; Clamp and Doak 2012; Daly and Proietti-Scifoni 2011).

Reconciliation is another contested and complex concept which is central to a number of models of transitional justice and, I would argue, intrinsically linked to restorative justice. While restorative justice practices may or may not produce reconciliation – this is not seen as an essential goal (Zehr 2005) – the same cannot be said in reverse. Reconciliation is an essentially restorative process and can be defined as the restoration of relationships or restoration of community (Lambourne 2004). Reconciliation can also be defined as a transactional process of apology and forgiveness, but I would argue that this definition reflects a narrow culturally framed Western and Christian practice and the origins of the word and concept in English. When exploring the concept of reconciliation in other religious, cultural and language contexts, it becomes clear that there are different practices and meanings of reconciliation (Galtung 2001), but that underneath there may be some more common experience of *what* reconciliation is, even if we differ in explaining *how* it is achieved. This arguably common human experience reflects a deeper essence of the meaning of reconciliation that is a psychosocial or psycho-spiritual process of coming to terms with something, which may or may not involve an apology or forgiveness or a transactional encounter with other human or spiritual beings.

In Cambodia, for example, there are several terms in the local language of Khmer that relate to the English word reconciliation. One means a more business-like transaction of dispute resolution, while another can be translated most closely as being about attaining 'peace in my heart'. The English word 'reconciliation', meanwhile, is seen as meaning something more like political compromise or betrayal because of the context in which it had been used in Cambodia in relation to providing amnesty for former Khmer Rouge leaders (Lambourne 2002). The use of the concept of national or political reconciliation in the context of transitional justice can thus undermine the significance of what is an essentially personal, individual process (Crocker 2002). There is one thing that most scholars agree: that reconciliation is a process and that it cannot be imposed or rushed. In Rwanda, for example, the government's policy of national unity and reconciliation is leading social and political change in the country, but there is still a need over time for psychological and relationship transformation at local community levels to support Rwandans in experiencing a sustainable peace and reconciliation (Lambourne and Gitau 2014).

Earlier models of transitional justice, such as the TARR model first proposed by Parmentier (2003) and the approach advocated by Boraine (2006), explicitly include reconciliation as a key pillar in place of institutional reform, and they also include broader conceptions of justice and truth than the UN model. For example, both identify accountability as the 'justice' pillar rather than prosecutions per se. Neither precludes the option of prosecutions, but neither do they require it. Mani (2002), while not providing a model of transitional justice as such, does identify several types of justice – legal, rectificatory and distributive – that go beyond retribution. She proposes a more integrated concept of 'reparative justice' that addresses the political, socioeconomic and psychosocial deficits identified by Oliver Ramsbotham as being required for peacebuilding (Mani 2002: 17–18). In the model I developed of transformative justice, I similarly define justice and truth in broader and more inclusive terms, and highlight the need for socioeconomic and political justice as well as a combination of retributive and restorative justice in order to provide accountability (Lambourne 2009). I also suggest the need for acknowledgement as well as knowledge in order to produce the four types of truth proposed by the SA TRC, and the need for relational as well as structural transformation in order to build peace after mass violence and violations of human rights (Lambourne 2009).

I argue that the exclusion of reconciliation as a key pillar of transitional justice, and its elevation to an overarching goal in the model of transitional justice produced by swisspeace as representing the Joinet principles, has undermined the inclusion of restorative justice as part of transitional justice. The more expansive interpretation of justice as including both restorative and retributive elements, as implied in the other models discussed above, is more consistent with the UN's overarching goals of achieving peace and reconciliation, I argue. By contrast, defining the right to justice more narrowly as the right to prosecutions has precluded the implementation of a more comprehensive and holistic approach to transitional justice that recognises the interdependence of the key pillars of justice, truth, reparations and institutional reform. In order to devise a transitional justice mechanism in any one context, an overemphasis on the need for prosecutions at the expense of methods designed to promote reconciliation and restoration of community is unlikely to build a sustainable peace. And vice versa, an overemphasis on restorative justice without also taking into account the need for retribution can also undermine the rebuilding of a society that respects the rule of law as a means of preventing the use of violence. However, if punishment is seen as the central purpose of transitional justice, then the past is given priority over the future, and the goals of peace and reconciliation are likely to prove elusive.

For example, in Burundi the 2000 Arusha peace agreement called for the establishment of both a truth and reconciliation commission and prosecutions of those responsible for mass human rights violations during the civil war and genocides that had devastated the country for more than 30 years. When the Burundian government finally took steps to establish the truth and reconciliation commission in 2014, the UN insisted that a TRC implying reconciliation without prosecutions could not proceed because it would undermine the right to justice. However, if the UN were to place more emphasis on restorative justice as a pillar of transitional justice it might accept the TRC as a valid mechanism, at least in the interim, understanding that in practice prosecutions may need to wait for a change in the national political context. In other words, the question here is not about whether prosecutions are required, but rather whether a restorative process designed to promote reconciliation is also desirable in the process of transitional justice.

A major challenge for transitional justice illustrated by the Burundian example is not only the Western legal emphasis on retribution, but also the dominant liberal peace paradigm that may be imposed on transitional states (Sriram 2009). Together these normative influences determine the priorities of transitional justice which can result in marginalisation of national governments and other local actors, their political priorities, psychosocial needs and cultural approaches. An important aspect of a restorative justice process is to be inclusive and participatory, and to support transformative peacebuilding through contextualisation and empowerment (Lederach 2000). In practice this is not a straightforward process, as the Burundi example again illustrates. While the government is insisting on reconciliation, civil society actors are split between those calling for prosecutions and those who support reconciliation, or both, while the UN is emphasising prosecutions as the number one priority. My argument in this paper is that a major impediment to transitional justice is thus the separation of retributive and restorative justice, while in other traditions we can see how these two aspects of justice may be combined into one method or practice.

Learning from other traditions

Restorative justice practice in Western criminal justice contexts derives from biblical understandings of justice and from the adaptation of traditional indigenous justice and conflict resolution processes. Zehr (2005, first published in 1990) explained how covenant justice derived from the Bible and the need to return to 'shalom' underpin restorative justice principles of community justice in contrast to how modern justice has evolved. Consedine (1995), meanwhile, outlined the restorative justice principles and methods existing in various traditional cultures around the world, including the Maori in New Zealand and Aboriginal Australians, which he combined with an understanding of biblical justice to propose an approach to restorative justice that could transcend cultural differences.

Both foundational authors in the field contrast restorative justice with criminal and retributive justice and, even though Zehr admits the potential for punishment to be part of restorative justice, he does advocate the replacement of the criminal justice system with a restorative approach. This either/or thinking has taken over the philosophy and practice of restorative justice in both domestic criminal justice and transitional justice settings. In some cases this manifests as an advocacy of restorative justice in place of criminal justice, such as the promotion of a healing ritual or truth and reconciliation commission in place of legal trials as in the Burundi example above, but in others the two processes are seen as complementary – such as a TRC or a victim–offender mediation to accompany trials. Yet, even in this latter scenario, there is a separation of methods that fails to take into account the interdependence of the two approaches to justice. For example, sentencing circles in which the community members decide the appropriate punishment for the offender combine both retributive and restorative elements in the one process (Pranis 2005). Similarly, many traditional indigenous mechanisms combine retributive and restorative justice rather than separating them as has occurred in the Western legal tradition, where punishment has come to be treated as an end in itself (Lambourne 2010b).

For example, the community reconciliation process (CRP) that was part of the Commission for Reception, Truth and Reconciliation (CAVR) in Timor

Leste incorporated the grassroots Timorese reconciliation process of *nahe biti*. *Nahe biti* refers to the symbolic rolling out of a mat at a venue to discuss and settle an issue among interested parties through consensus (Babo-Soares 2005). The process involved voluntary acceptance of culpability and agreement on reconciliation acts such as reparation, community service or public apology, and was usually finalised with a symbolic exchange of 'betel nut' ceremony to show sincerity and commitment. The significance of the mat is that it cannot be rolled up again until the conflict has been resolved. The sanctions or compensation requested by the victims more often than not involved a heartfelt confession and public apology, along with symbolic payments. Reconciliation in this manner is traditionally seen as a bridge to achieve a much greater aim of harmony and peace in the society (Babo-Soares 2005). As a result, the CRP resonated with traditional values in its emphasis on the community rather than the individual, and the opportunity for the perpetrator to engage with the community in an exchange which was both ceremonial and practical, and to be reintegrated into the community.

Both the CRP, as part of the Timorese truth and reconciliation commission and the *gacaca* process in Rwanda also illustrate how adapting an indigenous traditional approach to justice can address the need for reintegration that is a core principle of restorative justice. In other words, in both *gacaca* and the CRP, the perpetrator or offender is encouraged to accept responsibility and to make amends in return for reintegration into the community, rather than being banished or incarcerated. Transitional justice mechanisms otherwise do poorly with this aspect of restorative justice because of the challenges involved in a post-mass violence context. The adversarial courts which reinforce the judgement and ostracism of individual perpetrators and perpetrator groups are much more likely to undermine than to support reintegration.

If punishment is seen as a means to an end – of restoring peace and order in society – and the basic principles of restorative justice are not explicitly addressed, then the pursuit of punishment will lose its efficacy as a peacebuilding tool. The interpretation of the right to justice as the right to prosecution has served to reinforce this separation and undermine the ability of the UN model of transitional justice to achieve its goals of peace and reconciliation.

Restorative justice and reconciliation

As suggested earlier in this chapter, definitions and understandings of restorative justice and reconciliation overlap in the context of transitional justice. This is seen especially in analyses of the South African TRC, which seem to equate the TRC's goal of reconciliation with the method of restorative justice employed. Scholars and practitioners have also made links between reparation as a key pillar of transitional justice and restorative justice as both have repair of harm as a central goal. But, as explained by Laplante (2014: 71–74), reparative justice is not necessarily restorative unless the process by which it is implemented is also reparative in terms of showing respect for the dignity of the beneficiaries.

While agreeing that reconciliation along with peace should be seen as core goals of transitional justice, I have suggested that, by not including reconciliation explicitly as a key pillar, the UN model of transitional justice is lacking a key element required to ensure peacebuilding. This is reflected in the narrow definition of justice as the right to prosecution employed by the UN in its first key pillar, which in itself is incomplete and inconsistent with the achievement of peace and reconciliation. Similarly, the swisspeace model of transitional justice, also based on the Joinet principles, minimises any reference to restorative mechanisms under any of the key pillars required for dealing with the past (swisspeace 2012).

The concept of restorative justice assumes many of the same processes as might be required for reconciliation: an encounter with the 'other' in which the focus is on acknowledging the hurt caused and addressing the needs of the victim (Zehr 2005). However, as noted earlier, reconciliation is not a required outcome of restorative justice (Zehr 2005). Both restorative justice and reconciliation involve letting go of the demonisation and dehumanisation of the other, and no longer seeing the individual perpetrator or perpetrator group as the enemy but rather as part of the same shared moral community (Parent 2010). Retribution, by contrast, is not directly concerned with reconciliation and does not require a process of de-enmification or rehumanisation, hence the common perception that transitional justice must pursue justice or reconciliation, and not both – or, at least, not both at the same time.

Reconciliation can thus be understood as a process of breaking down the barriers between victims and perpetrators, where the perspective of the other is acknowledged and the decision is made to move forward with a future relationship that is based on mutual trust (Crocker 2002). Hamber and Kelly (2009: 291–292) propose a five-stage model of reconciliation that moves from development of a shared vision to acknowledging and dealing with the past, building positive relationships, and cultural, social, political and economic change. For some, this describes peaceful coexistence, rather than 'thick reconciliation' (Crocker 2002) which entails recognition of mutual suffering and forgiveness that promotes healing and a transformative process combining restorative justice with truth, mercy and peace (Lederach 1997).

Restorative justice on its own, however, at least as practised in the West and as part of transitional justice in addition to many traditional indigenous contexts, as with the Western retributive justice system, is not concerned with breaking down the division between perpetrator and victim. The offender is required to acknowledge the harm caused and to recognise an obligation to repair the harm in order to restore community relationships. This may or may not involve a psychosocial transformation akin to reconciliation as described above. While the perception of the perpetrator as the enemy or less than human may be achieved through restorative justice, the distinction of the perpetrator from the victim often remains, without the need or potential for recognition of mutual suffering and victimhood as might be required for reconciliation.

In the context of transitional justice where there have been reciprocal cycles of violence over time, a mutual process of reconciliation is required that goes beyond the concept of repairing harms implied by restorative justice. While restorative justice brings another element to the table beyond the retributive justice highlighted in the UN model of transitional justice, it is in itself insufficient to promote reconciliation in the context of mass violence and human rights violations. To achieve the goals of peace and reconciliation, transitional justice needs explicitly to include mechanisms designed to promote reconciliation rather than assuming that the required psychosocial transformation will somehow magically be achieved through addressing the four key pillars of prosecutions, truth telling, reparations and institutional reform.

On the other hand, as discussed above, restorative justice is more likely than retributive justice to promote reconciliation because it has the potential to restore the humanity of the perpetrator (Parent 2010). My research suggests that the ability to get perpetrators to acknowledge their crimes and the harm caused is a significant missing element in transitional justice, which could be encouraged by supporting community-based processes that combine retributive and restorative elements (Lambourne 2009). Even when truth and reconciliation commissions are established, and certainly when there are trials, the perpetrators have little incentive, and in many cases a strong disincentive, to acknowledge their crimes. For the victims, while punishment through a trial or obtaining the truth through a truth commission may be achieved, their potential healing and recovery is left incomplete when the perpetrators themselves do not acknowledge the crimes and the harms they have caused.

For example, the SA TRC required the full confession of crimes and a political motive in order to grant amnesty to the perpetrators, which went some way towards promoting national reconciliation, but for many victims the lack of apology or expression of contrition prevented a personal experience of reconciliation (Hamber 2009). The type of restorative justice promoted by the SA TRC did not include all of the features required of a restorative justice process, far less reconciliation, for many of the participants and the vast majority of South Africans who did not take part directly in the TRC. Encounter was a central feature but not universal, and reparations were promised but not delivered (Clamp and Doak 2012: 359).

When these state-run transitional justice mechanisms failed to provide a meaningful restorative process, community-based programs such as *Fambul Tok* in Sierra Leone have arisen to address the missing restorative justice and reconciliation elements in the truth and reconciliation commissions established as part of the national transitional justice process. In Burundi, in the absence of a formal transitional justice mechanism, civil society actors have focused on community healing and reconciliation processes, which they see as important as a basis for maintaining peace in the country (Lambourne and Niyonzima 2015). In Sierra Leone, the truth and reconciliation commission, as in South Africa, held hearings in major towns and provided an opportunity for a restorative process, but did not penetrate deeply into rural communities; and many victims and perpetrators were unable to participate (Lambourne 2008). Furthermore, the process of public hearings failed to fully engage with the local traditions and rituals that could have assisted with restorative justice and reconciliation, and because of the coexistence of the Special Court for Sierra Leone many of the perpetrators were reluctant to participate for fear of being prosecuted (Lambourne 2008). Disappointed by the TRC process, local human rights activist John Caulker joined with Mennonite practitioner Elizabeth Hoffman and her US-based NGO Catalyst for Peace to develop a more locally oriented transformative process – known as *Fambul Tok*, or 'family talk' – that is promoting reconciliation and peacebuilding in local communities (Lafton 2014; Schotsmans 2012).

Fambul Tok, in some ways like the examples of the Rwandan *gacaca* and the Timorese *nahe biti* processes, includes a strong emphasis on truth-telling and restoring community. Based on reviving communal traditions of confession, forgiveness and restorative justice, the process is designed to promote healing and peace in local communities as a basis for healing and peace in the country. Victims and perpetrators come together around a bonfire, surrounded by their communities, to testify about crimes – to acknowledge responsibility and to ask for forgiveness. Cleansing rituals for victims and perpetrators are performed, as well as the pouring of libations to ancestors, to ask their blessings on the community's attempts to reconcile. As with other traditional informal mechanisms, the context of community acceptance and potential for forgiveness provides an opportunity for perpetrators to acknowledge their crimes in a way that is designed to promote reconciliation, a process that is missing in most formal transitional justice mechanisms.

The examples discussed serve to illustrate how transitional justice practice has promoted the truth and reconciliation commission as a mechanism for promoting restorative justice and reconciliation when trials are seen as inadequate or not politically feasible. However, the key principles of restorative justice identified in the domestic criminal justice context have not been sufficiently incorporated into the design and implementation of these mechanisms. Truth and reconciliation commissions may be more restorative than courts which focus on retributive justice, because they enable an encounter between the perpetrator and victim and focus more on addressing the needs of victims. Yet they may still fail to fully engage with victims and perpetrators in ways that encourage acknowledgement of the harms and acceptance of the obligation to repair those harms, thus failing the test of a fully restorative process that produces restorative outcomes. Instead, community-based processes, some of which combine elements of both restorative and retributive justice, have been suggested as complementary or alternative approaches to achieving reconciliation as part of transitional justice.

Conclusion

As I have argued in this chapter, if it is to achieve its aim of peacebuilding in addition to dealing with the past, transitional justice needs to reengage with the concept and method of restorative justice in order to operationalise what it considers to be the 'messy' concept of reconciliation. Scholar–practitioners from law and political science need to engage with social psychologists and peace practitioners in order to understand and support the realisation of a holistic and transformative transitional justice process that incorporates restorative justice methods specifically designed to promote reconciliation and reintegration. While transitional justice is mired in the dominant Western paradigm of international law and the Joinet principles of the right to know, justice, reparation and non-recurrence, it will fail to engage meaningfully in the human needs for reconciliation, restoration and reintegration which are necessary for peace and stability.

The sheer magnitude of community involvement in genocide and mass crimes suggests that a fully restorative process that brings together victims, perpetrators and key stakeholders in the community may not be possible in the transitional justice setting. Certainly, formal state-run mechanisms such as the truth and reconciliation commissions have only in rare instances succeeded in penetrating local communities to enable encounters on a more inclusive scale. One such example was the CAVR in Timor Leste which conducted community reconciliation processes in all of the local areas, incorporating traditional rituals that produced both a restorative process and outcome (Lambourne 2010a). In other transitional justice settings it may be more feasible to incorporate community-level processes as a complementary approach, as illustrated by the example of *Fambul Tok* in Sierra Leone. Addressing harms – physical, material, psychological, social, moral and spiritual – and the potential for healing, possibly through forgiveness, as in the Christian ritual, but also through exchange of gifts, sharing of food and drink, or otherwise celebrating community as in Pacific societies such as Bougainville and Timor Leste, are examples of restorative justice and reconciliation in action as part of transitional justice.

It seems that a more locally driven process is required in order to tap into local traditions and approaches to justice and reconciliation that will enable rehumanisation of the other and a restoration of community in order to build a more sustainable peace, as in the *Fambul Tok* example discussed above. An integrative restorative justice process, such as the Community Reconciliation Process in Timor Leste, which includes elements of retribution as well as reparations and a focus on healing relationships, may be seen as the most effective contribution to transitional justice at the local community level. The question remains, however – how can this be interpreted and implemented at the national or international level where there are competing paradigms of justice embedded within a model of transitional justice that is essentially punitive rather than restorative, and where the possibility of encounter and provision of reparations is unlikely to be feasible except at the symbolic level. One positive step would be to reinstate reconciliation as an explicit goal and restorative justice as a value, even if not a process, in order to harness the transformative potential of transitional justice.

Notes

1 See Lambourne (2004, 2009) for definitions of these different types of justice.
2 See also Hoyle (2012) who argues that prosecutions can provide restorative justice through material and symbolic reparations, and that they are necessary along with

separate restorative justice mechanisms if societies in transition are to achieve peace, stability and restoration.

3 As I have argued elsewhere (Lambourne 2012), local ownership and civil society participation through a process of 'in reach', or what Clamp (2014: 36) refers to as 'engagement' in the context of restorative justice practices, are critical to achieving the transformative potential of transitional justice. It is as yet unclear how successful national consultations practised by the UN can be in achieving such engagement of key stakeholders. The evidence in the case of Burundi is not encouraging – see Lambourne (2014).

4 The ability to elicit a personal/narrative truth is changing as Western courts more often allow for victim impact statements to be provided.

5 As discussed by Clamp (2014: 71–76), the potential for attaining such truths through a transitional justice mechanism such as a truth commission is fraught with challenges, uncertainties and risks. My point here is to indicate how understanding the relationship between these four types of truths in theory can maximise the opportunity of realising the benefits of truth-telling as part of transitional justice in practice.

References

Babo-Soares, D. (2005) 'Nahe Biti: grassroots reconciliation in East Timor' in E. Skaar, S. Gloppen and A. Suhrke (eds) *Roads to Reconciliation*, Lanham, MD: Lexington Books.

Boraine (2006) 'Defining transitional justice: tolerance in the search for justice and peace', in A. Boraine and S. Valentine (eds) *Transitional Justice and Human Security*, Cape Town: International Centre for Transitional Justice.

Braithwaite, J. (1989) *Crime, Shame and Reintegration*, Cambridge: Cambridge University Press.

Braithwaite, J. and Strang, H. (2001) 'Introduction: restorative justice and civil society' in H. Strang and J. Braithwaite (eds) *Restorative Justice and Civil Society*, Cambridge: Cambridge University Press.

Burton, J. (1990) *Conflict: Resolution and provention*, London: Macmillan.

Clamp, K. (2014) *Restorative Justice in Transition*, London: Routledge.

Clamp, K. and Doak, J. (2012) 'More than Words: Restorative justice concepts in transitional justice settings', *International Criminal Law Review*, 12(3): 339–360.

Consedine, J. (1995) *Restorative Justice: Healing the effects of crime*, Lyttelton, NZ: Ploughshares Publications.

Crocker, D. (2002) 'Democracy and Punishment: Punishment, reconciliation and democratic deliberation', *Buffalo Criminal Law Review*, 6(4): 509–549.

Daly, K. and Proietti-Scifoni, G. (2011) 'Reparation and restoration', in M. Tonry (ed.) *The Oxford Handbook of Crime and Criminal Justice*, Oxford: Oxford University Press.

Galtung, J. (2001) 'After violence, reconstruction, reconciliation and resolution: coping with visible and invisible effects of war and violence', in M. Abu-Nimer (ed.) *Reconciliation, Justice and Coexistence: Theory and practice*, Lanham, MD: Lexington Books.

Hamber, B. (2009) *Transforming Societies after Political Violence: Truth, reconciliation, and mental health*, Dordrecht: Springer Verlag.

Hamber, B. and Kelly, G. (2009) 'Beyond coexistence: towards a working definition of reconciliation' in J. Quinn (ed.) *Reconciliation(s): Transitional justice in post conflict societies*, Montreal: McGill-Queen's University Press.

Herman, J. (1992) *Trauma and Recovery*, New York: Basic Books.

Holmes, T. and Ramji-Nogales, J. (2011) 'Participation as reparations: the ECCC and healing in Cambodia' in B. Van Schaak, D. Reicherter and Y. Chhang (eds) *Cambodia's Hidden Scars: Trauma psychology in the wake of the Khmer Rouge*, Phnom Penh: Documentation Centre of Cambodia.

Hoyle, C. (2012) 'Can international justice be restorative justice? The role of reparations', in N. Palmer, D. Palmer and P. Clark (eds) *Critical Perspectives in Transitional Justice*, Cambridge: Intersentia.

Johnstone, G. (2007) 'Critiques of restorative justice', in G. Johnstone and D. Van Ness (eds.) *A Handbook of Restorative Justice*, Cullompton, Devon: Willan.

Johnstone, G. (2011) *Restorative Justice: Ideas, values, debates*, New York: Routledge.

Kamatali, J. (2003) 'The Challenge of Linking International Criminal Justice and National Reconciliation: The case of the ICTR', *Leiden Journal of International Law*, 16: 115–133.

Lafton, B. (2014) 'Fambul Tok Helps Heal Sierra Leone', *Peacebuilder*, Spring/Summer: 24.

Lambourne, W. (2002) 'Justice and reconciliation: Post-conflict peacebuilding in Cambodia and Rwanda', PhD Thesis, University of Sydney.

Lambourne, W. (2004) 'Post-conflict Peacebuilding: Meeting human needs for justice and reconciliation', *Peace, Conflict and Development*, 4(April): 1–24.

Lambourne, W. (2008) 'Towards Sustainable Peace and Development in Sierra Leone: Civil society and the Peacebuilding Commission', *Journal of Peacebuilding and Development*, 4(2): 47–59.

Lambourne, W. (2009) 'Transitional Justice and Peacebuilding after Mass Violence', *International Journal of Transitional Justice*, 3(1): 28–48.

Lambourne, W. (2010a) 'Unfinished Business: The Commission for Reception, Truth and Reconciliation and justice and reconciliation in East Timor', in L. Barra and S. Roper (eds) *Development of Institutions of Human Rights*, London: Palgrave Macmillan.

Lambourne, W. (2010b) 'Transitional justice after mass violence: Reconciling retributive and restorative justice', in H. Irving, J. Mowbray and K. Walton (eds) *Julius Stone: A study in influence*, Sydney: Federation Press.

Lambourne, W. (2012) 'Outreach, inreach and civil society participation in transitional justice' in N. Palmer, P. Clark and D. Granville (eds) *Critical Perspectives in Transitional Justice*, Cambridge: Intersentia.

Lambourne, W. (2014) 'What are the Pillars of Transitional Justice? The United Nations and the Justice Cascade in Burundi', *Macquarie Law Journal*, 13: 41–60.

Lambourne, W. and Niyonzima, D. (2015) 'Breaking cycles of trauma and violence: psychosocial approaches to healing and reconciliation in Burundi' in P. Gobodo-Madikizela (ed.) *Breaking Cycles of Repetition: A global dialogue on historical trauma and memory*, Cologne: Budrich Academic Press.

Lambourne, W. and Gitau, L.W. (2014) 'Psychosocial Interventions, Peacebuilding and Development in Rwanda', *Journal of Peacebuilding and Development*, 8(3): 23–36.

Laplante, L. J. (2014) 'The plural justice aims of reparations' in S. Buckley Zistel, T. Koloma Beck, C. Braun and F. Mieth (eds) *Transitional Justice Theories*, New York: Routledge.

Lederach, J. P. (1995) *Preparing for Peace: Conflict transformation across cultures*, Syracuse, NY: Syracuse University Press.

Lederach, J. P. (1997) *Building Peace: Sustainable reconciliation in divided societies*, Washington, DC: United States Institute of Peace Press.

Lederach, J. P. (2000) 'Journey from resolution to transformative peacebuilding', in C. Sampson and J. P. Lederach (eds) *From the Ground Up: Mennonite contributions to international peacebuilding*, Oxford: Oxford University Press.

Mani, R. (2002) *Beyond Retribution: Seeking justice in the shadows of war*, Oxford: Polity Press.

Minow, M. (1998) *Between Vengeance and Forgiveness: Facing history after genocide and mass violence*, Boston, MA: Beacon Press.

Orentlicher, D. (1991) 'Settling Accounts: The duty to prosecute human rights violations of a prior regime', *Yale Law Journal*, 100(8): 2537–2615.

Parent, G. (2010) 'Reconciliation and Justice after Genocide: A theoretical exploration', *Genocide Studies and Prevention*, 5(3): 277–292.

Parmentier, S. (2003) 'Global Justice in the Aftermath of Mass Violence. The Role of the International Criminal Court in Dealing with Political Crimes', *International Annals of Criminology*, 41(1): 203–223.

Pranis, K. (2005) *The Little Book of Circle Processes*, Intercourse, PA: Good Books.

Sanson, A. and Bretherton, D. (2001) 'Conflict Resolution: Theoretical and practical issues' in D. Christie, R. Wagner and D. Winter (eds) *Peace, Conflict, and Violence*, Upper Saddle River, NJ: Prentice-Hall.

Schotsmans, M. (2012) 'Blow your mind and cool your heart: can tradition-based justice fill the transitional justice gap in Sierra Leone?' in N. Palmer, P. Clark and D. Granville (eds) *Critical Perspectives in Transitional Justice*, Cambridge: Intersentia.

Sikkink, K. (2011) *The Justice Cascade: How human rights prosecutions are changing world politics*, New York: W. W. Norton and Co.

Sriram, C. L. (2009) 'Transitional justice and the liberal peace', in E. Newman, R. Paris and O. Richmond (eds) *New Perspectives on Liberal Peacebuilding*, Tokyo: United Nations University Press.

Stauffer, C. (2007) 'Narrating the spirit of justice', in E. van der Spuy, S. Parmentier and A. Dissel (eds) *Restorative Justice: Politics, policies and prospects*, Cape Town: Juta and Co.

swisspeace (2012) *A Conceptual Framework for Dealing with the Past: Holism in principle and practice*, Bern: swisspeace.

United Nations (2010) *Guidance Note of the Secretary-General: United Nations Approach to Transitional Justice*. DPA/UNSG/2010–00904 (10 March 2010).

United Nations Security Council (2004) Report of the Secretary-General, *The rule of law and transitional justice in conflict and post-conflict societies*, S/2004/616, 23 August 2004.

Walgrave, L. (2008) *Restorative Justice, Self Interest and Responsible Citizenship*, Cullompton, UK: Willan Publishing.

Zehr, H. (2002) *The Little Book of Restorative Justice*, Intercourse, PA: Good Books.

Zehr, H. (2005) *Changing Lenses: A new focus for crime and justice*, Scottsdale, PA: Herald Press.

5 Stalking the state

The state as a stakeholder in post-conflict restorative justice

Jonathan Doak

Introduction

Once viewed as a strategy to deal with low-level, interpersonal crime, largely affecting juveniles, the past two decades have witnessed the osmosis of restorative justice, and its associated terminology and discourse, far beyond the realms of orthodox criminal justice and criminology. This will not come as a surprise to proponents of restorative justice, many of whom have long identified its transformative potential as a regulatory mechanism across different social spheres (Wachtel and McCold 2001; Woolford and Ratner 2010). As the title of this collection implies, restorative justice discourses are now readily applied within the relatively nascent field of transitional justice. This is evident not only within the burgeoning body of academic literature in the area, but also by the official language adopted by archetypal transitional institutions, perhaps most famously in the context of the South African Truth and Reconciliation Commission.

In one sense, the confluence of restorative and transitional justice might be seen as something of an inevitability given the strong overlap between the two paradigms; both tend to draw heavily on the same core values such as truth, accountability, reparation, reconciliation, conflict resolution and participation (Clamp and Doak 2012). In practical terms, the narrative and interaction that is so central to restorative justice may act as tools by which the narrow identities of victim and perpetrator or repressor and insurgent are replaced with a new sense of 'self' and 'other' that makes a new relationship possible (Long and Breke 2003: 69). In this way, restorative justice holds the potential to (re)invigorate democracy and peacebuilding through building trust between the state and hitherto disenfranchised communities (Braithwaite 2006; Doak and O'Mahony 2011).

Notwithstanding its potential contribution to the transitional process, a degree of caution should nevertheless be exercised in translating both the labels and the concepts from 'orthodox' restorative justice discourse as regards 'ordinary' crime in 'settled' societies into post-conflict environments. The neat, tripartite separation of victims, offenders, communities – while not unproblematic in the former context (see e.g. Maglione 2014) – is considerably more complex in the latter. In a previous paper co-authored with the editor of this volume (Clamp and

Doak 2012), we highlighted a range of caveats associated with the 'portability' of certain terminologies, including the roles traditionally attributed to key stakeholders and specific difficulties in applying the concepts of restoration and reintegration. This chapter builds on that work by exploring in further depth some of the difficulties in delineating an appropriate role for the state vis-à-vis its role in restorative justice.

The state may play a role in post-conflict restorative justice in two main contexts. The first relates to its capacity as lawmaker, whereby the state is charged with framing the parameters of the criminal law and criminal justice system. It is not unusual for post-conflict criminal justice reforms to include aspects of restorative justice to deal with 'ordinary' crime; such reforms were introduced to the youth justice systems of Northern Ireland and South Africa (O'Mahony *et al.* 2012), while grassroots and non-state initiatives have also evolved in these jurisdictions, as well as in Colombia, Guatemala and Timor Leste (see generally McEvoy and McGregor 2008). To some extent, the proliferation of restorative justice in such environments may be attributable to a desire to move away from punitivism or to secure support from the wider international community (Clamp 2014), and much has been already written on the potential difficulties that may subsequently arise (see Clamp 2014; Doak and O'Mahony 2011; Eriksson 2013; O'Mahony *et al.* 2012).

The second focuses on the role of the state in a different sense, as (potentially) a direct stakeholder *within* restorative mechanisms. While some of the discussion relating to the state's broader role in overseeing interpersonal restorative justice initiatives is also applicable in this context, considerably less thought has been afforded to exploring the particular challenges that may arise when the state assumes a role of a direct participant, either as a perpetrator or a victim. First, a state may be regarded as a perpetrator in the sense that it ought to be held accountable for abuses of power carried out by its agents. It is worth underlining that such transgressions occur not only through large-scale violations of international humanitarian law by autocratic regimes, but also through less exposed activities such as failures to protect its citizenry, abide by human rights standards, or address structural inequality. Such perpetrations are not limited to the autocratic regimes of Latin America or sub-Saharan Africa, but are also found in so-called 'conflicted democracies', defined by Ní Aoláin and Campbell (2005: 174) as liberal democratic states 'that have experienced prolonged, structured, communal, political violence, even where the political structures could broadly be considered "democratic"'. Contemporary examples include the United Kingdom (vis-à-vis Northern Ireland), Spain (vis-à-vis the Basque Country), and Sri Lanka.

By the same token, the state may also be regarded as a victim in the sense that its agents may have suffered direct harm as a result of the actions of non-state actors. It is also a victim in the sense that its authority has been transgressed by the lawbreaker (Van Ness 2014). Indeed, such victimhood may arise not only through direct harm caused, but also in an indirect sense since its citizenry (who it purportedly embodies) will have suffered harms as a result of the conflict.

Although each offence may have a negligible impact on the state as a whole, the cumulative effect of the harm is axiomatic (Van Ness 2014). Such harms are not only civil and political in their nature, but may also be economic, social or cultural. As Moffet (2014) attests, it is overly simplistic to attribute sole responsibility for social and economic harms to agents of the state without addressing the horizontal or overlapping responsibilities of such non-state actors. Furthermore, it is also conceivable that the notion of victimhood might be applied in circumstances where an external third party state actor has been directly involved or exerted an influence within internal conflict. States such as Afghanistan, Iraq, Palestine or South Sudan, all of which have paid heavy prices as a result of war in recent times, might in some sense be regarded as victims as the result of the actions or inactions of external state actors, including the international community in a general sense.

This chapter seeks to shed conceptual clarity on some of the ambiguities surrounding the position of the state as an actor in both transitional and restorative theory. It begins by proffering some general remarks exploring the state's role as a stakeholder within restorative justice, with particular emphasis on efforts to make 'restoration' within this context. It is argued that many of the conundrums surrounding the role of the state can be attributed to two factors: first, the top-down orientation of the predominant transitional justice paradigm; and, second, the tendency to construe the state as a monolithic and rational actor. Arguing that both of these factors serve to underline the efficacy of many transitional mechanisms, some practical suggestions are then made in terms of how the state might play a more meaningful, effective and legitimate role within post-conflict restorative frameworks.

The state as a stakeholder

Once commonly associated with 'victor's justice' and the need to avenge wrongs through prosecution and retribution, transitional justice underwent something of a paradigm shift during the 1980s and 1990s. The ascendancy of truth commissions and the widespread publicity afforded to the apparent 'restorative' ethos which underpinned the South African Truth and Reconciliation Commission (SATRC) (see for example Tutu 1999) was instrumental – among other factors – in shifting discourse away from prosecution towards issues such as peacebuilding, reconciliation, amnesties, and the potential role of apologies and forgiveness (see generally Bell 2009). While more recent empirical research has raised questions concerning the actual extent of the 'restorativeness' of the SATRC (Backer 2007; Byrne 2004; Clark 2012; Kaminer et al. 2001; Stein et al. 2008), there is little doubt the TRC sparked widespread interest in alternative approaches to post-conflict justice. Thus restorative justice discourse has also been readily associated inter alia with transitions in Cambodia (Sperfeldt 2012) Rwanda (Clark 2010), Timor Leste (Nixon 2013), and Bougainville (Braithwaite et al. 2011).

Most transitions will inevitably involve some form of onus on the state to repeal or amend existing laws that prevailed as instruments of oppression during the conflict, as well as to introduce new laws covering issues such as constitution reform, democratisation, the accountability of state agents, lustration, the mainstreaming of human rights and so on. Herein lies a noteworthy paradox, for, while the state is effectively rendering itself subject to the authority of the law, it is simultaneously the creator and enforcer of the law (Ní Aoláin and Campbell 2005). The dangers of this position are clear; states in transition may be more likely to attempt to reassert their authority amid shifts in loci of power and a prevailing climate of political uncertainty (Clamp 2014; Clamp and Doak 2012; McEvoy 2000). This effect is exacerbated by the fact that many high-level public servants and policy elites may remain in office post-transition (Cunneen 2008). Recent years have witnessed considerable expansion in the 'top-down' critique of transitional processes. This stems from the prevailing normative framework, which tends to be dominated by legalistic agendas of policy elites at the expense of meeting the needs of victims and communities (Boesenecker and Vinjamuri 2014; Clamp 2014; Gready and Robins 2014; McEvoy and MacConnachie 2013). Drawing on James C. Scott's 2008 seminal work, *Seeing Like a State*, McEvoy (2007: 421) observes how transitional justice has tended to be institutionalised into 'expensive supra-state and "state-like" structures', which tend to over-simplify problems and impose solutions according to their own rationalities. Such structures are endemically much more powerful and better resourced than existing community and civil society institutions, which have been weakened by a wider erosion of 'community values' across much of the western world (Forrest and Kearns 2001), not to mention the damage inflicted by war or conflict.

It is thus unsurprising that empirical evidence across many former conflict zones tends to show considerable dissatisfaction among both the public generally, and victims in particular, in terms of both the process and outputs of transitional justice initiatives (see below). For present purposes, this normative orientation carries detrimental ramifications in terms of the potential role that a state might play as a stakeholder in restorative justice. The theoretical restorative ideal – namely that that stakeholders deliberate as equal, democratic partners in a non-coercive environment (Dzur and Wertheimer 2002) – is clearly difficult to realise in practice, given the state's central role in delineating the formal parameters of the transition. This role, in turn, may undercut the perceived legitimacy of any restorative process since it risks portraying disinterest on the part of state actors in the plight of victims and hitherto disengaged communities.

This tension pertaining to the legitimacy of the transitional process is particularly pressing as the question of making 'amends' or 'restoration' arises. According to classic restorative justice theory, direct and indirect harms should be broadly construed to include physical, psychological or proprietary harm experienced by victims and their communities (Mallinder 2014; Pavlich 2005). The task of repair is clearly complex, with different contexts requiring varied and multi-faceted reparatory efforts. Yet in the prevailing paradigm of transitional justice, the primary means of making amends tends to be through the implementation of reparations programmes, which may be based around the recommendations of a truth commission or some other form of independent body (Hayner

2011). For the most part, monetary compensation remains the common currency of justice, with some states putting in place collective programmes. These may provide funding – for example, to national or local projects which seek to advance healthcare, social services, commemoration, education or reconciliation (see generally De Grieff 2006). Other states – particularly the so-called 'conflicted democracies' – tend to favour individualised reparations programmes. Thus, following reunification, the Federal German government paid political prisoners of the former GDR €300 for each month they had spent in prison. In Northern Ireland, a working group proposed that the UK government pay £12,000 to families of the victims of the Northern Ireland conflict, though the proposal was never implemented due to the contested nature of who could claim to be a 'legitimate' victim.

With a few exceptions (noted below), the task of redress still tends to be overwhelmingly associated with financial payments. Even within settled societies, the principled basis for attaching a pecuniary value to a death or serious injury is far from straightforward, and the complexity of this task is greatly exacerbated in contexts where the abuse of power is systemic in nature and stems from large-scale civil and political conflict. In such settings, the nature of harms instigated by agents of the state may range from violations of privacy or arbitrary detention at one end of the spectrum, to torture, extra-judicial killings and crimes against humanity at the other. Seemingly innocuous one-off incidents involving interpersonal violence that is politically motivated are often interwoven with the wider, societal conflict. Such 'micro-level' incidents are thus difficult to separate from their 'macro-level' context (Rohne et al. 2008). Even if some form of normative framework is used to establish a proportionate link between the nature of the harm suffered and the extent of compensation due, it is difficult to envisage how cost-effective and efficient administrative processes could be put in place to deal with large numbers of victims in war-torn countries with very little in the way of financial resources. Across the developing world, in particular, problems which stem from the lack of financial resources, infrastructure, and logistical support mean that large-scale pecuniary reparation is simply not an option without substantial international donors. It is difficult to envisage, for example, how the sheer scale of mass killings in settings such as Rwanda, Cambodia or Darfur could be subject to a reparation programme based around individual monetary payments, given the war-torn state of the economy and the numbers of victims involved.

In the same way, it is hard to identify any principled basis on which the state is able to provide effective restoration for socio-economic harms and the broader structures of inequality they represent (Sharp 2012). Issues such as social, cultural or religious discrimination; the destruction and theft of property; the erosion of livelihoods through corrupt practices by a small elite; the denial of workers' rights to form or join trade unions; and interference with access to food, water, education and healthcare are often left untouched by conventional transitional processes. In many cases, such abuses affect women and children most acutely (Ní Aoláin 2006). The people of Tunisia during the Arab Spring were not solely protesting against civil and political rights violations. Rather, the protests began when authorities confiscated a man's unlicensed vegetable cart and his means to earn a livelihood (Mabrouk 2011). In Egypt, the motto of the 2011 revolution was similarly 'bread, dignity, social justice' and a majority of participants cited economic hardship as the main reason for protesting (Gunning and Baron 2014). Many of the Latin American transitions have failed to tackle institutional corruption (Cavallaro and Albuja 2008), whilst similar criticisms have been directed towards the Timor-Leste Commission for Reception, Truth and Reconciliation (Stanley 2008). In South Africa, it has been argued that the transition fundamentally failed to tackle structural violence brought about by apartheid (Mamdani 2002). Such examples underline the need to address socio-economic harms in transitional justice processes, as they are crucial to broader transitional goals such as increasing social justice, democratisation, conflict prevention and peacebuilding (Turner 2015). Moreover, a failure to confront them may well prove socially divisive in the longer term, generating and perpetuating mistrust between social groups as well as in the institutions of the state, leading, in many cases, to the reinforcement of structural exclusivity and the recurrence of violence.

On the basis of the above, it would appear that effective restoration for both political and structural forms of violence cannot be fully realised within a legalistic paradigm which seeks to evaluate the question of redress through a purely pecuniary lens:

> In some cases ... the meaning of compensation is powerfully shaped by the larger frame: other gestures of recognition, acknowledgment, atonement, memorializing, social support and guarantees of prevention determine whether financial compensation sends an acceptable and dignifying message to victims and perpetrators, as well as to society generally.
>
> (Walker 2006: 380)

As such, monetary-based corrective justice appears to have fallen out of favour in recent years, and has been replaced by an 'atonement model' of reparations premised on 'the post-Holocaust vision of heightened morality, victim-perpetrator identity, egalitarianism, and restorative justice' (Brooks 2006: 283). The task of reparation is much broader than merely restitution or attempting to restore the *status quo ante*. Rather, it is a much more deeply symbolic process which constitutes a form of acknowledgement or vindication that may prove more effective than money alone in building social cement (Villa-Vicencio 2014). This broader vision of reparation has long been embedded in restorative justice theory, and is also now reflected in the United Nations' *Basic Principles and Guidelines on the Right to a Remedy and Reparation for Victims of Gross Violations of International Human Rights Law and Serious Violations of International Humanitarian Law* (van Boven 2005), which stipulates that material reparations (such as monetary compensation, proprietary restitution and development programmes) ought to be offered in addition to symbolic reparations, which include concepts such as 'rehabilitation', 'satisfaction' (including truth recovery mechanisms, official apologies, judicial sanctions against violations, and acts of commemoration) and 'guarantees of non-repetition' (which may include entrenching international human rights standards and putting in place mechanisms to monitor conflict resolution).

State apologies, in particular, have become relatively commonplace in recent times; it seems we now live in 'the age of apology' (Gibney *et al.* 2008). Although usually communicated by a head of state, apologies are often conceived as a form of collective, official regret over past actions, as opposed to personal regret on the part of the leader. Recent years have witnessed, inter alia, apologies by the leaders of Argentina and Chile for their countries' respective 'Dirty Wars'; apologies by Germany and Japan for their actions in the Second World War; President Clinton's apologies for western indifference over the Rwandan genocide and for previous US support for repressive regimes in Guatemala; the apology of the President of Montenegro, Milo Djukanović, to the Croatian people in 2000; New Zealand's apology to the *Ngai Tahu* in 1998; Tony Blair's 1997 statement of 'remorse' for Britain's role in the Irish Potato Famine, and Queen Elizabeth's apology in 1995 to the Maori people for the 'crippling impact' colonial policies had on their way of living (for further examples, see Gibney *et al.* 2008). There is, of course, a risk that symbolic forms of reparation, including apologies, may ring hollow and appear 'nothing more than a cheap effort at assuaging lingering guilt concerning some misdeeds from the past and, at the same time, to make those issuing the apology feel morally superior to those who came before them' (Gibney and Roxstrom 2001: 513). While it would certainly be foolhardy to suppose that the legacy of civil conflict could be negated through a few choice words from political leaders, it is also clear that apologies which are perceived to be sincere carry a deep moral resonance for many victims and matter a great deal more than the payment of compensation. This was arguably the case with the Australian government's 2008 apology to the stolen generations, and the British government's 2010 apology for the killing of 13 unarmed civilians on Bloody Sunday. Verdeja (2010: 569–570) cites three key reasons why victims tend to place such a high value on such apologies:

> First, apologies promote the restoration of victims' sense of moral value.... Second, apologies can generate public reflection and debate about social norms.... Third, apologies can make critical reinterpretations of history necessary by reframing the past and consequently undermining apologist historical accounts.

The form and extent of many state apologies have been the subject of considerable debate on various levels. Questions abound concerning what constitutes/ ought to constitute an apology; which acts are suitable/unsuitable for apologies; and whether they may be used by states in a cynical effort to divert attention away from prosecutions or, indeed, from more pressing socio-economic concerns (see, for example, Gibney and Roxstrom 2001; Nobles 2008; Parmentier and Weitekamp 2007). Indeed, Clamp (2014) suggests that institutional responses of this nature may carry greater symbolic value for the state and international community than for affected communities on the ground.

Notwithstanding, it is clear that the implications of official apologies may have a very significant impact upon the politics of the transition. In addition to their symbolic function, they also arguably play a form of 'communicative action' (Dzur and Wertheimer 2002) through humanising the 'other' and, in doing so, may be capable of meeting one of the primary needs of victims through placing on public record an acknowledgement of wrongdoing (Gibney and Roxstrom 2001). Provided that they are sincere, few would dispute that state apologies are a good thing; certainly they complement and enhance other transitional justice mechanisms. In this sense, they might be regarded as a form of *reparative* justice, but it is questionable whether they ought to be regarded as a form of *restorative* justice, even in the broadest sense of the term. This follows from the fact that the apology need not (and often does not) emerge from any form of encounter between the parties, nor need there be any form of participation on the part of victims. It is, after all, the state which decides whether, when, and on what terms to offer an apology. Certainly, there is no tangible 'core sequence' of apology and forgiveness which often forms part of a typical restorative process (Retzinger and Scheff 1996: 316).

In enunciating its official regret over past actions, the popular perception of the state as an homogeneous actor arguably means that such apologies carry a particular resonance over and above interpersonal apologies. This arguably reflects Manners' (2002) reflections on the 'normative power' of the state, referring to its capacity to shape what can or should be regarded as 'normal' within any given society. On the one hand, this normative power may be channelled in a more positive manner to propel the transition through promulgating positive values, such as democracy, human rights and the rule of law, and might thereby articulate a futuristic vision of a prosperous and settled society. It may also be used to create social capital between ex-combatants, and potentially to build trust with disaffected communities. On the other hand, such power may be undesirable in that it may be used to frame an overarching state-centric narrative of both the conflict and transition, as well as define key concepts such as 'victimhood' which may have a direct bearing on the roll-out of legal and other practical measures, including development and reparations programmes. In addition to the above-mentioned controversy regarding payments to victims of the Northern Ireland conflict, the Colombian Justice and Peace Law of 2005 also created widespread social tensions since it constructed the notion of 'victimhood' around those who had suffered as a result of the actions of non-state actors, with the vast majority of victims of state violence unable to benefit (Moffet 2014). The exclusion of grassroots and civil society from the process of framing such legislation may serve to further alienate those most acutely affected on the ground. In doing so, states may create the illusion of transitional processes being more participatory and more restorative than praxis might suggest.

Approaches solely based around a top-down framework are ultimately likely to fail because the state is unable to engineer significant social and attitudinal change within communities in which it is commonly viewed as a flawed entity. This may lead to feelings of disillusionment, resentment, or being 'left behind' in a peace process which have been widely reported from inter alia the Democratic Republic of Congo (Vinck and Pham 2008); Rwanda (Brounéus 2008); South Africa (Backer 2007; Byrne 2004; Clark 2012; Kaminer *et al.* 2001); Cambodia (Mohan 2009; Pham *et al.* 2011); Kenya and Uganda (Tenove 2013); and Timor Leste (Stanley 2008; Robins 2012). If the interests and needs of these communities are not sufficiently woven into the process, evidence tells us that the risks of failure and an eventual return to conflict are all too real (Laplante 2008).

As such, the best restorative justice tools – as with all post-conflict mechanisms – tend not to rest on linear assumptions on how best to deal with conflict and tend not to be overly institutionalised or imposed from above. Instead, they are often multi-faceted, cutting across the formal and informal, the top-down and the bottom-up, and making the most effective use of social capital and the civil society to build consensus around political and structural change (Woolford and Ratner 2010). By the same token, it is worth heeding the caveat posed by Daly and Immarigeon (1998): not all that is 'good' stems from community (vigilantism, lack of accountability, punitivism); and not all the bad stems from state (embedding human rights and the rule of law, ensuring social and economic development). Only an effective partnership between the formal and informal sectors can develop the capacity of state institutions to develop diversified strategies that are capable of addressing the complex needs of victims and grassroots communities (Arsovska *et al.* 2008; Backer 2003; Clamp and Doak 2012; McEvoy 2007; Woolford and Ratner 2010). Such idealistic language may appear somewhat aspirational, but successful partnerships between civil society and state institutions were forged during a number of transitions, including in Argentina, Uruguay, Poland and the former Czechoslovakia (see Backer 2003). For example, a number of reparations programmes have attempted to blend individualised and collective responses, as well as 'top-down' and 'bottom-up' approaches. Thus a dedicated healthcare system was established for survivors and victims' families in Chile alongside a pension scheme, while, in Argentina, compensation operated alongside a programme designed to locate the children of political detainees who had been forcibly removed from their families. The Timor-Leste Commission for Reception, Truth and Reconciliation oversaw a scheme which involved perpetrators working on community development projects, such as repairing buildings, planting trees or cleaning local facilities (Mallinder 2014). There has also been fruitful collaboration between the Peace Foundation and the government in Bougainville (Braithwaite *et al.* 2011) and between the government and community restorative justice schemes in Northern Ireland (Doak and O'Mahony 2011). It is only through building partnerships of this nature that transitional justice institutions can start to address the most pressing concerns of grassroots communities.

At a conceptual level, transitional justice discourse needs to be expanded in order to become more responsive to local contexts and the importance of individual agencies. While the state can and must play a role in leading, facilitating and resourcing the transition, this must not be at the expense of grassroots victims and their communities. In short, power and ownership over the transitional process need to be redistributed on micro and mezzo levels, as well as on a wider societal level. Writing in the South African context, the ideal proposed by Skelton and Batley (2006: 125) is that civil society organisations undertake the lion's share of service delivery, with the state enabling such programmes through the provision of resources and oversight of quality of practice. However, the practical means of realising such realignment are rarely straightforward. To begin with, there is often a lack of consensus not only among state actors, but also among community and victim representatives who may hold very diverse conceptions as to the nature of any working relationships (Boesenecker and Vinjamuri 2014). Effective partnerships between state and community organisations are often difficult to realise, given that the state-based agencies are often hierarchical and are not naturally attuned to working with those outside their formal parameters, and that there is relatively little evidence to demonstrate how such a partnership might operate on a practical level with any level of success for a sustained period (Clamp 2014). Indeed as Braithwaite (in this volume) highlights, the long-term sustainability of transitional justice mechanisms is key to delivering an effective and legitimate means of redress for victims. Likewise, it is important to consider the long-term role of international donors and supranational institutions in the delivery of reparations programmes. Short-term projects of a collective nature often fail to target the complex and very specific needs of affected communities and, in doing so, may lack any perceived remedial impact (Moffet 2014).

The monolithic state

There is, however, a further underlying issue which needs to be unpacked in order to maximise the prospects of these types of partnership working effectively in practice. As Ami Harbin and Jennifer Llewelyn helpfully explain in this volume, some of the difficulties stem from the application of 'community', as a collective entity, to a group of individual moral agents who comprise it. Similar issues arise in considering the nature of the state, the crux of the problem being that the state is frequently construed as a monolithic entity, with the actions, rights and interests of individual actors often being subsumed therein. While advocates of restorative justice are rightly keen to point out its flexibility in being able to disentangle complex relationships (particularly compared with conventional legal processes), it is clear that there are a number of issues that are yet to be satisfactorily addressed in both the restorative justice and transitional justice literatures.

The nation state may well be politically recognised as a unified entity, and is often portrayed as such in both academic and non-academic literature. This is particularly evident in the legal sphere, with the state afforded legal personality in both international and domestic law. States – like corporations and individuals – are regarded as having certain rights, duties and privileges which may be enforced through the courts. This implies that the state is thereby capable of undertaking cost–benefit analyses, and makes rational choices on that basis. There may be clear pragmatic advantages in viewing the state in such a light; its legal personality provides a mechanism whereby states can be held to account for breaches of human rights and international law. As a result, many communities and individuals have been able to pursue avenues of legal redress which may not otherwise have been open to them. In the same way, as suggested above, the public perception of the state as a unified actor may also serve to bolster the legitimacy of certain transitional justice mechanisms, including apologies.

However, the logical consequence of perceiving the state in such a light rests on somewhat shaky foundations. The very notion that states are capable of making rational choices seems inherently absurd, and has been subject to considerable criticism within political science literature (see, for example, Green and Shapiro 1994; Friedman 1996). As Mercer (2005) reminds us, political decisions tend to be based on a wide range of factors, including environmental variables, bureaucratic procedures, groupthink, emotions, and even sheer chance. In other words, the state cannot exercise any form of rational choice of its own accord. Like all collective entities, the state is heterogeneous and fluid, comprising a wide range of individual actors who are moral agents only in and of themselves. Moreover, in a Foucauldian sense, the realpolitik of the post-modern world means that state power is not wielded in isolation from other persons, both collective (in the form of local, national and supra-national organisations, NGOs and corporations) and natural (in the form of individuals working both within and beyond the state parameters). The paradoxical forces of globalisation and localisation have resulted in the power of the state both transcending upwards (towards international and transnational bodies such as the United Nations, regional human rights fora, and groups of nations with common interests such as the European Union, NATO, the Organization of Petroleum Exporting Countries, etc.), downwards (towards civil society, community actors and volunteers) as well as horizontally, across a range of public servants and officials.

The state then comprises a range of different individuals exercising a variety of roles at various levels in and beyond government. According to the 'bureaucratic politics' model, state actions and policies tend to be the product of a power struggle between different bureaucracies vying for power and funding (Allison and Halperin 1972). Thus, even within the state, there is considerable conflict between different communities of practice, with similar conflicts occurring at a micro-level among individuals within those bureaucracies. Such individuals have their own vested interests which may overlap, run parallel to, or even conflict with the interests of other state actors. Moreover, organisational process theorists argue that 'standard operating procedures' mean that these bureaucracies and the individuals within them are often wedded to standardised decision-making procedures which become entrenched and ingrained over time, making it difficult for policymakers to 'think outside the box' (Considine 2012). Although not a unitary actor, it is, however, clear that rules, traditions and 'standard operating procedures' may overreach the capacity of the many individuals and bureaucracies that comprise the state's decision-making processes.

In summary then, while an 'official' action or policy response is notionally carried out in the name of the state, it does not necessarily reflect the interests or desires of all the players who comprise it. Rather, the agendas of those individuals who are best placed to influence or manipulate law and policy at the highest levels will hold greatest influence in shaping or manipulating the 'official' actions and responses which are carried out in the name of the state.

A tentative proposal: 'surrogates' of the state

If, as argued above, apologies and other reparative measures are not, in and of themselves, to be regarded as forms of restorative justice, the question then arises as to whether it is possible to conceive of a form of restorative justice in which the state plays a role as a stakeholder, in light of what we understand of its collective nature. While the language of restorative justice is often invoked in relation to truth commissions, questions have rightly been raised as to how restorative they actually are in practice given that interpersonal deliberation only occurs between a tiny minority of both victims and perpetrators, and that victims often report feeling dissatisfied with both the process and the outcome (Clamp and Doak 2012). On one level, it is difficult to envisage how the state, as a governing body, might be party to a fully restorative process; clearly, as a nebulous entity, it is unable to be seated in a conference room or before some form of panel. However, if we disaggregate the state – through decoupling the roles of various actors at various levels of authority – we are then left essentially with a range of individuals with different backgrounds who have their own moral and political standpoints. While such individuals might have been accountable for certain specific actions or decisions while in power, their individual agency means that they can only be held accountable for their own rational choices. Where the person concerned was, for example, a member of the political elite, or a senior military commander who made a specific decision or gave a specific order, a restorative event might be operationalised in a similar manner as occurs within 'ordinary' criminal justice in respect of 'ordinary crime', since such persons would ultimately be accountable for their actions. Indeed, such restorative encounters have already occurred in many post-conflict arenas as part of truth recovery mechanisms (Braithwaite *et al.* 2011; Nixon 2013; Tutu 1999). It is problematic, however, to envisage how such an approach might work on a societal level, given the sheer numbers of victims and offenders in many post-conflict societies, many of whom will have long since passed away. More fundamentally, it is difficult to imagine quite how they might speak for the state as a whole in this capacity. Such individuals will have had little or no role in the formulation of laws and policies that may have resulted in political repression or structural inequality over the course of many years or generations. Even if an individual were prepared to offer such an apology on 'behalf' of the state, this would hardly be desirable since it would effectively mean that the process would be holding one person to account for the actions of others. In this sense, it is unlikely to be satisfactory for victims, since it would serve to depersonalise the very notions of individual agency and accountability, which are seemingly fundamental to restorative justice philosophy.

Restorative justice is, of course, conventionally used for 'traditional' offences committed by natural persons (i.e. individually discrete victims and offenders). There is thus a need to 'to broaden our vision of restorative justice beyond a concern with individualised concepts of crime and criminal responsibility' (Cunneen 2001: 83). Indeed, there have been some innovative practices which have evolved in recent years which may be instructive to the state's role in a transitional context. Many programmes deal with offences committed against corporate actors such as, for example, a public utility company which has sustained criminal damage. In these circumstances, many restorative justice programmes make use of victim representatives, who participate in a restorative process in order to help explain the consequences of the harm to the offender. For example, in our previous evaluation of youth conferencing in Northern Ireland, it was not uncommon for a store–owner, who was not the direct victim of theft, to attend a conference to convey how the offender's actions would ordinarily affect a similar retailer (Doak and O'Mahony 2011). This 'surrogacy' device was also used in instances involving the state; in another conference, we observed that a police officer acted as a surrogate victim where a fellow officer was unable to attend the conference due to the extent of his injuries. Although the use of surrogates tends to be applied in cases where the victim is unable or unwilling to attend in conventional criminal justice, I argue below that the practice of using surrogates (for both victims and offenders) provides a potentially valuable tool in the quest to recalibrate restorative justice for application within transitional processes, even where the primary stakeholders are unable or unwilling to participate.

In a similar vein, informative insights on how collectives might make restoration can be gleaned from some recent high-profile legal cases in the United States. While these cases were resolved through orthodox civil and criminal procedure as opposed to any form of mediation or restorative justice, the *outcomes* might nevertheless be regarded as broadly restorative insofar as they reflect the collective nature of corporate liability and the need to provide forms of redress that are more effective and meaningful for those directly affected by the harm. For example, in 2013 Wal-Mart was famously sentenced by a US court to pay $20 million into a community fund, including a $6 million 'Retail Compliance Centre', which was established to help retailers learn to handle toxic waste appropriately. Likewise, following the *Deepwater Horizon* oil spill, the BP Gulf of Mexico settlement involved hundreds of millions of dollars being diverted into local community projects and environmental protection initiatives (see further Spalding 2014).

Drawing on the above examples, there seems to be no reason in principle as to why such a corporation (or indeed a state) could not nominate a 'surrogate' representative to attend from the organisation, who would assume the role of 'the offender'. This would operate much along the lines of a typical conference or circle. Trained facilitators, acting through local civil society forums, would arrange for a state representative – perhaps a public servant, police officer, judge or politician – to attend a conference involving an individual victim or group of victims. Again, as in 'standard' restorative conferences, the facilitator would invite contributions from both parties, ensuring that they have an equal opportunity to participate, enter into dialogue and ask questions. At the end of the meeting, participants would discuss how to move forwards collectively, and there may be some symbolic gesture of reparation offered by the surrogate on behalf of the state. This would provide a forum for localised and personalised accountability and would create a space for deliberative democracy. This system might either supplement or supplant national forms of truth recovery, but would arguably be more legitimate in that it would provide locally and personally relevant 'micro-/mezzo-truths' on a face-to-face basis, which would be qualitatively distinct from the grander narratives or 'macro-truths' that tend to emerge from mechanisms at national level. In the longer term, such acts may assist in establishing new moral norms and may also build social capital and public trust between disengaged communities and state actors.

Admittedly, this proposal is not unproblematic. First, the use of surrogates means that the process would clearly fall short of the restorative ideal; it would be infinitely better if the perpetrators were to meet their victims in person. Realistically, however, this will only be feasible in a small number of cases where specific perpetrators can be identified in relation to specific incidents and, of course, consent to their involvement. Nonetheless, it is contended that an interpersonal encounter with a surrogate representative of the state would be better than no encounter at all. Secondly, the imbalance of power would be seemingly ingrained in the process. This, however, is a common critique of restorative justice, and in most restorative encounters there will be a power imbalance at some level. While equality is rightly regarded as a sacrosanct principle of restorative justice, it should be borne in mind that the type of equality that is valued is not equality of resources or equality of power. Inequality is often deeply ingrained in transitional societies, and such disparity cannot be ignored and is unlikely to be overcome in a short timeframe (Villa-Vicenzio 2014). However, the use of the term 'equality' within the restorative justice paradigm generally refers to *relational* equality, which might be defined as 'equality of respect, dignity and mutual concern for one another' (Llewelyn and Philpott 2014). Used in this sense, there is no reason why equality cannot be achieved within the parameters of a restorative conference. Thirdly, the proposal might also appear to give rise to the same conundrum as outlined above, namely that a surrogate acting as a state representative would not (usually) be directly responsible for the offence in question. However, under this proposal the surrogate would not be assuming *personal* responsibility for the harm; rather, he or she would be charged with communicating an acceptance of collective responsibility on behalf of the state.

It is thus contended that such an arrangement might be made to work effectively providing certain conditions were in place. First, it is clear that best practice would need to be followed in terms of going thorough pre-encounter checks and preparation. The importance of such preparation is widely acknowledged in terms of 'ordinary' restorative justice, and would be all the more pressing in a transitional context. Careful planning and facilitation can – to some extent at least – minimise the effect of inherent power imbalances. The key here is that the needs of the victim ought to be placed at the centre of the process, that they are given time to express themselves in a non-coercive environment and that measures are put in place to protect their safety (Dzur and Wertheimer 2002; Morris 2002). All parties involved would need to have clarity from the outset about what the process could realistically achieve. Victims, in particular, would need to be made aware that the surrogate was in attendance in the capacity of a representative of the state, rather than as an offender in his or her own right. For their part, surrogate offenders might be selected from the ranks of politics, the civil service, the police, the army, or the judiciary. They would need to be thoroughly briefed about the nature and extent of the harm caused to the victim, and the causal relationship between such harm and the actions of the state. They should approach the encounter with as many facts as possible, and be prepared to answer questions the victim may have in relation to a specific historical incident or in relation to state policy more generally.

Second, careful thought would need to be afforded to the nature of any outcome. Since – for reasons outlined above – it would be inappropriate for surrogates to offer a *personal* apology (unless they themselves were actually implicated), the best that might be hoped for is that they could communicate a *collective* apology, on behalf of the state, in person. This would inevitably need to be tied to the wider programme of transition and might involve, for example, reiterating a formal public apology that had been made by the leadership of the state. The interpersonal communication of the apology may render it more sincere in the eyes of the victim, and they may also gain a better understanding of the fact that the state is ultimately comprised of human actors who – like all of us – are ultimately fallible in their judgements. They may also gain an insight into the reasons behind the state's actions, even if those may seem unpalatable. By the same token, it would evidently not be appropriate for the surrogate to offer any form of personal reparation, but he or she might communicate those aspects of broader reparations or DDR (demobilisation, disarmament and reintegration) programmes that might be of direct benefit to the victim.

Third, and following from the above, the process would need to dovetail with a much larger transitional package which may include, inter alia, trials, a truth commission, collective reparations and DDR initiatives. For example, depending on the context, courts or truth commissions might operate a referral process whereby certain cases are assigned to restorative conferencing, not dissimilar to that which already operates in the youth courts of New Zealand and Northern Ireland. Alternatively, such a programme may operate 'in reverse', whereby localised processes are utilised to harness grassroots economic and political priorities which could then form the basis of a genuinely 'bottom-up' effort to shape the broader transitional arrangements at national level. Thus, for example, the nature and extent of any amnesty or lustrations laws, or the remit of a national truth commission, could be directly informed by deliberative dialogue between grassroots representatives and state surrogates.

Finally, steps should be taken to reintegrate and rehabilitate the state, as is done with 'ordinary' offenders in the criminal justice system. The process of acknowledgement and truth-telling may, in itself, be constructive to this end, but it is also possible that the very fact that victims are able to put a 'face' to the state and make a connection on a human level may play a role in building trust in the longer term. As part of our evaluation into youth conferencing in Northern Ireland, there was some evidence that coming face-to-face with a police officer assisted in alleviating a sense of suspicion of the police that prevails among certain communities in the province (Doak and O'Mahony, 2011). The social contact hypothesis, while not unproblematic (see Clamp, 2014), posits that this form of encounter may assist the transition process in the longer term by humanising the 'other', and thus challenge the pre-existing prejudices and collective stereotyping (Doak and O'Mahony, 2011; Rohne *et al.* 2008).

In order for this proposal to work effectively, considerable investment would obviously be required. As John Braithwaite outlines in this volume, one of the major problems that has beset transitional justice is that there are simply more victims than transitional mechanisms can handle within their temporal limits. In a similar vein, Villa-Vicenzio (2014: 206) has warned that such time-limited efforts are essentially akin to 'a one-off holiday before returning to an exploitative world where the playground bully goes home with the prize'. For that reason, serious consideration ought to be afforded to the establishment of long-term structures which would enable many more victims to be able to access these types of processes. There would obviously have to be widespread 'buy-in' from public servants who would assume the role of a state representative, and it would probably be the case that some form of financial or work-based incentive would be required to encourage their participation. As ever, of course, the feasibility of such a project would ultimately depend upon the political and economic priorities of the donor community, with the need for increased investment and appropriate targeting of its financial and logistical resources. It is equally important, if not more so, that the process is perceived as legitimate in the eyes of victims and grassroots communities. As noted above, transitional justice has been dogged with failed attempts to superimpose mechanisms from above and it is therefore vital that victims and ex-combatants are involved at all stages of the process, from its conception and design through to its management, implementation and day-to-day operation.

Conclusions

Our conceptual understandings of both restorative justice and transitional justice have not yet developed sufficiently to delineate a normative role for the state in the aftermath of civil conflict. To some extent, an inherent tension will always exist between the overriding desire for a 'successful' transition at a societal level and the needs and desires of communities and survivors most acutely affected by the conflict. In some respects, there are reasons to be optimistic. Restorative justice and transitional justice are both relatively nascent fields of study and praxis, and a recent proliferation in empirical research has served to stimulate innovative and creative thinking around how solutions to conflict might be better attuned to meet the needs of victims and communities. International and state actors are apparently – in some cases at least – more responsive to the concerns around perceptions of legitimacy and the associated dangers of ignoring the inputs of grassroots stakeholders. There are signs that more flexible forms of transitional justice arrangements are emerging, and the value of state–community has become apparent through co-operation on aspects of the transition in (among others) Timor Leste, Northern Ireland and Argentina. Notwithstanding the above, there is clearly still much to be done in order for the effects of innovative academic and policy contributions to translate into an increased sense of legitimacy on the ground.

The proposal here is for a participatory and inclusive restorative justice process that would be interwoven with other elements of a context-specific transitional package. The envisaged process would give victims an opportunity to meet and interact with representatives of the state, find answers to their questions, and receive an apology in person. It would clearly be counterproductive to present this proposal as a uniform blueprint; there may very well be communities where, for whatever reason, it would not be broadly accepted. However, it is hoped that the proposal might offer a broad framework that would be sufficiently flexible to allow it to be adopted in a variety of transitional contexts. This suggestion is not intended to downplay the deeper structural and political legacies of conflict that cannot possibility be resolved through individual, case-by-case encounters of this type. However, as initiatives in Bougainville and Timor Leste have demonstrated, restorative justice has a vital role to play in complementing (rather than replacing), other more established accountability mechanisms such as truth commissions or trials, as well as other forms of reparation and DDR. Undoubtedly, a number of conceptual and pragmatic challenges remain, and some have argued that transitional justice may become 'analytically overstretched and impractical' if it tries to include too much and that efforts to have it tackle broad socio-economic harms may create unrealistic expectations (Lambourne 2009; Waldorf 2012). However, if transitional justice is to be regarded as a forward-facing, as well as a backward-facing endeavour, creative thinking around such questions is surely to be encouraged.

References

Allison, G., and Halperin, M. (1972) 'Bureaucratic Politics: A paradigm and some policy implications', *World Politics*, 24(1): 40–79.
Arsovska, J., Valiñas, M., and Vanspauwen, K. (2013) 'From micro to macro, from individual to state: restorative justice and multi-level diplomacy in divided societies', in

I. Aertsen, J. Arsovska, H.-C. Rohne, M. Valiñas and K. Vanspauwen (eds) *Restoring Justice after Large-scale Violent Conflicts: Kosovo, DR Congo and the Israeli–Palestinian case*. Cullompton, UK: Willan.

Backer, D. (2003) 'Civil Society and Transitional Justice: Possibilities, patterns and prospects'. *Journal of Human Rights*, 2(3), 297–313.

Backer, D. (2007) 'Victims' responses to truth commissions: evidence from South Africa', in M. Ndulo (ed.) *Security, Reconstruction, and Reconciliation: When the wars end*. London: University College London.

Bell, C. (2009) 'Transitional Justice, Interdisciplinarity and the State of the 'Field' or 'Non-field', *International Journal of Transitional Justice*, 3(1): 5–27.

Boesenecker, A. and Vinjamuri, L. (2014) 'Charting the path of justice in peacebuilding', in J. Llewellyn and D. Philpott (eds) *Restorative Justice, Reconciliation and Peacebuilding*, Oxford: Oxford University Press.

Braithwaite, J. (2006) 'Building legitimacy through restorative justice', in T. Tyler (ed.) *Legitimacy and Criminal Justice*, New York: Russell Sage.

Braithwaite, J., Charlesworth, H., Reddy, P. and Dunn, L. (2011) *Reconciliation and Architectures of Commitment*, Canberra: ANU Press.

Brooks, R. (2006) *Atonement and Forgiveness: A new model for black reparations*, Berkeley, CA: University of California Press.

Brounéus, K. (2008) 'Truth-telling as Talking Cure? Insecurity and retraumatization in the Rwandan Gacaca courts', *Security Dialogue*, 39(1): 55–76.

Byrne, C. (2004) 'Benefit or Burden: Victims' reflections on TRC participation', *Peace and Conflict*, 10: 237–256.

Cavallaro, J. and Albuja, S. (2008) 'The lost agenda: economic crimes and truth commissions in Latin America and beyond', in K. McEvoy and L. McGregor (eds) *Transitional Justice from Below. Grassroots activism and the struggle for change*, Oxford: Hart Publishing.

Clark, P. (2010) *The Gacaca Courts, Post-genocide Justice and Reconciliation in Rwanda: Justice without lawyers*. Cambridge: Cambridge University Press.

Clark, J. (2012) 'Reconciliation via Truth? A study of South Africa's TRC', *Journal of Human Rights*, 11(2): 189–209.

Clamp, K. (2014) *Restorative Justice in Transition*, London: Routledge.

Clamp, K. and Doak, J. (2012) 'More than Words: Restorative justice concepts in transitional justice settings', *International Criminal Law Review*, 12(3): 339–360.

Considine, M. (2012) 'Thinking Outside the Box? Applying design theory to public policy', *Politics & Policy*, 40(4): 704–724.

Cunneen, C. (2001) 'Reparations and restorative justice: responding to the gross violations of human rights', in H. Strang and J. Braithwaite (eds) *Restorative Justice and Civil Society*, Cambridge: Cambridge University Press.

Cunneen, C. (2008) 'State crime, the colonial Question and Indigenous peoples', in A. Smeulers and R. Haveman (eds) *Supernational Criminology: Towards a criminology of international crimes*. Oxford: Intersetia.

Daly, K. and Immarigeon, R. (1998) 'The Past, Present, and Future of Restorative Justice: Some critical reflections', *Contemporary Justice Review*, 1(1): 21–45.

De Greiff, P. (2006) *The Handbook of Reparations*, Oxford: Oxford University Press.

Doak, J. and O'Mahony, D. (2011) 'In Search of Legitimacy: Restorative youth conferencing in Northern Ireland', *Legal Studies*, 31(2): 305–325.

Dzur, A. and Wertheimer, A. (2002) 'Forgiveness and Public Deliberation: The practice of restorative justice', *Criminal Justice Ethics*, 21(1): 3–20.

Eriksson, A. (2013) *Justice in Transition*, London: Routledge.

Forrest, R. and Kearns, A. (2001) 'Social Cohesion, Social Capital and the Neighbourhood', *Urban studies*, 38(12): 2125–2143.

Friedman, J. (1996) *The Rational Choice Controversy: Economic models of politics reconsidered*, New Haven, CT: Yale University Press.

Gibney, M. and Roxstrom, E. (2001) 'The Status of State Apologies', *Human Rights Quarterly*, 23: 911–939.

Gibney, M., Howard-Hassman, R., Coicaud, J.-M. and Steiner, N. (2008) *The Age of Apology: Facing up to the past*, Philadephia, PA: University of Pennsylvania Press.

Gready, P. and Robins, S. (2014) 'From Transitional to Transformative Justice: A new agenda for practice', *International Journal of Transitional Justice*, 8(3): 339–361.

Green, D. and Shapiro, I. (1994) *Pathologies of Rational Choice Theory: A critique of applications in political science*, New Haven, CT: Yale University Press.

Gunning, J. and Baron, I. (2014) *Why Occupy a Square? People, Protests and Movements in the Egyptian Revolution*, Oxford: Oxford University Press.

Hayner, P. (2011) *Unspeakable Truths: Facing the challenge of truth commissions*, London: Routledge.

Kaminer, D., Stein, D., Mbanga, I., and Zungu-Dirwayi, N. (2001) 'The Truth and Reconciliation Commission in South Africa: Relation to psychiatric status and forgiveness among survivors of human rights abuses', *The British Journal of Psychiatry*, 178(4): 373–377.

Lambourne, W. (2009) 'Transitional Justice and Peacebuilding after Mass Violence', *International Journal of Transitional Justice*, 3(1): 28–48.

Laplante, L. J. (2008). 'Transitional Justice and Peacebuilding: Diagnosing and Addressing the Socioeconomic Roots of Violence through a Human Rights Framework', *International Journal of Transitional Justice*, 2: 331–355.

Llewellyn, J. and Philpott, D. (2014) 'Restorative justice and reconciliation: twin frameworks for peacebuilding', in J. Llewellyn and D. Philpott (eds) *Restorative Justice, Reconciliation and Peacebuilding*, Oxford: Oxford University Press.

Long, W. and Breke, P. (2003) *War and Reconciliation: Reason and emotion in conflict*, Boston: MIT Press.

Mabrouk, M. (2011) 'A Revolution for Dignity and Freedom: Preliminary observations on the social and cultural background to the Tunisian revolution', *Journal of North African Studies*, 16(4): 625–635.

Mamdani, M. (2002) 'Amnesty or Impunity? A Preliminary Critique of the Report of the Truth and Reconciliation Commission of South Africa (TRC)', *Diacritics*, 32(3–4): 33–59.

Maglione, G. (2014) 'Discursive Fields and Subject Positions: Becoming "victim", "offender" and "community" in restorative justice'. *Restorative Justice* 2(3): 327–348.

Mallinder, L. (2014) 'Amnesties in the pursuit of reconciliation, peacebuilding and restorative justice', in J. Llewellyn and D Philpott (eds) *Restorative Justice, Reconciliation and Peacebuilding*, Oxford: Oxford University Press.

Manners, I. (2002) 'Normative Power Europe: A contradiction in terms?', *Journal of Common Market Studies*, 40(2): 235–258.

McEvoy, K. (2000) 'Law, Struggle, and Political Transformation in Northern Ireland', *Journal of Law and Society*, 27(4): 542–571.

McEvoy, K. (2007) 'Beyond Legalism: Towards a thicker understanding of transitional justice', *Journal of Law and Society*, 34(4), 411–440.

McEvoy, K. and McConnachie, K. (2013) 'Victims and Transitional Justice Voice, Agency and Blame', *Social & Legal Studies*, 22(4), 489–513.

McEvoy, K. and McGregor, L. (2008) *Transitional Justice from Below: Grassroots activism and the struggle for change*, Oxford: Hart Publishing.

Mercer, J. (2005) 'Rationality and Psychology in International Politics', *International Organization*, 59(1): 77–106.

Mohan, M. (2009) 'The Paradox of Victim-centrism: Victim participation at the Khmer Rouge Tribunal', *International Criminal Law Review*, 9: 733–775.

Moffet, L. (2014) *Navigating Complex Identities of Victim-perpetrators in Reparation Mechanisms*. Queen's University Belfast Research Paper No. 13, 11 September, 2014.

Morris, A. (2002) 'Critiquing the Critics: A brief response to critics of restorative justice', *British Journal of Criminology*, 42(3): 596–615.

Ní Aoláin, F. (2006) 'Political Violence and Gender during Times of Transition', *Columbia Journal of Gender and Law*, 15(3): 829–849.

Ní Aoláin, F. and Campbell, C. (2005) 'The Paradox of Transition in Conflicted Democracies', *Human Rights Quarterly*, 27(1): 172–213.

Nixon, R. (2013) *Justice and Governance in East Timor: Indigenous approaches and the new subsistence state*, London: Routledge.

Nobles, M. (2008) *The Politics of Official Apologies*, Cambridge, Cambridge University Press.

O'Mahony, D., Doak, J. and Clamp, K. (2012) 'Reforming Youth Justice in Transitional Societies: Northern Ireland and South Africa compared', *Northern Ireland Legal Quarterly*, 63(2): 267–290.

Parmentier, S. and Weitekamp, E. (2007) 'Political Crimes and Serious Violations of Human Rights: Towards a criminology of international crimes', *Sociology of Crime, Law and Deviance*, 9: 109–44.

Pavlich, G. (2005) *Governing Paradoxes of Restorative Justice*, London: Routledge.

Pham, P., Vinck, P., Balthazard, M., Strasser, J. and Om, C. (2011) 'Victim Participation and the Trial of Duch at the Extraordinary Chambers in the Courts of Cambodia', *Journal of Human Rights Practice*, 3(3): 264–287.

Retzinger, S. and Scheff, T. (1996) 'Strategy for community conferences: emotions and social bonds', in J. Hudson and B. Galaway (eds) *Restorative Justice: International perspectives*, Monsey, NY: Criminal Justice Press.

Robins, S. (2012) 'Challenging the Therapeutic Ethic: A victim-centred evaluation of transitional justice process in Timor-Leste', *International Journal of Transitional Justice*, 6: 83–105.

Rohne, H.-C., Arsovska, J. and Aertsen, I. (2008) 'Challenging restorative justice– state-based conflict, mass victimization and the changing nature of warfare', in I. Aertsen, J. Arsovska, H-C. Rohne, M. Valiñas and K. Vanspauwen (eds) *Restoring Justice after Large-scale Violent Conflicts: Kosovo, DR Congo and the Israeli– Palestinian case*, Cullompton, UK: Willan.

Sharp, D. (2012) 'Addressing Economic Violence in Times of Transition: Toward a positive-peace paradigm for transitional justice', *Fordham International Law Journal*, 35(3): 780–814.

Skelton, A. and Batley, M. (2006) *Charting Progress, Mapping the Future: Restorative justice in South Africa*, Pretoria, Institute for Security Studies.

Spalding, A. (2014) '*Restorative Justice for Multinational Corporations*'. Available at SSRN: http://ssrn.com/abstract=2403930.

Sperfeldt, C. (2012) 'Collective Reparations at the Extraordinary Chambers in the Courts of Cambodia', *International Criminal Law Review*, 12(3): 457–490.

Stein, D., Seedat, S., Kaminer, D., Moomal, H., Herman, A., Sonnega, J. and Williams,

D. (2008) 'The Impact of the Truth and Reconciliation Commission on Psychological Distress and Forgiveness in South Africa', *Social Psychiatry and Psychiatric Epidemiology*, 43(6): 462–468.

Stanley, E. (2008) *Torture, Truth and Justice: The case of Timor-Leste*, London: Routledge.

Tenove, C. (2013) *International Criminal Justice for Victims? Assessing the International Criminal Court from the Perspective of Victims in Kenya and Uganda*, Africa Portal, Research Paper No. 1, September 2013. Available: www.africaportal.org/articles/2013/09/24/international-justice-victims-assessing-international-criminal-court-perspective.

Turner, C. (2015) 'Transitional Constitutionalism and the Case of the Arab Spring', *International and Comparative Law Quarterly*, 64(2): 267–291.

Tutu, D. (1999) *No future Without Forgiveness*, NewYork: Random House.

van Boven, T. (2005) *Basic Principles and Guidelines on the Right to a Remedy and Reparation for Victims of Gross Violations of International Human Rights Law and Serious Violations of International Humanitarian Law*, New York: United Nations.

Van Ness, D. (2014) 'Accountability', in J. Llewellyn and D. Philpott (eds) *Restorative Justice, Reconciliation and Peacebuilding*, Oxford: Oxford University Press.

Verdeja, E. (2010) 'Official Apologies in the Aftermath of Political Violence', *Metaphilosophy*, 41(4): 563–581.

Villa-Vincencio, C. (2014) 'Pursuing inclusive reparations: living between promise and non-delivery', in J. Llewellyn and D. Philpott (eds) *Restorative Justice, Reconciliation and Peacebuilding*, Oxford: Oxford University Press.

Vinck, P. and Pham, P. (2008) 'Ownership and Participation in Transitional Justice Mechanisms: A sustainable human development perspective from Eastern DRC', *International Journal of Transitional Justice*, 2(2): 398–411.

Wachtel, T. and McCold, P. (2001) 'Restorative justice in everyday life', in H. Strang and J. Braithwaite (eds) *Restorative Justice and Civil Society*, Cambridge: Cambridge University Press.

Waldorf, L. (2012) 'Anticipating the Past: Transitional justice and socio-economic wrongs', *Social & Legal Studies*, 21(2): 171–186.

Walker, M. (2006) 'Restorative Justice and Reparations', *Journal of Social Philosophy*, 37(3): 377–395.

Woolford, A. and Ratner, R. (2010) 'Disrupting the Informal–Formal Justice Complex: On the transformative potential of civil mediation, restorative justice and reparations politics', *Contemporary Justice Review*, 13(1): 5–17.

6 Participation as restoration

The current limits of restorative justice for victim participants in international criminal trials

Ray Nickson

Introduction

Justice in transitional contexts is expected to respond to a variety of needs and imperatives. In these responses, transitional justice efforts have employed both restorative and retributive frameworks. Yet, following the creation of the ad hoc tribunals for Rwanda and the former Yugoslavia, official and international responses to justice in transition have often adopted prosecutorial mechanisms, the primary function of which has been to deliver retributive justice. These include the special courts in Sierra Leone and Lebanon; the War Crimes Court in Kosovo; the Bosnian War Crimes Chamber; the tribunal for prosecutions of Khmer Rouge leaders; and the International Criminal Court. While these international criminal justice institutions have primarily embraced a retributive response, some have also sought to work with more restorative institutions (such as truth commissions) or employ restorative approaches (such as victim participation). In particular, schemes that allow for the participation of victims during international criminal trials have been promoted as significant restorative justice initiatives because including victims, it is claimed, leads to empowerment, restoration of dignity, healing and reconciliation (Bair 2009; Baumgartner 2008; Chung 2008; Jasine and Phan 2011; McGongigle 2009; Mohan 2009; Pena and Carayon 2013; Van den Wyngaert 2011).

At face value, the participation of victims reflects the restorative justice imperative to 'deprofessionalise' justice. Yet, legal elites dominate the practice of international criminal justice: a cadre of jurists and legal professionals now exist who are ready to staff newly created institutions. In interviews conducted with a variety of international courts and tribunals, it was easy to find both senior and junior staff in all areas of the courts who had previously worked at one or more other international courts or tribunals (see Nickson 2013). Given that international criminal trials are a major feature of justice in transitional contexts, this contributes to the dominance of legalism in transitional justice. For McEvoy (2008: 28), a strong positivistic legal trend exists in transitional justice practice, in which legal elites may develop a perception of serving 'higher goals' such as rebuilding the rule of law, with the consequence that 'victims or violence affected communities [are treated] as constituencies which must be managed, rather than citizens to whom they [legal elites] must be accountable'. When coupled with what McEvoy observes as an emphasis on punishment in international criminal justice, it is difficult to conceive of how restorative justice might occur in such heavily professionalised institutions.

Yet, this is what victim participation at the International Criminal Court (ICC) and the Extraordinary Chambers in the Courts of Cambodia (ECCC) has, at least partly, sought to achieve: a restorative justice dimension within elite-controlled retributive institutions. This chapter examines victim participation as a restorative initiative at the ICC and ECCC with a view to critically evaluating just how 'restorative' these victim participation schemes have been. This chapter argues that this restorative justice initiative fails to restore because it does not give sufficient process control and opportunity for expression to non-elites, and more specifically victims. It then suggests ways in which restoration could be enhanced at the ICC and ECCC, as well as in future attempts to incorporate restorative justice into prosecutorial responses in transitional societies more generally.

The importance of process control in restorative justice

While victim participation represents a positive step toward a more holistic approach to transitional justice, the restorative potential of such initiatives remains untapped. In other words, the potential to truly incorporate victims into the process, so that their voices are heard and they have a genuine influence on how the harms they suffered and the causes of those harms will be addressed, has not been realised in practice. Marshall's (1999: 5) oft-cited definition of restorative justice: 'a process whereby parties with a stake in a specific offence collectively resolve how to deal with the aftermath of the offence and its implications for the future' indicates the importance attached to participation and empowerment by restorative scholars. As such, one would expect that, where a process claims to be restorative, and in reality lives up to its claim, it should seek to involve stakeholders in the process and empower them to influence decisions about how to repair the harm that has been caused.

Participation and empowerment are closely bonded in transitional restorative justice literature. This is because, as Clamp (2014) notes, the aspirational goal for transitional justice interventions should be the transformation of conflict into peace, built upon the transformation of stakeholders. One pathway for this transformation to occur is through a restorative justice process that embodies values including participation and empowerment. The participation necessary for restorative justice is more than mere inclusion in the process, however. It requires opportunities for victims to 'emote and to suggest ways in which the causes and consequences of the incident may be addressed' (Clamp 2014: 36). Consequently, we must distinguish between participation that contributes to restorative outcomes and participation that is insufficient to aid restorative endeavours. Drawing on Edwards's (2004) typology of participation, Clamp explains how the categories outlined do not adequately reflect the type of participation required in restorative justice processes: a power imbalance is evident when victims have sole control; stakeholders do not have decision-making power when simply consulted; victims have no active role when solely recipients of information; and the opportunity to express emotions can be disempowering when no follow-up action is undertaken. What these categories lack is engagement, which she argues offers the chance to express emotions, articulate needs and contribute solutions to addressing the harm, which are the central features of restorative justice.

Engagement can also be considered through Arnstein's (1971) ladder of participation. Arnstein identifies participation as ranging in eight categories from manipulation to actual control of processes. At the top of this ladder are three categories that should be understood as promoting engagement, which also provide a level of power in the process for participants. These three categories – partnership, delegated power, and control – provide for stakeholder engagement by allowing space for participants to express emotions, articulate needs and contribute solutions. These categories also describe participation where control of process and outcomes is, to varying degrees, in the hands of participants. As Mohan (2009: 750) has observed, in these categories participants are empowered through the ability 'to make decisions about [their] own life, have [their] own say before a formal judicial process, and be the author and arbiter of [their] own recovery'. Braithwaite and Mugford (1994) refer to this as 'process control'. Within the context of international criminal justice, this means that, to truly incorporate victims into the process or to give them a sense of process control, their voices have to be heard and they should have a genuine influence on how the harms they suffered and the causes of those harms will be addressed.

Process control is a central feature of restorative justice that distinguishes it from other types of justice approaches. Braithwaite and Mugford (1994) explain that degradation ceremonies privilege authorities with the role of denouncer and silence the voices of victims and other stakeholders. Most international criminal trials – with control in the hands of elites and operating primarily within a prosecutorial and retributive frame – would fit the description of degradation ceremonies. This privileging and silencing is usually deeply unsatisfactory for victims, and restorative endeavours seek to overcome this by giving victims and other stakeholders the opportunity to participate and by increasing the amount of control that they have in the process. Such participation is an important value of restorative justice, partly because it addresses the disempowerment victims (and even offenders) have experienced in traditional retributive approaches to dealing with crime and conflict.

Process control should, therefore, be seen as an important feature of restorative justice practice, as it addresses a key restorative objective: empowerment. Empowerment in restorative justice is about redressing the lack of stakeholders' control and the over accumulation of control among elites. For victims, but also other stakeholders, 'involvement in their own cases … can be an important way to return a sense of empowerment' (Zehr 2002: 15). Empowerment, then, is about returning control to stakeholders, while raising awareness among stakeholders about their own roles, capabilities and responsibilities (Clamp 2014).

This means supporting the decision-making power of stakeholders, providing opportunities to exercise that power and encouraging the confidence to do so. This contrasts with the disempowerment that arises by removing control and giving it to elites such as judges and prosecutors. Devolving process control to participants requires engagement, as it cannot take place when the expression of emotions or the contribution of solutions is not permitted. In this way, empowerment and engagement are inextricably linked: true participation that engages stakeholders cannot take place without their empowerment in the process, and empowerment cannot be achieved unless stakeholders are engaged through their participation.

While victim participation at the ICC and ECCC takes places within a primarily retributive institution, the dimension of restorative justice it offers is empowerment for victims through engagement. The restorative dimension and the restorative potential of both the ICC and ECCC can be evaluated according to the extent that 'parties with a stake' are truly permitted to participate and influence how the harms caused by an offence will be addressed. The following section provides an overview of the opportunities for victim participation within the ICC and ECCC. What becomes apparent is that the usual justice process, replicated in most international criminal justice institutions, often fails to meet the needs of victims, offenders and other stakeholders, in large part because these groups are not active players in the process. This lack of process control afforded to victim participants constrains the restorative potential of these endeavours, as ownership of the response is vested almost entirely with elites.

The failure of the ICC and ECCC as restorative models of transitional justice

While this chapter argues that victim participation at the ICC and ECCC is not particularly restorative in practice, these schemes have been claimed as restorative justice measures (Bair 2009; Baumgartner 2008; Chung 2008; Jasine and Phan 2011; McGongigle 2009; Mohan 2009; Pena and Carayon 2013; Van den Wyngaert 2011). Although the inclusion of victims in proceedings at the ICC and ECCC was heralded as an important advance in transitional justice, restorative justice in transitional societies is not new. The South African Truth and Reconciliation Commission (SA TRC) represented a peak for official restorative transitional justice, before a decline with the advent of ad hoc criminal tribunals in the mid-1990s. Despite its promotion as a model of restorative justice in transition, Clamp (2014) notes that the SA TRC has been criticised for failing to live up to its restorative claims. A problem with the SA TRC was its elite-driven nature, top-down operation (Lundy and McGovern, 2008) and very formal procedures and practices, with some elements resembling court hearings and adopting a distinctly judicial and accusatorial nature (Allan and Allan 2000). This elite-driven context meant that the SA TRC did not realise its restorative justice potential, with a restricted level of participation that permitted only a few to tell their stories. In turn, this failed to highlight the stories of the 'victims of the generalised system of Apartheid itself' (Clamp 2014: 80).

Although the SA TRC was a prominent transitional justice response at the time, the model was not adopted when responding to war crimes in the former Yugoslavia and the genocide in Rwanda. In part, this reflected the growing dominance and influence of legalism in transitional and international criminal justice (Nickson 2013). The International Criminal Tribunal for the former Yugoslavia (ICTY) and the International Criminal Tribunal for Rwanda (ICTR) were distant institutions, remote from the people whose lives had been damaged in the violence that prompted their creation. The proceedings were decidedly legal and formal, permitting victims of mass atrocity to participate only as instruments of the prosecution. In this role they were often subject to rigorous cross-examination in the adversarial proceedings, an experience that hindered healing. The communities that were affected directly by the violence also had little involvement and no ownership of proceedings – indeed the choice of what would be investigated and prosecuted was not something communities had been able to participate in or influence directly.

When future opportunities to design justice responses for societies in transition appeared, it was recognised that the ICTY and ICTR had been poor models for providing justice for victims. As a consequence, the elites who were tasked with designing new international criminal justice institutions looked for alternatives that would enhance the sense of justice afforded to victims. One of the solutions adopted by subsequent institutions was victim participation. Whereas the ad hoc tribunals were primarily based on an adversarial system of justice, victim participation schemes mirrored the inclusion of victims in inquisitorial systems. Not only was this seen as more inclusive, but also articulated as a restorative initiative.

Victim participation in the ICC

The dominance of elites within the current design of the ICC diminishes the restorative value of participation for victims in a number of ways. First, the terms of participation are set by elites. So, while victims' theoretical rights to participate are quite extensive (see Van den Wyngaert 2011), this is constrained by procedural hoops through which their legal representatives need to navigate. For example, legal representatives of identified victims (not those who elect to remain anonymous) may question witnesses. They must first, however, seek leave to do so, demonstrate that the witness' testimony affects the interests of the victim and provide a list of questions in advance, having 'identified and anticipated' in their application the parts of the proceedings relevant to the victims' interests (Pena 2010: 505). In this way, the terms of participation imposed on victims establish hurdles that limit the ways in which participation can be undertaken.

Second, elites evaluate and determine who may access participation and the spaces where participation is performed. Restrictions on victim participation appear almost immediately in the scheme, as the application process to participate as a victim in ICC proceedings is lengthy, administrative, and complicated. Initially, victims of crimes that were both charged and not charged were allowed to participate at trial. The appeals chamber, however, later limited the right of participation to only those who were victims of crimes charged for that trial (Van den Wyngaert 2011). The entire process of application has not been designed to suit the needs of victims – the people who will almost always be the least empowered in this process (Pena and Carayon 2013). Application forms, for instance, are complex and frequently require assistance for victims to complete. Compounding these problems is the snail's pace of application (Pena 2010), meaning victims must wait on the sidelines while elites determine their participatory rights.

Indeed, the application procedure is not just complicated, but needlessly so, requiring the balancing of a broad right to participate with an individual assessment of the impact that victims' participation will have on proceedings (Chung 2008). The ICC does not merely determine as part of this application that the applicant is a victim; the court must also agree that the victim's personal interests are affected and that it would be appropriate for the victim to participate in that stage of proceedings (Cohen 2009: 370). In addition, the three elements in section 68(3) of the *Rome Statute* that outline the broad principles of victim participation must be continually reassessed for each victim participant at each stage of proceedings. For example, despite being granted the status of victim participant at the pre-trial stage, the same victim participant must have their application reassessed at the trial stage (Baumgartner 2008). These factors are as likely to reinforce disempowerment and frustration as they are to facilitate involvement and recognise the worth or dignity of victims. In particular, they serve to underscore that the process is controlled by elites and the role of victims is a marginal addition to proceedings.

Third, the participation of victims is mediated and controlled by others. Victims are unlikely to be on the same continent as, let alone attend any proceedings of, the ICC. Instead, participation is undertaken by victims' legal representatives. As a result, Van den Wyngaert (2011) has asked whether victim participation can ever be anything other than symbolic. In this symbolic act, victim voices are translated and interpreted through their legal representatives, in the representative's voice. In effect, legal representation serves to modify and transform the nature of victim participation, shaping it into a legal rather than a personal act: 'rather than being emotive, victim participation at the ICC centers on the expression of victims' legal interest and concerns' (Wemmers 2010: 641). This legal lens elevates restricted, judicially manageable interests and values as opposed to restorative values of engagement and empowerment.

Not only must victims be represented by lawyers to enjoy the full (though limited) extent of participation the ICC affords them (Baumgartner 2008), but victims are often required to be jointly represented by the same lawyers. While this requirement makes sense from a procedural and efficiency perspective, it elevates those considerations above the interests of victim participants. When the court unilaterally groups victims together it can serve to obscure the real differences in their needs, hopes, experiences, harms and paths to restoration. Not only might victims' interests not align, but, as Trumbull (2008) has observed, they may be in conflict. This potentially artificial collation of victims may serve to provide the court with only a generic picture of the needs and concerns of victims, reinforcing a top-down approach, instead of an approach where the ICC genuinely considers and addresses the concerns of victims (Pena and Carayon 2013).

One of the least restorative elements of joint legal representation for victims at the ICC is the appointment of lawyers. As Pena and Carayon (2013) explain, this is often conducted by the court without consulting, or seeking input from, the victims. This is problematic because appointment of legal counsel will often be the first encounter victims have with ICC proceedings. When that counsel is appointed without the meaningful participation of victims in their selection, it serves to reinforce victims' lack of power and control over the process, consequently diminishing the restorative potential of the process. This, Pena and Carayon claim, can inform the expectations that victims have about how much the ICC will consider their views and concerns. This generic approach also reflects the way that counsel is appointed for indigent defendants, but given that the needs of defendants and victims are diverse, and because victim participation is in practice completely different to that of defendants at the ICC, a more tailored appointment system would be appropriate (Pena 2010).

Elite control also operates to exclude participation in determining what crimes will be charged. Involvement in these decisions can be important for restorative justice as it goes to the heart of recognition for the harms that victims have suffered and how they can be empowered or disempowered by the institution. Of course, charging a crime is not the only way to recognise victimisation, but, after guilty verdicts, it is the most potent way to recognise victims in a prosecutorial system. Pena and Carayon (2013) observed that victim participants at the ICC expressed considerable dissatisfaction with their lack of influence regarding the charges against an accused. A lack of process control has meant that victims exercise no direct influence at the pre-trial stage or on the charges against the accused, so that the crimes charged do not necessarily reflect the victims' experience of crimes (Pena and Carayon 2013). This diminishes the engagement and empowerment of stakeholders by excluding their role in an important part of proceedings.

Lack of process control over which crimes are prosecuted contributes to further restrictions on the restorative potential for victims. This is especially the case considering the strategy of ICC prosecutors to pursue symbolic, exemplary or educative prosecutions. This selection, which is often undertaken to pursue a crime of novel jurisprudential interest to the international legal fraternity – such as establishing a particular form of conduct as a war crime – clearly evidences elite control and a preference for the legal and formal aspects of proceedings over their restorative function. For instance, in the ICC's Lubanga trial (for crimes committed in the Democratic Republic of the Congo) the prosecution focused on specific acts related to child soldiers, much to the dismay of victims groups who felt this approach ignored other important crimes such as sexual violence committed by militias (Pena and Carayon 2013). Given that participation is limited to victims who were harmed by the specific crimes charged in the indictment, the number of victims who might ever participate in proceedings is further restricted. While this makes sense from a formal legal perspective, it has less relevance when viewing the needs of victims through a restorative lens. This restriction, in practice, means that the prosecution by default determines which victims can participate in proceedings (Gillett 2009).

Fourth, the attitude to victim participation at the ICC has relegated this restorative justice tool to a secondary position after the rights of the defendant and the need for fair and expeditious trials. Indeed, the ICC has been at pains to ensure that victim participation does not negatively affect the rights of the accused (Baumgartner 2008; Cohen 2009). It need not be this way. The ICC could think more innovatively and give greater weight to the restoration of victims when balancing these concerns. Or, more radically, it could eschew a zero-sum understanding of victim participation, rights of the accused, and expeditious and efficient trials.

This preference in many ways reflects other elite attitudes that have constrained the participation of victims at the ICC. For example, in interviews with staff at the ICC about their views of victim participation, Wemmers (2010) noted that the role of victims was perceived as aiding the more traditional court actors, and certainly not as exercising any control in proceedings or outcomes. These views evidenced a conception of participation that reflected the non-restorative categories in the typologies of participation of Edwards (2004) and Arnstein (1971). Indeed, elite attitudes may act to temper and sanitise the input of victims. As noted earlier, the channeling of victim participation through legal representatives can serve to reduce their input to the acknowledgement, recognition and occasional enforcement of legal and procedural rights, as opposed to any emotional response. This attitude is expressed by Van den Wyngaert (2011: 489), a judge at the ICC, who states that ICC trials 'are not the appropriate forum for victims to express their feelings, as this would detract from the serenity of the trial and would not serve a useful purpose from the perspective of a criminal proceeding'. This is a clear preference for the sanctity of trials over the perceived messiness of the victim experience.

Although the ICC bench has been considered to have taken an expansive view of victim participation (Van den Wyngaert 2011), elite reluctance to think broadly about the role of victims in proceedings is evident. In particular, both the prosecution and defence at the ICC have sought to constrain the scope of victim participation (Trumbull 2008). The prosecution has, for instance, opposed participation at the investigatory stage of proceedings (Chung 2008). The basis for this opposition was concern that it would be unfair to, and disappoint the expectations of, victims to permit participation when those matters may not proceed to trial (Chung 2008). While the ICC did rule in favour of victim participation at the pre-trial stage (Baumgartner 2008), it is worth considering how restorative any participation can be when a significant party to proceedings is hostile to victims' involvement.

As an experiment in victim participation, the ICC scheme has arguably failed to live up to the restorative rhetoric that has been applied to it. In its current format, this may have been inevitable. While restorative justice esteems initiatives that seek to return disputes to stakeholders, the ICC continues to remove disputes from those most affected. Thus, despite the inclusion of victims' legal representatives – in an institution on a different continent to most victims – the ICC has failed to provide any more engagement or empowerment than the ad hoc tribunals that came before it. By continuing to preference 'professional', distant and legalistic responses, the ICC has not given sufficient scope for victim participation to be truly restorative in practice.

Victim participation in the ECCC

Against the backdrop of the less than impressive outcomes of victim participation at the ICC, the ECCC developed its own model of victim participation in a prosecutorial institution. At face value, victim participation is a 'better fit' at the ECCC than the ICC, as the former is primarily based on an inquisitorial system that already provides for victims to participate as civil parties. Additionally, ECCC proceedings are conducted near the scene of crimes and the residence of potential participants, greatly enabling their presence at the court. As civil parties, victim participants at the ECCC enjoy enhanced participatory rights (in theory) over victims at the ICC. But despite greater rights, proximity and fit, many barriers to restorative participation still exist for victims at the ECCC.

In proceedings at the ECCC, civil party victims are frequently grouped together, reflecting the ICC's practice and replicating many of the same concerns. Indeed, according to McGonigle (2009), the ECCC's jurisprudence has often reinforced the collective nature of victims. The ECCC has, for instance, noted that victims could be encouraged or required to join their submissions (ECCC Pre-Trial Chamber 2008). But as Mohan (2009) points out, collectivisation is also reductionist: it conflates the individual experiences of victims into a generic meta-narrative. For Mohan, this process of narrative reduction at the ECCC preferences stories of helplessness over responsibility and victimisation over victimhood. These preferences can act to diminish the individuality of victims by focusing on the crime rather than the harm it caused and the act of the offender rather than the inviolability of the harmed. This is particularly an issue in transitional justice, where many victims may have been harmed by one of many individual acts that have been charged as a single offence, with the effect that their individual experiences and needs are lost in a sea of collective victimisation. Similarly, it limits the power and active engagement of victims (particularly as the language reinforces disempowerment) and can discourage efforts to think inventively about how to restore in such contexts.

Collectivising victims is just one element of how elite control has diminished the restorative effects of victim participation at the ECCC. After initially granting quite extensive rights to civil parties, the ECCC restricted civil parties' rights in a series of decisions and judgments, primarily out of concerns for efficiency and judicial manageability. For example, because of the numbers of victims who wanted to join as civil parties once the first trial commenced, the ECCC ruled that no leave would be granted for applicants to join as civil parties after proceedings had begun (Jasini and Phan 2011). Again this failed to recognise the individual nature of victims and that many may not be ready to seek participation at times arbitrarily determined by the court. Many victims may be sceptical of proceedings, fearful of retaliation or scared of the formalities and elite-driven nature of trials. This is especially true when the experience of citizens with domestic courts and authorities may be less than encouraging of trust and participation, such as in Cambodia where judicial corruption is common (Ratner 1999).

Artificially constraining when victims can participate fails to give many the chance to seek restoration through participation and empowerment, as it excludes all those who are not ready or able to participate at a given time: the traumatised, the young, the imprisoned, the unwell (Nickson and Braithwaite 2014). Many of the reasons that might prevent potential participants from being ready or able to participate at an arbitrarily determined time could be the result of the very actions being addressed. Telling victims and other stakeholders when they should be ready to, and directing them over when they can, participate in justice efforts makes the needs of those individuals and communities subservient to the needs of abstract justice. The decision to limit participation in this way is primarily about efficiency, less about fairness, and not about enhancing restorative justice.

Like their counterparts at the ICC, victim participants at the ECCC do not have a right to address the court themselves. Instead, their interaction with the court is usually channeled through their legal representatives (or mediated when giving testimony as a witness) (Bair 2009; McGonigle 2009). Observers watched closely in 2008 when the first real test of how participative the ECCC's victim participation scheme would be arose. It was then that civil party Theary Seng sought to address the court directly in an appeal by the defendant Ieng Sary against an order of provisional detention (McGonigle 2009). The court ruled that, because Theary Seng was represented by a lawyer, she could only address the court through her legal counsel. Theary Seng was legally trained, so she dismissed her lawyer and again sought to address the court herself. As a result of the judges' frustration with Theary Seng's attempt to enjoy the legal standing her position as a civil party should have afforded, the Chambers curtailed the direct participation that victims could have in proceedings (McGonigle 2009; Mohan 2009), limiting participation to the legal representatives of victims. As McGonigle (2009) points out, the ECCC was ill prepared to deal with an assertive civil party and failed to manage the situation effectively. This, of course, not only served to underline the control that legal elites have over when, how, and what victim participation is appropriate, it also channeled the voices of victims through legal elites. This example of the thwarting of victim participation is not an isolated one. The decision to limit the *actual* participation of victims in proceedings was made despite the fact that victim participants are supposedly parties to the proceedings (Mohan 2009), and presumably equal in standing with other parties.

The illustrative example of Theary Seng is not the only occasion when the ECCC ruled in ways that diminished the empowerment, and therefore restorative potential, of victim participation. The ECCC has, for example, determined that victim participants cannot question the accused on character or other matters pertinent to sentencing, which Sokol (2011: 167) suggests is the result of 'too much emphasis on the perceived need to increase the efficiency of the trial proceedings', neglecting the goal of national reconciliation and undermining the healing power of fuller victim participation. Sokol (2011: 181) further suggests that this has the effect of 'diluting' Cambodians' ability to claim ownership of ECCC trials. As the Chambers' judgments have effectively restricted actual participation by victims in proceedings, it has been argued that the role of civil parties in proceedings may have been reduced to simple tokenism, or even manipulation (Mohan 2009, applying Arnstein's ladder of participation).

Judgments restricting participation tend to illustrate a preference or an elevation of the retributive, due process aspects and the efficiency concerns of the ECCC over the restorative dimensions of participation and empowerment (Sokol 2011). Indeed, the favouring of efficiency and retribution at the ECCC has diminished the restorative potential of victims' roles as civil parties. For example, Stover *et al.* (2011: 541) observed that many civil parties were 'frustrated' because of the requirement to produce evidence of their victimisation to the satisfaction of the court. Given the circumstances of the Khmer Rouge crimes and the inability of many potential civil parties to provide documentary evidence of the harms they suffered, this intimates a preference for (arguably necessary) legal procedures and formal evidentiary requirements above the restorative values of engagement and empowerment.

This provides further evidence that the ECCC has focused too much on the retributive dimension of its function to the detriment of victim participation (Sokol 2011), and ultimately the restorative dimension. This preference went so far as the Chambers ruling that civil parties did not have the right to equal participation with co-prosecutors (Stover *et al.* 2011), despite a reasonable inference that this standing should be granted given the civil party status of victim participants. Stover *et al.* (2011) note that, throughout the ECCC's first trial, the court took such a restrictive view of civil party participation that it could legitimately be asked whether victim participants should really be considered civil parties to proceedings. Although at the beginning of the ECCC's first trial the victim participation scheme demonstrated significant promise, by the end of the trial victim participation had been severely curtailed (Werner and Rudy 2010).

One explanation for the failure of these restorative justice measures is that, as an addition to a primarily retributive institution, they are in practice overshadowed by the retributive focus of prosecutions and trials. Stover *et al.* (2011), in interviews with victim participants, observed several features of civil party participation that suggest the practice was not particularly restorative. They note that, although civil parties appeared to have experienced some potential for restoration at the ECCC's first trial, questions by the accused that interrogated victims about their identities, connection to deceased victims, and other matters often served to derail the restorative potential of participation and encounters with the defendant. This questioning was not limited to the defendants, but was also conducted by the defendant's legal counsel and the judges, who 'picked apart' the victims' testimonies. Similarly, Stover *et al.* noted in their interviews with civil parties after the first trial that many felt the admissions made by the defendant were part of a bargaining ploy to win favour with judges. Furthermore, despite identifying the initial motivations of civil parties to participate as non-retributive, participants subsequently expressed considerable dissatisfaction with the quantum of punishment the sentence delivered. This reflects what Braithwaite and Mugford (1994) observe as the dissatisfaction of victims with a system that provides little opportunity to express anything other than a desire for more severe punishment. In this context, however, the quantum of punishment is never satisfying, because the pain inflicted on the offender does not address the needs of the victims, particularly for engagement and addressing the disempowerment caused by an offence.

It is possible, then, that this could partly be explained by the overshadowing of restoration by retribution. As Braithwaite and Mugford (1994: 149) have noted 'even in traditional stigmatic punishment systems, victims are not as vengeful as popular preconceptions suggest'. In the context of victims of widespread violence, Clifford Shearing found most wanted justice as a 'better future', which was less about retribution and more about restoration (Shearing and Froestad 2007). Of course, we should not attempt to speak definitively for what victims want, lest we produce the same problems of elite-control that we are trying to avoid. Considering, however, that the initial motivations of civil parties at the ECCC appeared to be non-retributive, it is worth considering whether attempting to incorporate restorative justice in this way serves to 'taint' it with a more retributive flavour.

The restorative potential of victim participation at the ECCC to empower and permit meaningful engagement has, as at the ICC, been constantly diminished through elite control of the process and the favouring of retributive features and the desire for efficiency. Consequently, in respect of victim participation there is much room for improvement at the ECCC (Jasini and Phan 2011), which has struggled so far to marry its retributive and restorative components (McGonigle 2009). Its restrictive approach to victim participation may evidence that it is not actually up to the task of providing restorative justice (Bair 2009; Sokol 2011). As most participants in the ECCC's first trial pointed out, they were most dissatisfied with elite control of the process that limited their own role as civil parties (Stover *et al.* 2011). Additionally, the limited level of direct participation at the ECCCs first trial may be impossible to replicate in subsequent trials as the number of victims is enlarged and the direct connection between victims and perpetrators is reduced (Stover *et al.* 2011).

This section has demonstrated that the lack of process control, the elite-driven nature of proceedings, and the overshadowing of restorative aspects by retributive aspects often work as barriers to restorative justice at the ICC and ECCC. Enabling greater process control – and therefore improving engagement and empowerment – is one way that these barriers could be overcome. In the following section, transitional boards are suggested as one possible way of overcoming these limitations within international criminal justice. It is argued that they provide a platform and forum for stakeholder process control in transitional justice, enabling more meaningful engagement of participants.

Harnessing representative 'boards of transition'

The ICC and ECCC models significantly restrict who and how many victims can participate in proceedings. Within the legal and prosecutorial paradigms under which both institutions operate it may be difficult to overcome these restrictions. Yet, alternative models of greater participation and especially greater process control for victims and communities, even within prosecutorial structures, are available. Most notably, Rwanda's *gacaca* courts provide an example of how process control can be divested to communities in transition. *Gacaca* provide for both retributive and restorative justice by directly involving communities in proceedings, with laypeople acting as judges (following some training), and by encouraging admissions of guilt and outcomes that involve reparative actions such as community service (Meyerstein 2007). Judges in *gacaca* are elected by citizens (but subject to some vetting) and, as Clark (2007: 796) explains, *gacaca*

> relies heavily on popular involvement at all levels ... from the election of judges to these judges' sentencing of genocide criminals on the basis of communal discussions and provision of evidence [so that] the population often shapes *gacaca* according to the needs of each community.

Importantly, *gacaca* does not include the participation of elites such as police and lawyers, to ensure that ownership of proceedings remains with community members (Clark 2007). Of course, *gacaca* has had its own problems (see further Brounéus 2008, 2010; Rettig 2008; Wierzynska 2004), but it does indicate how greater process control, or at least reduced elite control, can be achieved in transitional justice.

Yet, turning the ICC and ECCC over to the masses, such as has occurred with *gacaca*, is probably not a feasible solution to enhance restoration. It must be remembered that *gacaca* complements the work of the ICTR, which is the institution dealing with defendants of comparable profile to those who appear at the ICC and ECCC. Additionally, *gacaca* has direct cultural relevance to Rwanda, and would not necessarily be culturally relevant in other transitional societies. It has been noted previously that transitional justice responses should ideally be culturally relevant to the society where they take place (Iyer 2007; Reissman 1996). This is especially true for restorative justice, which would likely be more effective the more it reflects local restorative traditions. Instead, it is worth considering possible solutions that can complement and enhance victim participation at the ICC and

ECCC, endeavours that will expand the restorative efforts that these institutions currently undertake.

The restorative justice that these, and similar, institutions can deliver could be improved in several ways. First, and perhaps the simplest, would be to provide as much process control to affected parties, and primarily victims, as possible. It should be possible to consult victims on various aspects about the operation of courts and the conduct of their trials. This might include victim representation at meetings that create rules of procedure and evidence, and at least a level of direct consultation with victims on these matters before and during the operation of courts. Rather than provide a system adapted to the practical needs of victims and the restorative values that their participation is supposed to embody, the system at both the ICC and ECCC has required that participants function within its overly legal procedures. This could be improved by better design of victim participation, particularly in the design of applications to participate. Currently, these processes reflect an 'inside-out' design that preferences the administrative purposes and needs of the system and the elites operating it, which can frequently be too inflexible (Braithwaite 2005). What would be better is an 'outside-in' design of these processes that 'reflects the needs and preferences of users rather than administrators' (Nickson 2013: 380). This argument has been made for the design of transitional justice responses generally (Nickson 2013), but can also apply to discreet components such as victim participation applications.

In terms of better application procedures, for example, such a system would ideally take into account the context within which victims make their applications. This would mean considering what documents they might reasonably be expected to have or obtain, or, more radically, eschewing the need for documents to prove victim status and exploring alternative ways to establish status. It might simply mean applications that are more 'user friendly' and less legalistic in their form and content, or applications that are not paper based but utilise other media. Indeed, it is difficult to predict what an 'outside-in' design would look like, as this requires consultation and input from the individuals who are likely to use it. This can also have further restorative benefits, particularly by creating a more inclusive process (Nickson 2013), refocusing the purpose of such activities to facilitating the restorative involvement of victims and adhering to the values of engagement and empowerment.

A broader 'outside-in' approach that allowed stakeholders to contribute to a dialogue on possible transitional justice responses would advance engagement and empowerment even further. If this only provided a small measure of input for victims and the wider community, it could still have significant restorative dimensions by divesting process control from elites to those most affected by the offences. This could serve to empower individuals who are likely to have been disempowered by crimes and are likely to be disempowered by elite-controlled responses to crimes. Because restorative justice preferences processes that are inclusive and collaborative, leading to outcomes based on consensus (Zehr 2002), designing institutions 'outside-in' gives greater scope for inclusion, collaboration and consensus. Should a judicial, prosecutorial model of justice without further broad participation be chosen by consensus, then participation in that selection still constitutes an opportunity for an inclusive, collaborative and empowering process of sorts. It may also have flow-on effects that are beneficial to restorative justice by enhancing participation and the sense of community ownership of proceedings.

Second, in addition to looking for greater opportunities to enhance process control within the structure of criminal proceedings, the ICC and ECCC should seek to link their victim participation efforts to broader grassroots and civil society restorative justice efforts in transition. This might be done most effectively by encouraging victims' organisations to create links between participants, non-participant victims and communities more generally, ideally with some process control. A possible mechanism to achieve this is a type of representative board, modelled on peace committees from South Africa's transition, that would act as a forum for dialogue, providing a conduit for the sharing of information, views and concerns between communities and official institutions such as the ICC and ECCC (Nickson 2013). Peace committees were established at national, regional and local levels as part of South Africa's National Peace Accord in 1991 (US Agency for International Development 1998). The functions of these committees were:

> 1) opening channels of communication; 2) legitimizing the concept of nego-tiating; 3) creating a safe place to raise issues that could not be addressed in other forums; 4) strengthening accountability; 5) helping equalize the power balance; and 6) helping reduce the incidence of violence.
> (US Agency for International Development, 1998, p. vii)

All these functions have restorative dimensions, but of particular importance here is the value of providing a measure of process control to proceedings, reflected mostly in points four and five. By providing an officially recognised space, controlled by community members rather than elites, this can be achieved. This is especially true if the boards are considered genuine partners with institutions such as the ICC and ECCC and have some level of oversight of these institutions.

Boards would ideally be empowered to discuss and provide comment on the process of justice initiatives, including official institutions, allowing a measure of oversight that would constitute a more practical level of process control than direct control of legal proceedings. It has previously been observed that 'transitional justice could benefit from greater accountability' (Nickson 2013: 383) and boards could provide and promote that accountability through oversight, monitoring and by providing a space where unencumbered conversations can take place about the shortcomings of official responses and where feedback can be provided to the institutions themselves. Oversight and an opportunity to comment on the operation of institutions could constitute a meaningful form of process control for victims and wider community members. Done well, boards of this sort can act to enhance the restorative endeavours and complement the retributive efforts of courts. When there are procedural limits on how victims can participate in specific legal proceedings, this role could broaden participation and deepen involvement – two developments that are central to enhancing the justice citizens can receive in transition (Nickson and Braithwaite 2014).

Forums, such as boards modelled on peace committees, could also provide a measure of process control for victims and wider members of affected communities, particularly if entrusted with taking the partial restorative work of courts and building additional restorative activities from this foundation. This can also help to build links with efforts that have cultural resonance for the society in transition. This type of collaboration has been done well in Cambodia, where links between the ECCC and civil society groups have aided in broadening the justice that is provided to Cambodians, and included additional restorative practices within communities (Nickson 2013). If this collaboration were devolved to victims and other community members through representative boards, in addition to or instead of court staff and leadership of international NGOs, it could further empower victims. As the Rwandan *gacaca* experience has demonstrated, even in communities where widespread atrocities have taken place, there is an available cohort of suitable community members who can aid in steering restorative efforts to the wider benefit of victims and communities. It also provides scope for infusing a more culturally relevant dimension to activities. For example, boards can undertake or promote the sorts of spiritual activities that might be contextually appropriate for societies in transition, but that the ICC is unable to address in The Hague. These might be, for instance, the reconciliation ceremonies conducted in Timor Leste that addressed the spiritual needs of communities and the essential features that held those societies together (Braithwaite *et al.* 2012).

The role of such boards need not be limited to particular activities relevant to facilitating process control: there is a wide range of restorative activities that such boards could support. Importantly, boards can use institutional and official responses as platforms for developing ongoing measures to respond to mass atrocity, creating a dynamic form of transitional justice not limited in its restorative potential to a single forum (Nickson 2013). This could also overcome unforeseen problems when the scope of restorative measures, such as victim participation, are decided and set early, in transitional circumstances that might not apply to future needs for recovery. One way that justice can be more restorative is for it to be iterative in its function, continually learning and improving from previous experience. Boards could permit this level of flexibility into the design of transitional justice, at the same time empowering community members with control over how these efforts are shaped. The advantage of providing process control through boards is that they can exist alongside the official institution, without undermining legal proceedings where greater process control in the hands of communities is not usually possible.

Conclusion

The preceding discussion has focused on the limits of victim participation as a restorative justice initiative within international criminal trials. As noted earlier, one problem with these proceedings is that process control is in the hands of elites and insufficiently devolved to participants, who are most disempowered by official, institutionalised justice responses. This serves to limit participation in multiple ways, including restricting the number of victims who participate and the actions that those participants may take in proceedings. Process control is important for the realisation of restorative justice in victim participation schemes, as it greatly contributes to achieving restorative values of engagement and empowerment. But at the ICC and ECCC, process control is never relinquished by elites and provided to others. In both cases, officials such as judges, prosecutors, international jurists, and politicians control the selection of a particular transitional justice mechanism, its proceedings and its outcomes and also determine the extent and nature of participation in those proceedings by others. Thus, the dominance of legalism (McEvoy 2007, 2008) and the elite-driven nature of these institutions, means that control is centralised in official hands, removing disputes and their resolution from those most affected by the crimes and harms that are being addressed. If it is not permitted within the courtroom, then institutions of international criminal justice must look for complementary forums to enable some process control for victims, giving those who want restorative justice that opportunity for engagement and empowerment. Courts can provide greater process control for victims but, as institutions, they must think more broadly about how they can increase restorative justice by engaging and empowering victims.

Victim participation schemes fail to adequately empower victims and thus fail to sufficiently aid in their restoration. Instead, these schemes more often reinforce the elite nature of institutions, the lack of process control that those directly affected by crimes have, and the secondary position of restorative justice with regard to retributive justice. This imbalance needs to be addressed if restorative and retributive justice are to be effectively pursued in the same institution. To truly attempt justice that is restorative, many of the values and assumptions that underpin international criminal justice should be revisited. These include the preference of discreet and manageable legal issues over inclusive processes; strict adherence to formal rules of procedure over the ability of victims to communicate their needs in their own voice; and the importance placed on denunciation by authorities over dialogue among stakeholders aimed at repairing harms. Participation – particularly when it only constitutes space in a courtroom for a lawyer that you share with a thousand others – does not on its own provide restorative justice. The restorative purpose of inclusion is that it empowers and engages stakeholders with a meaningful role in responding to an offence and this is what a restorative justice victim participation scheme should seek to achieve.

This chapter has suggested one way of overcoming these limitations through the use of transitional boards. An advantage of boards is that they adopt a very different perspective of what constitutes justice and how it can be achieved. Unlike courts trying international crimes – where justice is embodied in the conviction (and occasional acquittal) of defendants – boards promote restorative justice by engaging stakeholders in a process that empowers them to generate their own responses to harms. And this difference hints at why restorative justice within retributive paradigms is at greatest risk of failing: the institutions and the elites that run them still view the operation of justice through a retributive lens. As Howard Zehr would suggest, restorative justice requires that we view these issues through a different lens. For this reason, victim participation schemes, represented here by the ICC and ECCC, demonstrate a misunderstanding about restorative justice: it is considered an accessory. As an accessory, it is never an equal or central focus. What is needed instead is to view the crimes, the harms they caused and all of the surrounding concerns, through both retributive and restorative lenses. When this is done, initiatives such as victim participation are far more likely to manifest values of engagement and empowerment, and provide a true restorative partner to retributive institutions.

References

Allan, A. and Allan, M. (2000) 'The South African Truth and Reconciliation Commission as a Therapeutic Tool', *Behavioural Sciences and the Law*, 18: 459–477.

Arnstein, S. (1971) 'A Ladder of Citizen Participation', *Journal of the American Institute of Planners*, 35(4): 216–224.

Bair, J. (2009) 'From the Number who Died to those who Survived: Victim participation in the Extraordinary Chambers in the Courts of Cambodia', *University of Hawai'i Law Review*, 31: 507–550.

Baumgartner, E. (2008) 'Aspects of Victim Participation in the Proceedings of the International Criminal Court', *International Review of the Red Cross*, 90(870): 409–440.

Braithwaite, J. (2005) *Markets in Vice, Markets in Virtue*, Annandale, NSW: Federation Press.

Braithwaite, J. and Mugford, S. (1994) 'Conditions of Successful Reintregration Ceremonies: Dealing with juvenile offenders', *British Journal of Criminology*, 34(2): 139–171.

Braithwaite, J., Charlesworth, H. and Soares, A. (2012) *Networked Governance of Freedom and Tyranny*, Canberra, ACT: ANU E-Press.

Brounéus, K. (2008) 'Truth-telling as Talking Cure? Insecurity and retraumatization in the Rwandan *gacaca* courts', *Security Dialogue*, 39(1): 55–76.

Brounéus, K. (2010) 'The Trauma of Truth-telling: Effects of witnessing in the Rwandan *gacaca* courts on psychological health', *Journal of Conflict Resolution*, 54(3): 408–437.

Chung, C. (2008) 'Victims' Participation at the International Criminal Court: Are concessions of the court clouding the promise?', *Northwestern Journal of International Human Rights*, 6(3): 459–545.

Clark, P. (2007) 'Hybridity, Holism, and 'Traditional' Justice: The case of the gacaca courts in post-genocide Rwanda', *George Washington International Law Review*, 39: 765–837.

Clamp, K. (2014) *Restorative Justice in Transition*, New York: Routledge.

Cohen, M. (2009) 'Victims' Participation Rights within the International Criminal Court: A critical overview', *Denver Journal of International Law and Policy*, 37(3): 351–377.

Edwards, I. (2004) 'An Ambiguous Participant: The crime victim and criminal justice decision-making', British Journal of Criminology, 44(6): 967–982.

Extraordinary Chambers in the Courts of Cambodia Pre-Trial Chamber (2008) 'Decision on Civil Party Participation in Provisional Detention Appeals', *Nuon Chea case*, Case No. 002/19–09–2007-ECCC/OCIJ (PTC01).

Gillett, M. (2009) 'Victim Participation at the International Criminal Court', *Australian International Law Journal*, 16: 29–46.

Iyer, V. (2007) 'Of Prosecutions and Amnesties: Does Fiji's experience suggest a reconsideration?', *Australian Journal of Asian Law*, 9(1): 1–43.

Jasini, R. and Phan, V. (2011) 'Victim Participation at the Extraordinary Chambers in the Courts of Cambodia: Are retributive and restorative principles enhancing the prospect for justice?', *Cambridge Review of International Affairs*, 24(3): 379–401.

Lundy, P. and McGovern, M. (2008) 'Whose justice? Rethinking transitional justice from the bottom up', *Journal of Law and Society*, 35(2): 265–292.

Marshall, T. (1999) *Restorative Justice: An Overview*, Home Office: London.

McEvoy, K. (2007) 'Beyond Legalism: Towards a thicker understanding of transitional justice', *Journal of Law and Society*, 34(4): 411–440.

McEvoy, K. (2008) 'Letting go of legalism: developing a thicker understanding of transitional justice', in K. McEvoy and L. McGregor (eds) *Transitional Justice from Below: Grassroots activism and the Struggle for change*, Portland, OR: Hart Publishing.

McGonigle, B. (2009) 'Two for the Price of One: Attempts by the Extraordinary Chambers in the Courts of Cambodia to combine retributive and restorative justice principles', *Leiden Journal of International Law*, 22(1): 127–149.

Meyerstein, A. (2007) 'Between Law and Culture: Rwanda's *Gacaca* and postcolonial legality', *Law and Social Inquiry*, 32(2): 467–508.

Mohan, M. (2009) 'The Paradox of Victim-centrism: Victim participation at the Khmer Rouge Tribunal', *International Criminal Law Review*, 9: 733–775.

Nickson, R. (2013) 'Great expectations: managing realities of transitional justice', unpublished doctoral thesis, Canberra: Australian National University.

Nickson, R. and Braithwaite, J. (2014) 'Deeper, Broader, Longer Transitional Justice', *European Journal of Criminology*, 11(4): 445–463.

Pena, M. and Carayon, G. (2013) 'Is the ICC Making the Most of Victim Participation', *The International Journal of Transitional Justice*, 7(3): 518–535.

Pena, M. (2010) 'Victim Participation at the International Criminal Court: Achievements made and challenges lying ahead', *ILSA Journal of International and Comparative Law*, 16(2): 497–516.

Ratner, S. (1999) 'The United Nations Group of Experts for Cambodia', *The American Journal of International Law*, 93(4): 948–953.

Reissman, W. (1996) 'Legal Responses to Genocide and other Massive Violations of Human Rights', *Law and Contemporary Problems*, 59(4): 75–80.

Rettig, M. (2008) 'Gacaca: Truth, justice, and reconciliation in postconflict Rwanda', *African Studies Review*, 51(3): 25–50.

Shearing, C. and Froestad, J. (2007) 'Beyond restorative justice – Zwelethemba, a future-focused model using local capacity conflict resolution', in R. Mackay, M. Bosnjak, J. Deklerck, C. Pelikan, B. van Stokkom and M. Wright (eds) *Images of Restorative Justice Theory*, Frankfurt: Verlag fur Polizeiwissenschaft.

Sokol, D. (2011) 'Reduced Victim Participation: A misstep by the Extraordinary Chambers in the Courts of Cambodia', *Washington University Global Studies Law Review*, 10: 167–186.

Stover, E., Balthazard, M. and Koenig, K. (2011) 'Confronting Duch: Civil parties participation in Case 001 at the Extraordinary Chambers in the Courts of Cambodia', *International Review of the Red Cross*, 93(882): 503–546.

Teitel, R. (2003) 'Transitional Justice Genealogy', *Harvard Human Rights Journal*, 1(6): 69–94.

Trumbull, C. (2008) 'The Victims of Victim Participation in International Criminal Proceedings', *Michigan Journal of International Law*, 29: 777–826.

US Agency for International Development (1998) 'Managing Conflict: Lessons from the South African Peace Committees', *USAID Evaluation Special Study Report No. 78.*

Wemmers, J. (2010) 'Victims' Rights and the International Criminal Court: Perceptions within the court regarding the victims' right to participate', *Leiden Journal of International Law*, 23(3): 629–643.

Werner, A. and Rudy, D. (2010) 'Civil party representation at the ECCC: Sounding the retreat in international criminal law?', *Northwestern Journal of International Human Rights*, 8(3): 301–309.

Wierzynska, A. (2004) 'Consolidating Democracy through Transitional Justice: Rwanda's gacaca courts', *New York University Law Review*, 79: 1934–1970.

Van den Wyngaert, C. (2011) 'Victims before International Criminal Courts: Some views and concerns of an ICC trial judge', *Case Western Reserve Journal of International Law*, 44: 475–496.

Zehr, H. (2002) *The Little Book of Restorative Justice*, Intercourse, PA: Goodbooks.

7 Working across frontiers in Northern Ireland

The contribution of community-based restorative justice to security and justice in local communities

Tim Chapman and Hugh Campbell

Introduction

Northern Ireland is in transition from being engaged in an extended period of violent conflict towards becoming a modern democratic state. Structural reform of government and criminal justice has resulted in substantially reduced levels of violence. However, difficult cultural and relational issues in Northern Irish society continue to generate inter-communal conflict. This chapter will argue that the structural change and institutional justice processes associated with transitional justice are unlikely to address these conflicts effectively. Rather, we suggest that community-based restorative justice is a resource which should be harnessed for its potential for resolving conflict and reducing violence in working-class communities. Yet, this very resource is being limited by the tendency of a more confident state system to colonise civil society through its power to regulate and to allocate funding.

The ALTERNATIVE research programme[1] aims to develop alternative ways of understanding and responding effectively to conflicts within and between communities in intercultural contexts. The research team has examined how restorative justice may operate in the areas in which transitional justice measures are falling short and, in doing so, it is identifying and developing alternative understandings of the relationship between the state and civil society, and of the key concepts of community, identity, and justice. While the state and its agencies can support or hinder the resolution of conflict and reconciliation, restorative justice directs our attention primarily to the engagement and facilitation of those closest to and most affected by harmful conflicts in active participation in their resolution. The ALTERNATIVE project focuses on the work of community-based restorative projects operating in the most deprived areas of west and south Belfast and Derry/Londonderry.

West Belfast is largely working class, Catholic (92.5) and republican.[2] Less than 2 per cent of the population is from a minority ethnic or black community. Three wards fall within the 2 per cent of most deprived wards in Northern Ireland. South Belfast is an area which contains some of the most affluent as well as the most relatively deprived communities. The working class areas are predominantly Protestant and are generally perceived to be loyalist.[3] Approximately 5 per cent of the population identifies as belonging to an ethnic minority or black group. Contrary to general crime trends, hate crimes are increasing in south Belfast and this is one of the issues that the ALTERNATIVE research addresses.

Derry/Londonderry is the biggest city in Northern Ireland outside Belfast. It is located in the west and is literally a border town. 'It is a place that is in one sense parochial, quite separate from Belfast, remote from Dublin and yet also a very European city' explained Denis Bradley to the ALTERNATIVE team. 'The walled history of the city reflects the religious wars of Europe in the sixteenth and seventeenth centuries'. The population is predominantly white (98.2 per cent) and Catholic (75.8 per cent). The west bank of the river Foyle, (Cityside) is predominantly Catholic and the east bank (Waterside) is predominantly Protestant. Derry is an area of high disadvantage. Drug offending, while fluctuating, shows a slight upward trend. The focus of the study in Derry is drug dealing and drug use.

Community-based restorative justice is at a different stage of development in each of these sites. In Derry/Londonderry, no restorative justice response to the problems raised by drug use and drug dealing had emerged. A local organisation worked with the Ulster University team to undertake a community consultation process, which culminated in a community conference on the issue. In south Belfast, the ALTERNATIVE research involved monitoring the efforts of a very new community-based restorative justice organisation to engage with issues such as a major political protest over the flying of flags and race hate crime. Community Restorative Justice Ireland in west Belfast is a mature project with a history of effective restorative practices over 17 years. The focus of the research in this area was how a project previously under citizen control is gradually being co-opted by the state.

Wright (1987) referred to Northern Ireland as an 'ethnic frontier society' in that it was characterised by an uneasy tension between two competing nationalisms within its boundaries. In modern societies, there are many internal frontiers where different groups encounter each other. The most obvious frontier in Northern Ireland is between the Protestant/unionist/loyalist community and the Catholic/nationalist/republican community. These identities dominate the politics and social space of the country.

The intractability of the historical conflict in Northern Ireland is further complicated by the 'intersections' (Yuval-Davis 2011) of other frontiers. There is a class issue in the areas of the study. Most of the violent conflict is both perpetrated and suffered by people from working class areas. The people living in these areas, especially those from a Protestant background, feel abandoned by the political system and excluded from the economic and social benefits of the peace process. There is also a generational factor. Many young people are disaffected and become involved in violence, both as perpetrators and as victims. Those most involved in violence are generally male, suggesting a strong gender dimension to the various conflicts. Since Northern Ireland has become more peaceful and prosperous, there has been an influx of new ethnic minorities. This has resulted in conflict in local communities over access to housing and to an increasing incidence of hate crime.

The ALTERNATIVE study examines the conjunction of these intersecting tensions with strong community solidarity in the research sites, the presence of armed (paramilitary) groups and the legacy of violence. In such circumstances, it is difficult and potentially dangerous to work across these frontiers. The ALTERNATIVE study inquires whether restorative justice processes can provide a 'scaffolding', which provides a safe, neutral space and a process of dialogue to enable people affected by conflict to engage with the other constructively.

The Northern Irish context

The conflict was primarily a political struggle over the legitimacy of the state of Northern Ireland. During the conflict, the British state deployed the police, courts and prisons to counter violent actions, such as the destruction of buildings and the killing and wounding of people by bomb explosions and shootings, perpetrated by both republican and loyalist paramilitary organisations. The Royal Ulster Constabulary officers (the police) were predominantly Protestant. As a consequence, the criminal justice system was perceived by republicans as part of the state apparatus directed against their struggle (Ruane and Todd 1996).

Many of the most bitter and violent struggles have focused on the institutions of the criminal justice system. These included policing practices such as the use of emergency legislation to arrest and interrogate suspects and collusion with loyalist paramilitary organisations. Trial without jury introduced by emergency legislation, (the so-called 'Diplock' courts), and the use of 'supergrasses', (informers who had made a deal with the authorities to avoid to prosecution), to bring large numbers of people suspected of politically motivated offences to trial undermined the credibility of the rule of law. The prison system had to contend with internment without trial and a succession of protests against the practice of strip searches and to gain special category status for paramilitary prisoners (distinguishing them from other prisoners and including privileges that others were not entitled to) culminating in the hunger strikes (McEvoy 2001). In the course of the conflict many judges, magistrates, police officers and prison officers were killed by paramilitary organisations.

The peace agreement in Northern Ireland was made in 1998 (Northern Ireland Office 1998). The priorities were to establish a democratic government, strengthen human rights and equality and reform the criminal justice system, particularly policing. In addition to the political reforms, the Independent Commission on Policing in Northern Ireland (1999) and the Review of the Criminal Justice System in Northern Ireland (Criminal Justice Review Group 2000) set in train a process of fundamental reform of policing and criminal justice. These reforms have generally been welcomed and perceived as successful.

The criminal justice system in Northern Ireland has become increasingly sophisticated, strategically and technically. This has enabled it to manage conflict and disorder reasonably effectively and to control the risk of serious violence. However, this system struggles to address the more intangible cultural and relational issues, which underpin most of the current conflicts.

As a result of these reforms, which can be understood within the discourse of transitional justice, violence has reduced though has not been eliminated. However, the power-sharing arrangements institutionalised a politics in which power is derived from maintaining balanced but separate interests, thus sustaining the contentious cultural issues and the low level conflict between the communities.

Most people in Northern Ireland live in neighbourhoods that are almost exclusively made up of people from one religious tradition and most children attend schools, which are predominantly either Catholic or Protestant. Many of these segregated communities are situated very close to each other on 'interfaces', often protected by ten-metre-high 'peace walls' designed to keep them apart and to prevent stones, petrol bombs and other missiles from being thrown. Thousands of people continue to feel victimised and hurt by the conflict. This legacy of past hurts has not been addressed satisfactorily, and cultural identity remains contentious. The transformative potential of transitional justice has been limited by the politics of identity and the existence of communities that live apart from each other. In spite of the progress that the peace process has made over a relatively short period, internal 'frontiers' persist and sustain a form of identity politics that continues to generate conflicts, which disrupt political, economic and social progress in Northern Ireland.

One product of communities in conflict was the growth of vibrant and creative community and voluntary organisations. Community groups in the most deprived areas emerged to divert young people from offending (Chapman 1995; Chapman and Pinkerton 1987). At the same time, both republican and loyalist paramilitary organisations imposed an alternative punishment system to control criminal and anti-social behaviour. Sanctions included threats, beatings, shooting young people in various limbs ('kneecapping'), exiling young people from their communities and in some cases taking the lives of serious offenders. Paramilitary punishments were a product of the contested nature of the state and consequently of policing, fear of crime within beleaguered communities, and the strategy of the paramilitary organisations to be perceived as legitimate by their communities (McEvoy 2003; Monaghan 2004). These draconian punishments proved no more effective in reducing offending than the state's system of punishment.

Community-based restorative justice emerged in the mid-1990s in a number of mainly loyalist and republican areas. Eriksson (2010) traces their origins to disillusionment with paramilitary punishments. Community restorative justice projects dealt with neighbourhood disputes, anti-social behaviour and local crime. The schemes were funded by private philanthropy and run largely by volunteers from the local community. Most of the work related to complaints from local people and paramilitary organisations. The projects tended to focus on resolving conflict and repairing harm rather than reducing reoffending.

In addition to working on specific cases, the schemes in both the loyalist and republican communities invested time in educating their communities in human rights and restorative values and practices. This countered the prevailing culture of violence in relation to crime but also achieved a degree of community owner-ship of the restorative approach. McEvoy and Mika have argued strongly for the value of community-based restorative justice:

> when it is based upon a genuine commitment to the values and practice of restorative justice; located in politically organized and dynamic com-munities; well managed and staffed by committed volunteers; and guided by locally developed standards of practice which are based upon accepted human rights principles.
>
> (2002: 556)

While initiatives within the sphere of transitional justice have contributed to a sub-stantial reduction in political violence, community-based restorative justice has reduced the incidence of violence as a means of controlling crime and disorder in local communities. In 1998 when the key community-based restorative justice pro-jects, Community Restorative Justice Ireland (CRJI) and Northern Ireland Altern-atives, became active there were 144 beatings and 72 shootings, according to official police statistics. In 2014, this had reduced to 41 beatings and 24 shootings (The Detail 2015). The emphasis in restorative justice on relationships between ordinary people in conflict has the potential to address those areas of contention that structural reform may be too blunt an instrument to resolve.

However, this potential has been limited by the relationship between the reformed state and community-based restorative justice organisations. Because community-based restorative justice was associated with paramilitary punish-ments and because ex-prisoners were taking a lead in the projects, the govern-ment refused to fund the schemes or permit its agencies to cooperate with them. The issues that concerned government officials included fears that parties would be coerced to participate in restorative processes by armed groups and other pos-sible abuses of human rights.

In 2007, protocols for community-based restorative justice schemes were established between the government and the community-based projects, Com-munity Restorative Justice Ireland and Northern Ireland Alternatives. The proto-cols were drawn up to conform to the Human Rights Act 1998, the UN Convention on the Rights of the Child, equality legislation, and the UN *Basic Principles on the use of Restorative Justice in Criminal Matters*. The two organi-sations were required to agree to regular inspections by the Criminal Justice Inspectorate, to be subject to an independent, external complaints mechanism and to undertake accredited training. This enabled the organisations to apply for and to receive funding from the state and hence achieve the financial stability that they needed to develop their services.

The critical provision related to referrals. Community schemes had always taken referrals from members of their community. In 2006 this resulted in just over 1,000 cases referred to the CRJI scheme in west Belfast. Community or self-referral enabled the projects to respond quickly, flexibly and informally. The protocols required that all cases involving a criminal offence would have to be investigated and assessed by the Police Service for Northern Ireland and the Public Prosecution Service, which would then decide whether or not an individual case was appropriate for a community-based restorative process. Between 2007 and 2014, only two cases were referred to CRJI through the police and public prosecution services.

The efforts to restore the legitimacy of the criminal justice system in Northern Ireland have had the consequence of severely reducing the capacity of community-based restorative justice to provide a quick and effective response to local people's concerns about low-level crime and anti-social behaviour. The consequence of this restriction on referrals has been that the community-based organisations have become more involved in youth work, social work, community development and the mediation of disputes and conflicts in their communities. Their involvement in restoring justice between a victim and a perpetrator of harm has been severely curtailed.

The colonisation of community restorative justice by the state

This problem can be understood through the use of Habermas's (1987) theory of the colonisation of the lifeworld by the system. 'Lifeworld' corresponds to everyday social life in civil society, such as family and friends, and cultural and social activities. In these contexts, most day-to-day problems are addressed and solved through communication between ordinary people. It is on this basis that community-based restorative justice addresses the incidence of harm between people very effectively. Yet this form of doing justice is what the state seems to distrust and wishes to limit.

Habermas's (1987) concept of the lifeworld encompasses the idea of community in the sense of the informal and largely taken for granted norms and personal obligations, the networks of relationships, and the shared meanings of people's everyday lives in their world. Many people in Northern Ireland live in areas that they would describe as a community. The majority of the population live in communities that are predominantly Protestant or Catholic. They find that the concept of community provides them with a sense of belonging and identity. They live with people with whom they identify and this also provides them with a sense of security (Bauman 2001).

The lifeworld can be analysed as being made up of 'culture' through which meaning is generated and reproduced, 'society' or the relationships and identities that sustain social cohesion or solidarity, and 'personality' or the narratives, beliefs, values and capabilities that members of the community have internalised so as to function effectively in society. A healthy community is nourished through open and dynamic cultural transmission, through social inclusion and integration and through the effective socialisation of individuals. These levels of community are interconnected and interact through communicative action (Habermas 1987). While the outcomes of communicative action may be difficult to measure on a case by case basis, there is evidence that strengthening social cohesion and social capital are key factors in controlling crime (Braithwaite 1989; Bursik and Grasmick 1993; Putnam 2000).

These important resources to community life may be under threat in modern society. Habermas (1984) examines how the lifeworld is colonised by the state and market through their instrumental or strategic action. He states that: 'in modern societies, economic and bureaucratic spheres emerge in which social relations are regulated only via money and power. Norm-conformative attitudes and identity-forming social memberships are neither necessary nor possible in these spheres; they are made peripheral instead' (Habermas 1989: 189).

The colonisation of the lifeworld is characterised by the managerialism of state bureaucracies (Bauman 2001), by increasing economic inequality (Wilkinson and Pickett 2009) and a culture of control (Garland 2001) including a high level of imprisonment. Unlike the lifeworld, which is animated by communicative action, systems depend upon strategic action. The purpose of the lifeworld is to enable people to live together. The purpose of systems is to achieve planned outcomes, for example to realise political objectives, or to increase profits and market share.

Systems see groups of people as markets and individuals as consumers. Social needs are defined as problems or risks to be managed by professional experts. As McKnight and Block (2010: 30) write 'All that is uncertain, organic, spontaneous and flowing in personal, family and neighbourhood space is viewed in system space, and in science, as a problem to be solved'. Public services are standardised, commodified and depersonalised. This echoes Christie's (1977) thesis that state professionals steal conflicts from those who are involved in them. McKnight and Block (2010: 36) put it this way: 'Professionalisation is the market replacement for a community that has lost or outsourced its capacity to care'.

Sennett (2012) believes that economic inequality creates social distance and weakens the desire and capacity to cooperate with those who are different. He believes that the skills of paying attention to detail and listening, of empathy, of tentativeness so as to respect the other, of distinguishing between information sharing and communication, of understanding context and meaning are being eroded by modern society. This allows people with power to treat others in a way they would not wish to be treated themselves. Furthermore, people's capacities to solve their own problems are reduced. Habermas (1987: 143) refers to these as 'social pathologies'. The outcomes of these social pathologies in community life include the undermining of relationships of solidarity and an avoidance of personal responsibility.

The weakening of 'organic' communities in modern society does not extinguish people's need for belonging. As Young (1999: 164) observed: 'Just as community collapses, identity is invented'. Bauman refers to identity as a surrogate of community (2001: 15). Tajfel (1981: 255) defines social identity as: 'that part of an individual's self-concept which derives from his knowledge of his membership in a social group (or groups) together with the value and emotional significance attached to that membership'. The search for the security that an identity offers requires one to stand out and be different and as such can lead to ethnocentrism.

Staub (2001) has developed a model to understand violent ethnocentric conflict. The threat to basic human needs such as security, positive identity, effectiveness and control, connection to other people, and meaningful understanding of reality and one's place in the world is a critical factor to the escalation of intergroup conflict. It is important to note that these are the same needs that are addressed on a daily basis through the lifeworld. When these basic needs are not met, people feel a sense of injustice and grievance. Usually another group, which is perceived as competing for scarce resources, becomes the object of resentment.

To summarise the argument so far, the institutionalisation of identity politics through power sharing and the modernisation of the criminal justice system in Northern Ireland has reduced violence and improved services to local communities. However, in doing so, ethnocentric difference and conflict is sustained and the resources within civil society, including community-based restorative justice, which could contribute to greater harmony between the diverse communities in Northern Ireland, have been weakened through the process of the colonisation of the lifeworld by the state system. Is this an inevitable consequence of formal democracy and the modernisation of the state or can there be a balance between an effective state and a flourishing civil society? The next section contends that it is possible to distinguish the roles of the state in maintaining order and of civil society as represented by community-based restorative justice in sustaining peace.

How can community-based restorative justice address this impasse?

First, the institutional discourse that defines restorative justice must be challenged. Restorative justice has been largely developed in modern societies as a means of addressing individual acts of harm. Thus, many definitions of restorative justice are based upon the identification of victim and offender (Shapland *et al.* 2012; Walgrave 2008). These labels are a product of the criminal justice process. In the lifeworld of community, such distinctions are not so easy to make. Across ethnic frontiers, harm is often caused by groups and suffered by other groups, rather than individuals, and will likely be an event within an ongoing narrative of oppression and resistance.

Such harmful conflict represents to the state a breakdown in order and a challenge to its ability to impose its authority. As a result, the state will use its powers of coercion to restore order strategically. Van Ness and Strong (2010) maintain that government's responsibility is to maintain a just order, whereas community is responsible for establishing a just peace. Order can be measured by the absence of disorder. Peace is more difficult to quantify. It is a product of the quality of many diverse relationships between groups living in community and of how people resolve conflict and address breaches of norms. McEvoy and Eriksson (2008) raise the question of who owns justice and argue that, as long as the state prioritises control over justice and security, community-based restorative justice has a major part to play in any system of justice.

Both the criminal justice system and restorative justice share the aim of delivering justice. The system administers justice to reinforce the authority of the law and to keep order. The aim of restorative justice is to restore justice as a means of sustaining right relationships. Nevertheless, the two approaches are qualitatively different. Community-based restorative justice schemes have a very different orientation from the criminal justice system, as Abel makes clear: 'non-bureaucratic and relatively undifferentiated from larger society, (they) minimise the use of professionals, and eschew official law in favour of substantive and procedural norms that are vague, unwritten, commonsensical, flexible, ad hoc, and particularistic' (Abel 1982: 2). The Northern Irish state instinctively distrusts such challenges to its view of justice (McEvoy and Eriksson 2008).

Restorative justice and the criminal justice system can be further distinguished by how they go about their processes. The system adopts a strategic approach to its outcomes: detecting crime, prosecuting and defending a case, assessing risk, sentencing, implementing rehabilitation programmes and planning for reintegration. Each of these processes requires professionals thinking and acting strategically. In relation to community-based restorative justice the state does more than regulate referrals but presses the projects into supporting the strategic actions and values of statutory agencies, which often perceive restorative justice primarily as an opportunity to cut public spending and to reduce reoffending.

On the other hand restorative justice is facilitated through communicative action (Habermas 1987) between those most affected by the harmful incident. The purpose of communicative action is to achieve mutual understanding about an issue and consensus about what action to take. Other than agreement, there can be no preconceived outcome. The restorative process is similar to Arendt's (1958: 200) understanding of action and speech:

> power is actualised only where word and deed have not parted company, where words are not empty and deeds not brutal, where words are not used to veil intentions but to disclose realities, and deeds are not used to violate and destroy but to establish relations and create new realities.

The value of community-based restorative justice is that it provides a safe space for people to communicate honestly with each other about issues that they find threatening. In this context, safe means free from domination by political or economic power (Braithwaite 2001). Ultimately there needs to be an accommodation between the state and the community restorative justice sector through which certain types of cases are clearly the province of the state and other cases are recognised as being more effectively processed in the community. The following section provides an overview of the findings of the ALTERNATIVE project conducted in Northern Ireland where such an approach has been harnessed successfully within the community.

ALTERNATIVE: the Northern Ireland case studies

The ALTERNATIVE research project has worked in three sites – south and west Belfast and Derry/Londonderry – over the past three years. It has identified the issues that concern these communities and studied how community-based projects have responded to these issues. The following section describes case studies that demonstrate what community-based restorative justice can achieve more effectively than the state system.

Our research has found that current responses by both the state and most community organisations are largely based upon the strategic actions typical of systems rather than the communicative action of the lifeworld. Many young people in the deprived areas of south and west Belfast are engaged in anti-social behaviour and sectarian violence (which often takes the form of 'recreational rioting' arranged through social media). The community in west Belfast, previously deeply alienated from the police, has supported the police strategy to 'get tough' with gangs of youth. Youth organisations based in local communities are engaged in diverting young people from anti-social behaviour through youth work activities. Community groups from loyalist south Belfast and republican west Belfast have cooperated in bringing young people involved in sectarian violence together through the organisation of football training, delivered by coaches from Glasgow Rangers and Glasgow Celtic football clubs ('the 'Old Firm' traditionally divided by religion). The armed groups in Derry address the problem of drug dealing through coercive and often violent retribution. Serious inter-communal conflict along the interfaces of south and west Belfast is managed by a careful process of negotiation by community activists backed up by the strategic use of policing. Each of these strategies controls the problems that they are designed to address but fail to address the underlying relationships that cause and sustain the problems.

Cultural issues in loyalist communities

In recent years it has become clear that the loyalist community believe that their cultural identity is under threat as republicans become more confident in government. As one leading loyalist put it, 'the IRA has failed to expel the British people from Ireland. But now republicans are trying to take the Britishness out of the people'. For loyalists the military war has been transformed into a cultural war. The threat now is to identity rather than to territory and physical safety. Contentious issues such as the flying of Union flags on public buildings and the right of the Orange Order to march past Catholic neighbourhoods have stimulated intense conflict and some street violence.

Capacity building of community-based projects wishing to develop restorative responses to issues that concern them is part of the action research methodology that the ALTERNATIVE project has adopted. Ulster University enrolled 12 loyalist community activists to complete the Certificate in Restorative Practices. About half way through this six month part-time course, the majority of councillors in Belfast City Council voted to fly the union flag on a restricted number of days rather than every day of the year as had been done up to then. This sparked major protests in working class Protestant areas by large crowds of loyalists who saw this as an assault upon their national culture. These protests often descended into riots and violence against the police and neighbouring Catholic neighbourhoods.

During this period, several of those who had undergone the training in restorative justice acted as mediators between the protesters and the police and on many occasions succeeded in defusing conflict that could have led to more serious violence. They also spoke at local meetings called to discuss the crisis and urged the community to take democratic action to change the policy and to avoid violence. In doing so, they risked being accused of not demonstrating solidarity with the loyalist cause. Paramilitary organisations were organising the protests and were accused of encouraging its escalation into violence. Acting restoratively in these circumstances required considerable courage.

Politicians made political capital out of the protests and the police kept the protests under control. In contrast to these strategic responses, the community activists who were trained in restorative practices employed communicative actions such as mediation and urged non-violent and democratic responses to the conflict. In south Belfast there was very little violence. The community activists would say that restorative justice gave them the skills and the concepts to respond more effectively to this conflict.

Hate crimes

As violence between Protestants and Catholics has receded, hate crime against minority ethnic groups has increased, especially in loyalist areas. Through the ALTERNATIVE project, Ulster University has trained many community activists, many of whom are ex-combatants, in restorative practices. They have been using the processes and skills that they have learnt to 'nip conflicts in the bud'. The University has developed a restorative process appropriate to harmful conflicts between groups rather than individuals. Community restorative circles (Pranis 2005) are the appropriate form for communities to resolve their differences as they do not require the labels of offender or victim and can address inter-group harm. The following example illustrates their value by both defusing an escalating conflict and strengthening relationships in a community.

An east European family complained that their neighbour was allowing rubbish to come into their garden. This incident took place in a loyalist area during the Unionist Orange festival in July. In addition to the rubbish, the local neighbour had loyalist bunting flying from her house and it had become loose in the wind. Consequently it was invading the neighbour's territory. The local neighbour and her friends interpreted the complaint as disrespect to their culture. This situation was becoming quite threatening to the foreign national family and they sought support from their compatriots who perceived the conflict as racist.

A community activist who lived nearby and had been trained in restorative practices by Ulster University approached the foreign family to hear their side of the story. In doing so, he experienced a degree of hostility from the local people who accused him of taking the other's side and betraying them. He then spoke with the local neighbours. He also consulted other members of the minority ethnic community. Eventually all parties agreed to meet along with a police officer, a local politician and members of the foreign national's community.

They all met in a local community centre. They sat in a circle and each party was invited to give an account of what happened and the issues as they saw them. After a carefully facilitated dialogue the neighbours reached an understanding that the conflict was neither about cultural disrespect nor racism. They agreed to live as good neighbours. The local community invited the foreign nationals to their street party and they in turn offered to provide a barbecue. By providing a safe space in which those most affected by the dispute could communicate respectfully, the true issues emerged without being distorted by the politics of identity.

Drug use in Derry/Londonderry

In Derry the issue that ALTERNATIVE is studying is the harm that emanates from dealing and using drugs. The focus of the research is the community reaction, an aspect of which has been violent punishments inflicted by armed groups. Republican Action Against Drugs, replaced by the 'Irish Republican Army' in 2012, has taken upon itself the role of detecting and punishing people engaged in dealing and using drugs in the areas that it controls. Its methods include 'punishment shootings',[4] destroying the property of alleged dealers, often by arson, and ordering people to leave the community. In 2013, at least 85 people were shot in Derry by the IRA. The organisation claims community support for its activities. However, the involvement of armed groups prepared to use violence to protect their interests makes it difficult for local residents to challenge the brutality of shooting drug dealers. In such a narrative, the community sees itself as the victim of the harm caused by the use and dealing of drugs. The organisation working with Ulster University wanted to find a way to support the community to safely express their disapproval of the behaviours that are causing them harm and to discuss how the issues could be addressed without violence (Kennedy 2011).

To this end the ALTERNATIVE research team, in partnership with the Northland Centre, a drug and alcohol treatment facility, engaged in a series of consultations with a range of people connected with the problem of drug use. The purpose of this was to understand the various narratives about drugs in the communities of Derry. Within this context, a plurality of stories emerged. Some started with a sense of outrage at young deaths or with paramilitary violence while others started with poverty or a sense of anomie. Others have characterised drug and alcohol misuse as a legacy of the conflict, while some describe entirely new features, which reflect global trends, including the impact of the internet and easy access to 'legal highs'. What is unanimous is that harm is being caused. Life has been lost and damaged. Most of the discourse from statutory agencies and community and voluntary organisations has been framed in strategic terms: the need for more information about the problem through research, the need for better coordination of services, the need for new and tougher laws or regulations, and the need for more resources for better services.

Once these consultations had been completed a community conference was planned. The University, not wishing to dominate, offered to support a local community organisation to organise and facilitate the conference. Interestingly the local organisation eventually asked the University to facilitate the conference, as it was perceived as politically neutral and as providing a safe place for honest dialogue without political or paramilitary interference. The conference took place in a community centre in a working class community in Derry. It was attended by people whose relatives were drug users, by local politicians, by community activists, by representatives from both non-governmental organisations and statutory agencies. The process engaged local people in a restorative inquiry designed to enable them to define what the harm is and how it can be addressed and what support the community will need. What made this different was that the conference was not addressed by 'experts' and was not dominated by strategic concerns. It was facilitated in small groups through which ordinary people could tell their stories, raise their concerns and offer their ideas for solutions. They were speaking as representatives of a community that was being harmed by drug use and dealing and that was frustrated by the ineffectiveness of the experts and the formal agencies to address this harm. Significantly there was a consensus that the solution was not to press for more resources but for more effective relationships between and coordination of resources. The Ulster University team recorded the discussions and has completed a report which has been sent to all participants for approval. The next step will be to invite the key agencies to meet the community to agree a coordinated approach, which meets the needs of those who use drugs and their families. This exemplifies a restorative process that the state would find it difficult to replicate.

Discussion

Each of these examples demonstrates how community-based restorative justice can restore a sense of justice and greater security when local communities experience an injustice. For this to happen more often and more effectively, the ALTERNATIVE research has concluded that the state must accommodate and support a space within which ordinary people can be supported to resolve their issues without interference and domination. This involves accepting that the state and its criminal justice system do not have exclusive ownership of justice, particularly when it can be restored through communicative action rather than through strategic coercion or incentive. This requires transitional justice to recognise the importance of relational issues and communicative action in addition to structural reform and institutional procedures.

Sen (2009) asks the question: 'How would justice be advanced?' He is interested in outcomes for ordinary people rather than institutional arrangements. Sen (2009: x) writes that 'Justice is ultimately connected with the way people's lives go, and not merely with the nature of the institutions around them'. He connects the process of justice with a democratic orientation that requires the engagement of people in dialogue. To be active participants in a justice process, they need to develop the appropriate capabilities. For Nussbaum capabilities are the 'totality of the opportunities she has for choice and action in her specific political, social and economic situation' (2011: 21). This discourse of justice is based upon policies that protect and support human agency and participation, rather than upon services that treat people as passive recipients or consumers. 'In the absence of action, rights are mere words on paper' (Nussbaum 2011: 65)

Sandel (2005) believes that justice is intimately involved in membership of a community and the obligations owed to it. In return for fulfilling these obligations, the other parties will focus on how the perpetrators of the harm can be supported to have a good life free from harming others (Braithwaite 1989). Community-based restorative justice projects are an important means of providing a safe space and an inclusive structure for such communicative action. In such a model of justice, personal agency and collective solidarity interact. Community is not static nor is it merely a place to live in or a group of people with common interests. Community is in a constant process of change through negotiation and clarification. Just as justice is something that people do rather than receive, community is also participative. The ALTERNATIVE project, having studied community-based restorative justice, perceives community not as a static signifier of belonging or identity, but as an active and reflexive social and communicative practice on how to live equitably in interdependence with an increasingly diverse range of other identities.

Community-based restorative justice has the potential to address the harmful aspects of identity politics. By engaging people in a process of dialogue, they are offered an opportunity to conceive identity as multi-dimensional and open rather than singular and closed. Yuval-Davis (2011: 12) suggests that 'People can "belong" in many different ways and to many different objects of attachment'. Given these dynamics, a sense of identity is in a constant state of becoming and cannot be reduced to religion, nationality or ethnicity. As Sennett (2012: 4) explains: 'The "self" is a composite of sentiments, affiliations and behaviours which seldom fit neatly together: any call for tribal unity will reduce this personal complexity'. This way of conceiving identity is underpinned by a reflexivity and agency that can be activated through a process of encounter and dialogue which engage participants in striving to understand each other and to make moral choices.

Restorative processes ask people to listen to each other's stories of harm in a spirit of respect, to arrive at some level of mutual understanding and to come to an agreement on what needs to be done. Such moral choices are made not only on the basis of one's own identity but also in recognition of the identity of others. This requires a strong civil society: 'A healthy civil society is important not only because it promotes civility (though this may be a welcome by product) but because it calls forth the habits, skills and qualities of character that make effective democratic citizens' (Sandel 2005: 55). These skills and habits include thinking about the good of the whole, being responsible for others, dealing with conflicting interests and standing for your values while respecting the views of others.

There is a need in a pluralist and rapidly changing society to develop people's capacity to negotiate their way through the 'sometimes overlapping and sometimes conflicting obligations that claim us and to live with the tension to which multiple identities give rise' (Sandel 2005: 34). The resources that enable people to do so are found in 'the places and stories, memories and meanings, incidents and identities, that situate us in the world and give our lives their moral particularity' (Sandel 2005: 34). Restorative justice offers people the opportunity to gain access to these resources.

Sennett (2012: 39) distinguishes two versions of solidarity, one that emphasises the unity of the group, while the other values inclusion of difference. The first relates to politics, the second to society. Sennett writes of the social triangle which supports strong informal relationships between ordinary people outside of politics: earned authority, mutual respect and cooperation during a crisis, qualities which are at the core of restorative processes. Sennett states (2012: 6):

> the good alternative is a demanding and difficult kind of cooperation; it tries to join people who have separate or conflicting interests, who do not feel good about each other, who are unequal, or simply do not understand one another. The challenge is to respond to others on their own terms.

He says that such cooperation enables people to grasp the consequences of their own actions and gain self-awareness. Such cooperation requires skill, 'dialogic skills'. Sennett, inspired by the work of Sen and Nussbaum, states that 'people's capacities for cooperation are far greater and more complex than institutions allow them to be' (2012: 29).

This suggests that the restorative process in community should create an inclusive but apolitical space in which ordinary people can cooperate in resolving conflict through communicative action. Block (2008) perceives community as about the experience of belonging. However, his is not a passive belonging but an active membership. He points out that the word 'belong' also relates to owning, which he connects with responsibility, commitment and accountability:

> The essence of restorative community building is not economic prosperity or the political discourse or the capacity of leadership; it is citizens' willingness to own up to their contribution, to be humble, to choose accountability,

and to have faith in their own capacity to make authentic promises to create the alternative future.

(Block 2008: 48)

A restorative community is characterised, according to McKnight (1995: 165–167), by interdependence, by fallibility rather than the ideal, by diversity and a place for everyone, by many leaders, by quick responses to issues, by creative solutions, by individualised relationships, by caring, and by citizenship. A restorative community recognises and values the plurality of affiliations people have and offers opportunities for people to encounter each other and use reasoning to resolve differences and repair harm.

Conclusion

The purpose of this chapter is to establish through research that community-based restorative justice can play a much more significant role in contributing to a Northern Ireland that is democratic, socially and culturally inclusive and at peace. Northern Ireland is emerging from an extended period of violent conflict and is embarked upon a peace process designed to reconstruct a democratic form of inclusive government and a society based upon human rights, equality and a reformed criminal justice system. This process has been effective in substantially reducing violence. However, a low level of conflict continues to disrupt the stability of society, sustains distrust between communities and from time to time results in street disorder. Structural reform and security strategies have been effective in controlling the conflict and preventing it from escalating into serious politically motivated violence. However, the peace process has struggled to address the conflict's underlying relational and cultural issues. Indeed, the politics of identity that dominate the governance of Northern Ireland are more likely to exacerbate these issues

The ALTERNATIVE action research project has generated examples of how community-based restorative processes can address the relational and cultural issues that political and institutional reforms fail to resolve. These examples will add weight to the argument that the state, rather than marginalising community restorative justice organisations, should accommodate and support them to engage in and transform the conflicts that it can only seek to control. If it does so, society will recognise that community-based restorative justice can contribute to building a pluralist society at peace with itself and in which identity is multi-dimensional and not a source of harmful conflict.

Notes

1 ALTERNATIVE is a research programme funded through the European Commission's Seventh Framework Programme (FP7). It is a partnership between research organisations in Austria, Belgium, Hungary, Northern Ireland, Norway and Serbia. This chapter reflects only the authors' views and asserts that the European Union is not liable for any use that may be made of the information contained therein.

2 Irish republicanism is a political ideology based on the belief that all of Ireland should be an independent republic, in opposition to British rule.
3 Generally, the term loyalist in Northern Ireland refers to Protestant working class politics characterised by a militant opposition to Irish republicanism. An Ulster loyalist is a unionist who strongly supports the political union between Great Britain and Northern Ireland. Loyalism is also perceived to be associated with paramilitary organisations, such as the Ulster Defence Association, Ulster Volunteer Force and the Loyalist Volunteer Force.
4 'Punishment shooting' refers to the practice of armed groups attempting to control crime in their areas by inflicting punishments on offenders by shooting them through various limbs such as kneecaps, elbows and ankles. Occasionally drug dealers were shot dead.

References

Abel, R. (1982) *The Politics of Informal Justice Vol 1, The American Experience*, New York: Academic Press.
Arendt, H. (1958) *The Human Condition*, Chicago: University of Chicago Press.
Bauman, Z. (2001) *Community: Seeking safety in an insecure world*, Cambridge: Polity Press.
Block, P. (2008) *Community: The structure of belonging*, San Francisco: Berrett-Koehler.
Braithwaite, J. (1989) *Crime, Shame and Reintegration*, Cambridge: Cambridge University Press.
Braithwaite, J. (2001) *Restorative Justice and Responsive Regulation*, New York: Oxford University Press.
Bursik, R. and Grasmick, H. (1993) *Neighbourhood and Crime: The dimension of effective community control*, Lexington, MD: Lexington Books.
Chapman, T. (1995) 'Creating a culture of change: a case study of a car crime project in Belfast', in J. Maguire (ed.) *What Works: Reducing re-offending*, Chichester, UK: Wiley.
Chapman, T. and Pinkerton, J. (1987) 'Contradictions in Community', *Probation Journal*, 34(1): 13–16.
Christie, N. (1977) 'Conflict as Property', *British Journal of Criminology*, 17: 1–26.
Criminal Justice Review Group (2000) *Review of the Criminal Justice System in Northern Ireland*, Belfast: HMSO.
Eriksson, A. (2009) *Justice in Transition: Community restorative justice in Northern Ireland*, Cullompton, UK: Willan.
Garland, D. (2001) *The Culture of Control*, Oxford: Oxford University Press.
Habermas, J. (1984) *The Theory of Communicative Action, Vol. 1: Reason and the Rationalisation of Society*, Boston: Beacon Press.
Habermas, J. (1987) *The Theory of Communicative Action, Vol. 2: Lifeworld and system: A critique of functionalist reason*, Boston: Beacon Press.
Habermas, J. (1989) in S. Seidman (ed.) *Jurgen Habermas On Society and Politics – A Reader*, Boston: Beacon Press.
Independent Commission on Policing in Northern Ireland (1999) *A New Beginning: Policing in Northern Ireland*, Belfast: NIO.
Kennedy, D. M. (2011) *Don't Shoot: One man, a street fellowship and the end of the violence in inner-city America*, London: Bloomsbury.
McEvoy, K. (2003) 'Beyond the Metaphor: Political violence, human rights, and "new" peacemaking criminology', *Theoretical Criminology*, 7(3): 319–346.

McEvoy, K. (2001) *Paramilitary Imprisonment in Northern Ireland: Resistance, management and release*, Oxford: Oxford University Press.

McEvoy, K. and Eriksson, A. (2008) ' "Who owns justice?" Community, state and Northern Ireland transition', in J. Shapland (ed.) *Justice, Community and Civil Society: A contested terrain*, Cullompton, UK: Willan Publishing.

McEvoy, K. and Mika, H. (2002) 'Restorative Justice and the Critique of Informalism in Northern Ireland', *British Journal of Criminology*, 43(3): 534–563.

McKnight, J. (1995) *The Careless Society: Community and its counterfeits*, New York: Basic Books.

McKnight, J. and Block, P. (2010) *The Abundant Community: Awakening the power of families and neighbourhoods*, San Francisco: Berrett-Koehler.

Monaghan, R. (2004) 'An Imperfect Peace: Paramilitary "punishments" in Northern Ireland', *Terrorism and Political Violence*, 16(3): 439–461.

Northern Ireland Office (1998) *The Agreement*. [Online]. Available at: ww.nio.gov.uk/agreement.pdf.

Nussbaum, M. C. (2011) *Creating Capabilities: The human development approach*, Cambridge, MA: Harvard University Press.

Pranis, K. (2005) *The Little Book of Circle Processes: A new/old approach to peacemaking*, Intercourse, PA: Good Books.

Putnam, R. D. (2000) *Bowling Alone: The collapse and revival of American community*, New York: Simon and Schuster.

Ruane, J. and Todd, J. (1996) *The Dynamics of Conflict in Northern Ireland: Power, conflict and emancipation*, Cambridge: Cambridge University Press.

Sandel, M. J. (2005) *Public Philosophy: Essays in morality and politics*, Cambridge, MA: Harvard University Press.

Sen, A. (2009) *The Idea of Justice*, London: Allen Lane.

Sennett, R (2012) *Together: The rituals, pleasures and politics of cooperation*, London: Allen Lane.

Shapland, J., Robinson, G. and Sorsby, A. (2012) *Restorative Justice in Practice: Evaluating what works for victims and offenders*, Abingdon, Oxon: Routledge.

Staub, E. (2001) 'Individual and group identities in genocide and mass killing', in R. Ashmore, L. Jussim and D. Wilder (eds) *Social Identity, Intergroup Conflict and Conflict Reduction*, Oxford: Oxford University Press.

Tajfel, H. (1981) *Human Groups and Social Categories: Studies in social psychology*, Cambridge: Cambridge University Press.

The Detail (2015) www.thedetail.tv/articles/above-the-law-paramilitary-punishment-attacks-in-northern-ireland.

Van Ness, D. W. and Strong, K. H. (2010) *Restoring Justice: An introduction to restorative justice*, New Providence, NJ: LexisNexis.

Walgrave, L. (2008) *Restorative Justice, Self-interest and Responsible Citizenship*, Cullompton, UK: Willan Publishing.

Wilkinson, R. and Pickett, K. (2009) *The Spirit Level: Why more equal societies almost always do better*, London: Allen Lane.

Wright, F. (1987) *Northern Ireland: A comparative analysis*, Dublin: Gill and Macmillan.

Young, J. (1999) *The Exclusive Society*, London: Sage.

Yuval-Davis, N. (2011) *The Politics of Belonging: Intersectional contestations*, London: Sage.

8 Restorative justice in transitions

The problem of 'the community' and collective responsibility

Ami Harbin and Jennifer J. Llewellyn

Introduction

Restorative justice holds particular promise for transitional contexts that must confront the social/collective nature of harms and their causes in order to achieve the social transformation transition demands. It is little wonder that such energy and attention has gone into the development of restorative processes (e.g. some truth and reconciliation commissions and traditional justice mechanisms) in transitional contexts. Restorative justice has much greater potential for transitions than is often reflected in accounts of it as partial justice ('justice to the extent possible') or a kind of justice suited for transitions. It is about more than ensuring justice for victims by hearing stories, acknowledging suffering, and investigating the truth about what happened or providing an alternative justice mechanism to secure responses where prosecution and punishment is not optimal. Both views of restorative justice misunderstand its full potential for transitional contexts (Llewellyn 2007). Rather, restorative justice is a theory and approach to justice that is relational, comprehensive, holistic and future-focused (Llewellyn 2011). It is not focused on the individual ascription of blame and liability for past harms, but is committed to understanding the contexts and causes of individual harms and to securing the conditions for just social relationships in future (Llewellyn 2011). This focus on the future was captured in the South African Truth and Reconciliation Commission's mandate to 'promote unity and reconciliation in a spirit of understanding which transcends the conflicts and divisions of the past...' (TRC Act: s. 3(1)). The Canadian Truth and Reconciliation Commission is similarly motivated by 'a profound commitment to establishing new relationships embedded in mutual recognition and respect that will forge a brighter future' (Mandate Canadian Truth and Reconciliation Commission, *Residential Schools Settlement Schedule N)*.

Restorative justice is focused on establishing restored relationships as the foundation upon which transition to a just society rests. The goal of justice understood restoratively is fundamentally about *transition of relationship.* Restorative justice is concerned with ensuring equality of *social* relationships, not only in addressing harms to interpersonal or intimate relationships. Restorative justice strives to create the conditions of social relationship in which all parties might flourish and achieve meaningful, just and peaceful co-existence. Community is key to this goal. Community plays an essential role in meeting the re-integrative needs of both victims and wrongdoers, and to the recovery and rebuilding of societies. Restorative justice provides an opportunity for communities to understand the harms of past wrongdoing and to establish or re-establish a sense of community essential for transitioning to a just and peaceful future. The view that the community is both affected by social conflict and plays a fundamental role in its creation and resolution is central to restorative justice (Llewellyn and Howse 1998). The importance of public participation for restorative justice is perhaps most obvious in transitional contexts facing the challenge of recovery and rebuilding from conflict, violence and oppression. Indeed, the inclusion of 'reconciliation' in the name and mandates of transitional mechanisms reflects this larger ambition to deal with the past in order to secure a just future. Restorative justice is oriented to this goal of reconciliation as the establishment of peaceful and just future relationships in which individuals, groups and communities can live together with dignity, respect, care and concern for one another (Llewellyn 2008; Llewellyn and Philpott 2014).

This broader understanding of the goal of restorative justice in transitions poses the significant conceptual and practical challenge of understanding and operationalising the role of 'the community'. We suggest that part of what is challenging about future-oriented restorative justice processes is illuminated by what philosophers have referred to as 'problems of collective action'. Collective action is essential to the role of community in restorative justice and to the work of transition itself. Collective action depends significantly on appreciation of collective responsibility for injustices that require action to ensure response, redress and change. Given a pervasive tendency in the history of philosophical ethics to understand responsibilities as things that could only ever be ascribed to individuals, the potential responsibilities of groups or communities have been considered secondarily, where they have been considered at all. As we employ them here, the collective responsibility debates serve as one source of insight into the difficulties of conceiving of 'the community', and point to the need for a relational approach to restorative justice in transitional contexts.

This challenge of collective responsibility in restorative justice theory and practice often presents as dilemmas or problems related to the position and role of 'the community' in response to complex harms. The struggle to articulate the role of the community reveals the difficulty of moving beyond individualistic models in the implementation of restorative justice practices. Recognising the nuances of individualistic assumptions in the collective agency debates can help us better understand practical questions in restorative justice, including: Why is it so difficult to conceive of 'the community' as responsible for major harms? Why is it important to be critically aware of tendencies to neglect many important relationships when trying to isolate 'the community' who should be involved in restorative justice practices? How might restorative justice processes need to more explicitly prepare for the refusal of some parts of the community to see themselves as part of 'the community'? Answering these questions reveals and reinforces the need for a relational approach to the notion of collective responsibility and the community in restorative justice.

This chapter will proceed as follows. We begin by discussing the confusion surrounding the role of 'the community' in restorative justice theory and practice. We then turn to an analysis of philosophical debates about collective responsibility, using them to clarify how the persistent focus on individuals and a basic belief in the opposition of the individual and the collective continues to restrict restorative justice theory and practice. We then outline how the failure to adequately address the role of the community affects those in transitional contexts, often resulting in an inability to conceive of shared social responsibility for structural and systemic issues. As we conclude, the way forward will require instead developing a relational approach to restorative justice in transitional contexts, taking the development of relationships of trust and respect at collective, community and system levels to be a central objective.

Restorative justice and the problem of 'the community'

Restorative justice is often defined by its expansive inclusion of those affected by wrongdoing, as, for example, in Tony Marshall's early and influential account of restorative justice as 'a process whereby *all the parties* with a stake in a particular offense come together to resolve collectively how to deal with the aftermath of the offense and its implications for the future' (Marshall 1999: 5, emphasis added). Explanations of restorative justice that followed have generally reflected these elements. Howard Zehr, generally recognised as one of pioneers of restorative justice, explains that restorative justice 'involves the victim, the offender, and *the community* in a search for solutions which promote repair, reconciliation, and reassurance' (1990: 181, emphasis added). The triad – victim, offender and the community – is so familiar within restorative justice descriptions that it is mantra-like in its invocation. It reflects the different framework restorative justice offers to understand and respond to crime. Crime is understood by restorative justice as harm to individuals and communities, rather than simply a violation of abstract laws against the state. Those most directly affected by crime – victims, community members and offenders – are therefore encouraged to play an active role in the justice process.

This core formula often distinguishes restorative justice from the criminal justice system by virtue of the *centrality of victims*. While this difference warrants attention, it is not the only shift worthy of note and consideration.[1] Restorative justice relies equally heavily on *the community* in terms of participation, leadership, implementation and authority within these processes. Umbreit and Armour's recent work affirms: '[a] major pillar of the restorative justice approach is its emphasis upon the involvement of communities and respect for the needs of the community' (Umbreit and Armour 2011: 88). Surprisingly, despite this central place of the community in restorative justice, little attention has been paid to what is meant by 'the community' or its role in the process.

The term 'community' is used in vague and general ways throughout the literature, with only surface acknowledgements of its complexity. While most advocates of restorative justice agree that there are often many types or levels of community involved in a given situation, few attempt to identify these various communities or explain how they are different from one another. Two notable previous attempts were made by McCold (1996) and Van Ness and Strong (2006), both of which divide community into different levels or categories that might be relevant in a restorative processes. At times, within the restorative justice literature and practice generally, and particularly with respect to transitions, community is used as shorthand for society in general (read as 'the public'). In other instances it is intended to refer to the particular communities to which the offender and victim belong (for example, families, ethnic, or racial communities). The term is also used to denote the involvement of geographic communities, such as the immediate community in which the parties live, or where the wrongdoing took place.

As McCold, Van Ness and Strong recognise, there is sometimes acknowledgement of the difference between those communities we are a part of by virtue of proximity or space and those communities we belong to by virtue of intimate connection. Even as they try to identify possible communities, they all agree that the relevant community for a given restorative process will depend in large measure upon the context, the parties involved, and the nature of the harm at issue, rendering the question of 'who is the community?' a contextual one with no a priori answer. Neither account dwells, however, upon the role and significance of community within restorative justice. Indeed, operational questions of who the community is and who should be included have overshadowed more basic questions of *why the community is included at all*.

Some have paid more attention to the significance of community for restorative justice (Clamp 2014; Llewellyn 2011). Llewellyn, for example, has suggested that the focus on 'the community' reflects a commitment to a relational view of those involved or affected by a situation or those who can affect the outcome. 'The community' is then an idea that plays stand-in, demanding attention to the network or web of relationships that are relevant in a given situation. Its place in the mantra reflects a call to understand harms and people relationally (Llewellyn 2005, 2007, 2011; MacKenzie and Stoljar 2000).

Generally, however, the community is taken, within literature and practice, as either or both *agent* and *object* of restoration. Advocates claim that restorative justice is realised *in* the community and is, at the same time, potentially transformative of that community. Community is seen as an agent of restoration chiefly in a post-event sense: it plays host, facilitator, or support for restorative processes (as is familiar from community justice). It is clear from the literature that restorative justice is concerned with more than simply community *based* justice. Community justice and restorative justice are related in their commitment to locate justice as a concern of the community and to empower communities to undertake such work. In significant measure they both draw inspiration from similar sources, including the critique of the role of the state in the justice system and the professionalisation of dispute resolution (Christie 1977). While empowerment of the community is certainly significant for transitional contexts, community justice understood in this way does not offer a different way of understanding conflict or justice. Rather it simply speaks to the interest of community in this work and the opportunities it presents to influence justice outcomes. While the inclusion of the community in restorative justice entails more than this, its role and significance in the theory and practice is not as clear. The community is sometimes viewed as a party within individual processes, often as a victim or secondary victim of harm in need of restoration. The community as 'victim' itself is common in cases where the harm is in whole or in part to social order or social values, which are sometimes referenced as 'victimless' as in the case of drug use or membership in certain banned organisations or groups. In other circumstances, the community is the victim as the holder of collective interest or property – as in large scale environmental damage, financial crimes or denial of rights and entitlements for certain segments of society. In yet other situations, the community is a victim because of the conflict between its members or flowing through from the harm to its members. This is often referenced as the harm to the 'fabric' of the community by virtue of the tensions or divisions caused between its members. This dimension of harm to community is particularly clear in post-conflict/transitional contexts, where the impacts and effects of conflict on the fabric of society have a tangible effect through societal breakdown and its implications for individuals. In these respects the community seems to take the role and place held by the state in the traditional criminal justice system. In many transitional contexts, an enlarged role for community or civil society is even more common since the state may be failed, fragile or implicated in ways that prevent it from exercising moral authority to represent collective interests or lead justice processes (see Doak, this volume).

Association with the roles typically played by the state has had significant influence on the understanding of the role of the community and its operationalisation in restorative justice (Llewellyn and Howse 1998). Legal historian Harold Berman describes the insertion of the state into this realm of dispute resolution as a 'legal revolution' (1983). This revolution resulted in a reconceptualisation of the nature of disputes, and, by its end, the crown had proclaimed itself 'keeper of the peace' and as such would be the victim whenever the peace was violated. The role of the courts changed in suit; no longer was their task simply to referee between disputing parties who requested their involvement. Courts now took up the role of defending the crown. They began to play an active role in prosecution, taking ownership over those cases in which the crown was deemed victim (Zehr 1990: 110). Justice, pursued through the work of these courts, came to mean 'applying rules, establishing guilt, and fixing penalties' (Zehr 1990: 112). This new role of the crown resulted in devastating and lasting effects for the real victims harmed by wrongful acts. They were no longer parties in their own cause, having been effectively ousted from their own disputes. This remains largely the situation today, with their participation generally limited to their usefulness as crown witnesses. Evidence of this change in focus from victim-centred to state-centred justice can be found in the preference for fines (payable to the crown) instead of restitution, and for punishment over problem-solving and settlement. Punishment served the interests of the state as a show of power and authority, while doing nothing to address the harms caused by the wrongdoing. Crime was about law-breaking, not harm. As a result, attention was focused on the actions of the offender not the effects of his behaviour (Van Ness and Strong, 2006: 7). These developments clearly had the effect of marginalising the interests and role of individual victims within the justice process. But the effects extended beyond this to shape our very notions of responsibility with respect to the individual and community in service of these new developments in criminal justice. Nicola Lacey argues that, with these and later historical developments within the criminal law, came 'a broad movement from ideas of responsibility founded in character to conceptions of responsibility as founded in capacity' (Lacey 2001a: 250; also see Lacey 2001b; 2008).

As Lacey explains, responsibility used to be assessed by relying upon societal norms and knowledge. However, as the idea of individual responsibility developed, it became reliant on the agency and capacities of people to deliberate and choose. No longer, on this conception, are individuals responsible by virtue of who they are or their social status; according to Lacey, responsibility is now assigned according to what individuals choose to do. This conception of responsibility places significant emphasis on the subjective attitudes of individuals. As it moved away from the character basis for responsibility, the understanding of social or collective responsibility was marginalised by focus on the individual (Lacey 2001a: 255).

Understood in the historical context of the changing role of the state and the importance of individual responsibility in the legitimation and operation of criminal justice trial processes, it is perhaps not surprising that the role of 'the community' in restorative justice is bounded by the scope of the role of the state in criminal justice. Viewed as post-event agent or facilitator of restorative justice, or harmed/injured subject in need of restoration, there is little conception or attention to the idea of community as *agent responsible for the harm* (either itself or alongside individuals). The account of why this is so tends not to be rooted in collective responsibility or action but rather in the authority, entitlement or legitimacy of the community as opposed to the state to have a say or some control in the justice realm. Community is more typically in the role of host or facilitator. In this wider sense, the community ensures a connection to 'the public' and thus the legitimacy of such processes as more than private dispute settlement. While perhaps significant at this programmatic level, the role of community as host or facilitator of restorative justice does little to address community responsibility for harm or injustice nor their related obligations to act in response.

The failure to conceive of, and attend to, the role of the community as a responsible agent warrants significant attention by restorative justice theorists and practitioners alike. In a recent article, Umbreit and Armour (2011) acknowledge this failure in their identification of the issue of community responsibility as an opportunity for extending the vision of restorative justice. They suggest restorative justice should be developed to strengthen 'the fabric of community responsibility through increasing involvement of neighbors and citizens in restorative community-based justice initiatives. This kind of involvement provides opportunities for more frequent and meaningful contact with others in activities that benefit all of society' (2011: 83).

It is noteworthy that, even in their recognition of the need for more attention to the community in terms of collective responsibility, the example they offer of a project in a low socioeconomic area in San Antonio, Texas, falls more in line with community as support or resource without any careful consideration of the idea of collective community responsibility for harm (Umbreit and Armour 2011: 83). When it comes to determining responsibility for harm in restorative justice, the emphasis remains largely focused on the individual. This inattention to community responsibility at a practical level is somewhat curious given the focus on relationships within the restorative justice literature. The attention to relationship has led to the recognition that harms flow through to the community from the individuals involved by virtue of existing relationships, but it is still a strain to recognise the reverse flow of harms from the community to individuals beyond the generalised appreciation of the nature and social origin of harms.

Despite some theoretical accounts that have gone further than naming the centrality of relationships within restorative justice practice to offer it as a relational theory of justice (Llewellyn 2011; Llewellyn and Howse 1998), the focus on the triad of parties – victims, offenders and community – central to restorative justice theory and practice still reflects the individualistic approach deeply rooted in the individualism of the criminal justice system that is centrally focused on accountability for responsible individuals. While there is clearly effort, within restorative justice processes, to understand wrongdoers' intentions and motivations in more nuanced ways that consider the role of social inequality, such contextual analysis remains as explanation and context for individual responsibility rather than as relational understanding of responsibility at individual and collective levels. This approach to restorative justice theory and practice sees relationships between individuals as important but it does not take a *relational view of individuals*. While it takes into account the influence individuals have on one another, it does not require a different view of people qua individuals, nor of the significance of relationship as core to our understanding of harm and responsibility. The failure to do so has the field's understanding of the role of the community – the collective – for restorative justice, particularly with respect to collective responsibility. Doing so has created a challenge for restorative justice to realise its promise and potential for transitional contexts.

The problem with collective responsibility

Over the last 50 years of philosophical ethics, significant attention has been paid to the tensions that arise when groups are seen to be responsible for serious harms experienced by other groups.[2] There is by now a well-established spectrum of positions on the existence and character of collective agents, some arguing their impossibility, and others claiming they are possible but variously characterising them as similar or dissimilar to individual agents. Feinberg (1968) was among the first to suggest the need for nuanced consideration of the possibility of group responsibility for harms against others, and it opened up a number of the questions that have shaped the debate most significantly since: how to determine relevant groups, what relationships of solidarity or membership inhere in the groups, how to guard against unfair claims to responsibility, how to negotiate addressing group responsibility where 'fault' is not obvious, the voluntariness of group membership, and the status of those who have benefitted from harms against others. Most positions within the debate are cautious about making overly ambitious or sweeping claims about collectives being responsible, as the implications of such claims for real lives can be significant. As Larry May and Stacey Hoffman highlight:

> Revenge was sought against people who had not themselves perpetrated any harm. Rather, the people against whom retaliation was directed were simply members of a group, other members of which had committed violence. Implicit in all of this was the claim that the group, per se, was responsible for the harms, and that all of its members should pay compensation. As with many of the views we will examine, this is a misuse of the notion of collective responsibility. But the fact that such examples of guilt by association have been common in the history of human interaction may help explain why so many people have a visceral reaction to any form of collective responsibility.
>
> (May and Hoffman, 1991: 1–2)

Philosophers have articulated a wider variety of critical and sympathetic positions on the question of the status of collectives as moral agents than could be canvassed here. Against the backdrop of hesitancy in establishing collective responsibility, philosophers have offered starting points, some more critical, and others more optimistic.[3] In the camp of those more resistant to collectivist notions of responsibility, Narveson (2002) formulates some of the objections to the existence of collective agents most simply. At the heart of his arguments against the possibility of collective responsibility are the privileging of the direct connection between voluntary action and responsibility, the bedrock assumption that only individuals can act, and the insistence on a gap between group membership and actions for which individuals can be held responsible. He worries especially about an individual member of a group being accused of harming another group in the past or present, without sufficient evidence. A group then should only be said to harm another group if there is evidence of many members of the group regularly, or fairly often, causing such harm to individuals within the other group (2002). Narveson argues that individual agents are both the only meaningful objects of harm and the only reasonable subjects of responsible or irresponsible action (2002: 180–181), as he summarises, '[u]nderlying individualism is the only rational meta-theory for collective responsibility' (2002: 182).

Corlett more specifically evaluates the possibility of collective responsibility in light of the conditions that necessarily hold in a case where a group could be understood as responsible (2001: 574). Corlett acknowledges that three necessary conditions of collective responsibility – intention, voluntariness, and knowledge – may be said to 'wrongly [construe] collective moral responsibility in terms of what constitutes individual moral responsibility', but maintains that there are neither other options for analysing responsibility except through the conditions of intentional, voluntary, and epistemic action, nor reasons to seek such options (2001: 574–575). Having positioned these as the necessary conditions of collective action, Corlett argues that each will be difficult to the point of near impossibility for even highly organised collectives (such as corporations) to satisfy in everyday contexts.

On the other side of the spectrum, philosophers have offered accounts of collective responsibility that aim to clarify collectivist dimensions of action: aspects of agency that exist at the collective level, in ways distinct from how they operate for individuals. Virginia Held (1986: 164), Margaret Gilbert (2006), and Tracy Isaacs (2011) have explored aspects of agency that can be possible only when collectives exist. For example, Isaacs's approach could be considered to be a hybrid: she defends the possibility of genuinely collective responsibility and explores individuals' responsibilities in collective contexts. Contra Narveson and Corlett, according to Isaacs, collectives can be agents, with the possibility of collective intentions and the accompanying possibility of collective actions (see also Harbin 2014).

Across their differences though, these positions on collective responsibility reflect the persistent influence of the punitive framing of responsibility and the individualism that feeds it. This model of responsibility is what Iris Marion Young refers to as the 'liability model'. It seeks liable parties for the sake of doling out punishment or requiring compensation or redress. She suggests that practices conforming to this model are generally backward-focused. While Young concedes that this model is indispensible in our current criminal justice practices, focused, as they are, on individual culpability, she is clear it is inappropriate for dealing with systemic or structural injustice (Young 2010: 98–99).

A major thread running through the debates about the possibility of collective agency is the persistent focus on individuals: still much of the debates centre on solving puzzles about how a collective agent could believe, intend, commit, or be motivated. These accounts reveal the extent to which the debates over collective responsibility are founded in a basic belief in the opposition of the individual and the collective. In her effort to sketch a relational framework and its implications for autonomy, Jennifer Nedelsky notes that the independence often associated with autonomy is cast in opposition to the community and is, indeed, under threat from it (2011: 51). This underlying belief in the opposing stance of the individual and collective serves as a blinder, according to Nedelsky, to a relational view of autonomy, and it is likewise true for responsibility. She argues that, so long as this oppositional stance is maintained:

> a relational approach becomes relegated to exceptions [...] as a general concept it becomes an unproductive paradox or an unsolvable puzzle. The questions that arise out of the oppositional framework can never be satisfactorily answered. The framework of the question needs to be changed.
>
> (Nedelsky 2011: 52)

Attempts to make sense of collective responsibility as an enlarged version of an image we already have of individual responsibility neglects the ways collective agency, whatever it is, is likely to be significantly distinct from individualistic models of individual responsibility. Indeed, the problem we want to highlight in these debates is not just that many accounts of collective responsibility are referring to and modelling themselves after accounts of individual responsibility, but, rather, that those accounts of individual responsibility are *themselves* deeply individualistic and non-relational. They start with the question of 'how can X be shown to be responsible for harms against Y?' rather than 'how is X in relation with Y, and what does such a relationship call for?'

Many views of collective responsibility remain individualistic in senses that circumscribe conceiving of collectives relationally, which is to say, as shaped and structured by relations internal to the group (i.e., among individuals and groups), and by past and present relations among other groups. Deficits in relational thinking about collective agency should not, perhaps, be surprising given the history of philosophers' and social theorists' struggle to think relationally about individuals' agency. Yet, on some level, given the obvious relational dimensions of collectives, it is somewhat surprising that the limits of individualism have garnered such scant attention.

These challenges of collective responsibility are of central significance for restorative justice and are particularly poignant in transitional contexts. Many who consider the possibility of collective responsibility for major harms raise the worry about the *risks* of collective responsibility for individuals who do not see themselves as responsible. In large measure, such risks are produced because responsibility is viewed through the lens of individuals at risk of being blamed or punished. Concerns about the legitimacy of collective responsibility are thus shaped by the punitive criminal justice context in which responsibility operates. It is important, in our view, for the assumption of this context to be laid bare and examined to reveal its structuring and limiting effects on the possibilities for collective responsibility. In this respect, restorative justice as an alternative to this retributive/punitive frame for justice is an obvious and important site to consider collective responsibility anew.

A restorative approach to justice is focused on understanding and assessing responsibility for what happened in the past *not* in order to ascribe blame and legitimate punishment but to establish responsibility for future action – individual and collective – aimed at creating and sustaining conditions for just relations. The common focus on punishment as the natural outcome of collective responsibility is not surprising, given the central role of the criminal justice system in the development of our modern notions of individual responsibility (Lacey 2001a). Young describes our familiar practices of assigning responsibility as focused on finding 'who dunnit' and tied to being able to identify the cause of the harm. This approach, however, causes a significant problem for finding responsibility for structural injustice, often central in transitional contexts, because by their nature they are not typically authored or caused by an individual agent or agents (Young 2010: 95–96).

It is interesting that the sense of individual responsibility which developed in service of the needs of a modern criminal justice process to legitimise its individualised and punitive orientation is now taken as an argument for the necessity of that very system. As a theory of justice, restorative justice understands wrongdoing and harm in integrated and holistic ways. It attends to the complex multi-layered webs of relationships involving individuals, groups, communities and nations at play. Despite this relational approach, however, in practice, restorative processes often struggle to deal with collective responsibility and support collective action. Even as their mandates are often rooted in commitments to understand collective responsibility for the past and to foster collective action for a just future, in practice such processes are overly focused on collecting the truth (largely through individual testimony) in order to establish individual blame and entitlement (through findings, amnesty processes and victim reparations). Collective aspects of responsibility are generally represented by the liability of particular institutions or organisations. The broader ambition, to understand our collective social responsibility, is often left to officials of the process to reflect upon and offer in the form of a report and recommendations, as they seek to make sense of the sum of the parts of its findings on individual harms and responsibilities throughout the process. As a result, there is often a disconnect between the nature of the insights about collective responsibility that result from restorative justice processes and the application and operation of collective responsibility and action within the processes themselves. The problems of collective responsibility thus affect restorative justice despite the fact that it seeks to be relational and contextual, as evidenced by the central place of the community in its formulations and its forward-looking focus.

The limits of community and collective responsibility: a problem for transitions

The individualism influencing the notion of collective responsibility is clearly reflected in and impacts on the struggle to conceptualise and operationalise the role of the community within restorative justice. The lack of a relational conception and approach to responsibility has resulted in significant practical challenges for transitional restorative justice processes. This has resulted in issues and tensions with respect to the capacity of restorative justice processes to ensure both individual accountability and collective responsibility.

It is perhaps ironic that one of the implications of the employ of individualistic models of responsibility within restorative justice is a perception that such processes do not adequately ensure individual accountability. In some ways, this is expected and accepted as a trade off in favour of addressing collective responsibility. This was, for example, the position of the South African Constitutional Court in deciding a constitutional challenge to the amnesty provisions of the Truth and Reconciliation Act. The Chief Justice Mahomed in the AZAPO case[4] defended amnesty as a necessary trade off with justice. He found it was a justified balancing of the need for justice to victims in the form of individual liability and the need for national reconciliation. Indeed, restorative justice often stands for the proposition that, in order to move toward a better future, we must forego backward-focused blame and punishment.

The problem with individual accountability for restorative justice arises because, while the theory makes clear the need to shift our conceptions of responsibility to be relational and forward looking, the practice does not often reflect this shift. Restorative processes often focus largely on understanding the past and seeking a way through to the future through a focus on addressing individual harms and individual responsibility. The structure and operations of such processes reflect this focus by their emphasis on finding the truth of the past through the collection of individual testimony, documents and other information sources. While restorative processes generally move away from punishment, they do not move away from the liability model of responsibility that looks back and ascribes responsibility to individual actors or organisations. This liability model then generates expectations of what is required and owed to discharge responsibility – for what one is liable for – and restorative processes offer few ways of satisfying or paying this debt. Individuals are often left without ways to meet their responsibilities without imposed punishment or compensation.[5] Interestingly, the process generates the liabilities and, with them, related entitlements to those harmed, but then can only answer them by ensuring that the state or society pays what is owed. This usually takes the form of reparation paid by the state.

Such reparations do not often come as an acknowledgement of shared responsibility – they are sometimes reflective of collective responsibility because of acts by or failures of state institutions but more often than not they are explained as the state paying the debt that is owed in place of individuals who are responsible (Llewellyn, 2004). This issue is even more pronounced when individual compensation is provided to victims by the state in advance of a restorative justice process (as in the case of the Residential Schools settlement in Canada, see Llewellyn (2008) and Cunneen's chapter in this volume). This poses a challenge when individual compensation is viewed as the sum total of the reparation required to address the harms, even if it is later revealed as inadequate to address the collective harms identified within a restorative process.

Insofar as there is attention within processes to collective responsibility, it is often focused on collective agents that can bear individual responsibility (read: blame and liability). They rarely address the broader shared social responsibility for structural or systemic issues. Collective responsibility in this broader sense is left for comment and recommendations in final reports with the hope that the process itself will prove a catalyst and moral authority for shared social responsibility and future action. This does not, generally, receive significant attention within processes. In fact, the individualism that shapes the approach to responsibility for individual and collective agents within restorative justice processes can actually undermine the potential for collective responsibility and action within processes. As Young notes, the problem is that the application of individual responsibility actually functions to undermine collective responsibility by suggesting that the actions of the individual caused harm to an otherwise acceptable state of affairs, i.e. that the status quo ante was just (Young 2010: 106–107).

This danger is a familiar one for restorative justice, as it forms the basis for one of the most persistent critiques of the use of restorative justice in transitional contexts. The critique trades on what we view as a common misconception of restorative justice if understood as a relational theory. The misconception is perhaps understandable, though, given the common usage of the term 'restore' to indicate a return to a status quo ante. The critique is that restorative justice cannot restore relationships to a just state if no such state ever existed before. A related concern is that establishing just social relationships between individuals is not possible in the context of systemic or structural injustice (Llewellyn 2011; Llewellyn and Howse 1998). Indeed, some restorative processes do pursue this goal of repair or return. Notably though, it is those processes narrowly focused on addressing individual wrong and harm in the context of interpersonal relationships that tend to do so. The idea of 'return' is a particular problem for restorative justice processes in the context of transitions, since it locates justice in the past rather than building it for the future. Understood as a relational theory of justice, however, restorative justice is not just a response to the past. It is not like the liability model of responsibility, which pins liability to a departure from a normal set of background conditions and/or an ideal (Young, 2010). If the idea of responsibility in restorative justice does not turn on liability, and if it is future focused, it does not assume the existing baseline is just and worthy of a return; these models can then be more useful in transitional context. As Young explains:

> A model of responsibility derived from an understanding of the mediated connection that agents have to structural injustices, on the other hand, does more than just evaluate harms that deviate from the normal and acceptable; it also often brings into question precisely the background conditions that ascriptions of blame or fault assume to be normal. When we judge that structural injustice exists, we are saying precisely that at least some of the normal and accepted background conditions of action are not morally acceptable. Most of us contribute to a greater or lesser degree to the production and reproduction of structural injustice precisely because we follow the accepted and expected rules and conventions of the communities and institutions in which we act.
>
> (Young, 2010: 107)

The liability model of responsibility is also problematic, because assigning liability to individuals or entities often results in absolving others of responsibility. On one level, this may be attractive in transitional situations. Indeed, some have argued for the importance of criminal justice models on precisely these grounds – that determining individual responsibility can end the cycle of recrimination against groups for the harms of the past (Todorov 1996). Although attractive in its logic, there is little empirical basis for this claim (Llewellyn and Howse 1999). One might also equally worry that such ascription of individual responsibility for harms that are social/structural in nature may cause resentment at such an unfair burden and result in rejection even of that shared responsibility an individual ought to bear. For example, this seems, at least in part, to have been the issue that resulted in objections from both the National Party and the African National Congress against the release of the report of the South African Truth and Reconciliation Commission. After previewing the findings the Commission proposed for its final report, both objected to the responsibility ascribed to their political parties, because it seemed an uneven share of the collective responsibility for what occurred during the Apartheid. Read in the context of the entire report, though, the moral nuances of shared responsibilities within which the findings were made may have been more apparent. This was not, however, what was initially conveyed to the parties. The findings about their individual responsibilities were shared, abstracted from the broader context of shared responsibility.

The experience of the Canadian Truth and Reconciliation Commission provides another example of the problems generated by an individualistic approach to responsibility for the restorative justice process. In the Canadian context, compensation was paid to former students of residential schools in advance or alongside the Commission process. The government's compensation served as an expression of collective responsibility and liability for compensation. It did not, however, represent or produce the shared responsibility for structural injustice that Young describes. Instead, this was to be the task of the Truth and Reconciliation Commission. However, the Commission has struggled throughout its work with generating this shared responsibility. Its work has focused significantly on taking individual statements, investigating related claims and seeking to compile evidence of past wrongs. It has sought and received 'gestures of reconciliation' from groups and collective entities. Apart from the concern that many of these expressions constituted little more than gestures, the more significant issue for our purposes is that they generally served as expressions of the responsibility of collectives (governments, church entities and other organisations and groups) but not as expressions of shared responsibility that entail future collective action.[6] Instead, the general public has engaged most often with the Commission as audience/witness to the process.

A way forward: a relational approach to collective responsibility

As the lens of the collective agency debates have helped us clarify, the challenge of understanding the role of the community in restorative justice contexts reveals a fundamental struggle with the influence and weight of individualism. The way forward, as we have begun to chart, requires developing a relational approach to restorative justice in transitional contexts. Such an approach would require revisiting and revising notions of individual and collective responsibility. A relational understanding will highlight the significance of 'community' in the restorative justice mantra as a call to attend to relationships and interconnection as central to understanding responsibility for what happened and what needs to happen next.[7]

Young's social connection model provides an important starting point for describing the notion of responsibility needed for restorative justice. As she has argued, 'Being responsible in relation to structural injustice means that one has an obligation to join with others who *share* that responsibility in order to transform the structural processes to make their outcomes less unjust' (Young 2010: 96–97 emphasis added). Even so, it is important to acknowledge the limits of this model as she presents it.[8] The idea of shared responsibility is very helpful to the work of restorative justice in transitions for its attention to the background structural factors and social injustices connected to individual responsibility. It clearly offers a challenge to the individualism that structures and influences existing approaches to responsibility and which limits our imaginations and efforts within restorative justice to understand the role of community as central. Young's account is particularly helpful in this respect, as it can reveal and address the limits brought by this individualism to the implementation of responsibility within restorative justice, particularly within transitional contexts. An account of individual responsibility centred on liability is of limited value within transitional contexts, which often look to restorative justice precisely because of the limits and failures of backward-looking criminal and civil justice processes shaped by retributive or corrective accounts of justice. Where Young's account falls short, however, is in her failure to interrogate the influence of individualism on the responsibility of individual agents:

> I propose a social connection model of responsibility specifically for thinking about responsibility in relation to structural injustice. In proposing this model, I do not aim to replace or reject the liability model. I am claiming instead that the liability model is appropriate in some contexts but not all.
>
> (Young 2010: 100)

Given the limits and problems she identifies with the liability model, her assumption of it as essential for individual justice is curious. Indeed, her position seems to be determined by the structure and demands of the current criminal and civil justice systems, steeped as they are in the logic of individualism. Her account fails to consider that the problem may lie with these systems that focus on blame and liability, rather than with the notion of collective responsibility. For restorative justice to realise its promise and potential and serve the needs of transitional settings, it requires a relational approach to responsibility that is broadly capable of comprehending the interwoven nature of individual and collective responsibilities. Care must certainly be exercised when claims of collective responsibility are made. But any motivation for caution should be inspired less by desires to adhere to abstract standards motivated by suspicions about the very possibility of collective responsibility and more by desires to avoid making inaccurate claims about collective responsibility that may have further damaging effects on relationships and people. Caution for the sake of such relationships is justified. Having said this, the same relationships are just as easily damaged by failures to understand where responsibility is collective and shared.

A relational approach to responsibility helps overcome the conceptual and practical limits for restorative justice in relation to the role of the community. The involvement of the community is essential for restorative processes to support and facilitate the shared responsibility and collective action required for justice in times of transition. The way forward for restorative justice in transitional settings is to interrogate the operative notion of responsibility and consider the practical implications of this conceptual shift. Assumptions about the individual nature of responsibility and the limits of collective responsibility have significantly shaped restorative justice processes and their capacity to fulfil their promises for transitional contexts. The potential and implications of this conceptual shift for particular restorative justice processes will, of course, vary depending upon the context, but a number of general differences are likely to result.

A relational model of responsibility in transitional contexts would require action-oriented processes that seek to create the conditions for realising and expressing shared responsibility. Such processes would need to engage the public as more than witnesses to, or the subject of, harm. Rather, public engagement needs to be active and far reaching to develop the sense of shared responsibility required for collective action toward transition. Restorative justice processes would also have to do more than consider collective responsibility as simply the sum of individual statements and amnesties. Rather, individual responsibility should not replace or foreclose collective responsibility, but should demand explicit examination of the structural and systemic injustices to identify the connection to collective responsibility. Doing so would require central attention within the mandates of transitional restorative justice processes to structural and systemic issues as more than a contextual back story for individual liability. In practice, this would mean a move away from 'fact finding' as the orienting activity of such processes and toward processes capable of establishing relational truth (Llewellyn 2008; Llewellyn and Howse 1998). Such truth cannot be found simply by collecting testimonies and focusing on individual amnesties or liabilities. It requires sharing truth so that 'collective sense' might be made of them. This is work that must be undertaken by a wide range of affected or connected parties within restorative processes. It is not work that can be left for a few commissioners to do in a final report as an outcome of the process.

Assumptions about the individual nature of responsibility and the limits of collective responsibility have significantly shaped restorative justice processes and their capacity to fulfil their promises for transitional contexts. Understanding and accepting shared responsibility for injustice requires relationships of trust and respect at collective, community and system levels. These relationships are also essential for collective action to address such injustice. Restorative processes must, then, take the task of building such relationships as a central objective. It is in this work that the role and significance of community for restorative justice becomes clear. A focus on community for restorative justice is a focus on those relationships that are required to establish the shared responsibility and collective action upon which peaceful and sustainable transitions depend. This is the promise and potential of restorative justice that transitional contexts seek.

Notes

1 Indeed, it may require more nuanced attention than it has typically received within the restorative justice literature and movement. While it is true that the victim is a central part of a restorative process (in contrast to the traditional retributive justice-based systems which have generally sidelined the victim in favour of giving the state the central role), it is not accurate to describe restorative justice as 'victim-centred' if what is intended is a flipping of the tables whereby the victim's needs become central at the expense of the wrongdoer's or the community's. Rather, it is more appropriate, Llewellyn suggests, to say restorative justice is 'relationship-centered', as the focus of restorative justice is always broader than any individual party because of its goal of restoring relationships (Llewellyn 2007; Llewellyn and Howse 1998).
2 See Copp (2006); Feinberg (1968); French (1984, 1998); Gilbert (1997, 2000, 2006); Isaacs (2011); May (1987, 1992); Narveson (2002); Raikka (1997); Sadler (2007); Smiley (1992, 2010).
3 David Copp and Raimo Tuomela have since developed views of collective agency that resist the monopoly of the individual on agency. Copp defends the possibility of collective intentions, where collectives can have immediate access to their intentional states, even though they do not have consciousness of their intentional states (Copp, 2006: 198–200). Tuomela considers 'group will-formation' and 'authority systems' in which, by implicit or explicit process, collectives can establish the will to act in a particular way (Tuomela, 1995: 174–179).
4 *Azanian Peoples Organisation (Azapo) And Others v. The President of The Republic Of South Africa* (1996) CCT 17/96 South African Constitutional Court.
5 For example, one might consider the case of Brian Victor Mitchell, who was granted amnesty by the South African Truth Commission with respect to the Trust Feeds Massacre – Amnesty Application No. 2586/96.
6 Seemingly in response to public voicing of this concern, the announcement of the TRC's closing event in May 2015 referenced these as 'actions of reconciliation'. The timing is particularly interesting, coming at the end of the process and its recommendations for future action. Interestingly as this chapter goes to print the TRC released its final report and issued 94 'calls to action' in lieu of recommendations. In framing it this way the TRC invoked collective responsibility in terms of taking action in future.
7 The need for new thinking about collective responsibility is being recognised within the field of political science. Scholars are questioning the influence of individualism and seek forward-looking accounts (French and Wettstein 2014). Restorative justice as a relational theory and practice of justice may have much to offer this reconceptualisation, as much as it will benefit from it.
8 One must acknowledge in identifying the weakness or limits of this account that this work was completed and published after Young's death. As a result some of the ideas and implications may not have been developed fully.

References

Berman, H. (1983) *Law and Revolution: The formation of the Western legal tradition*, Cambridge, MA: Harvard University Press.

Christie, N. (1977) 'Conflicts as Property', *British Journal of Criminology*, 17(1): 1–15.

Copp, D. (2006) 'On the Agency of Certain Collective Entities: An argument from "normative autonomy"', *Midwest Studies in Philosophy*, XXX: 194–220.

Corlett, J. A. (2001) 'Collective Moral Responsibility', *Journal of Social Philosophy*, 32: 574.

Feinberg J. (1968) 'Collective Responsibility', *Journal of Philosophy*, 65: 674–688.

French, P. (1998) *Individual and Collective Responsibility*, Rochester, VT: Schenkman.

French, P. (1984) *Collective and Corporate Responsibility*, New York: Columbia University Press.

French, P. and Wettstein, H. (2014) *Forward-Looking Collective Responsibility*, Hoboken, NJ: Wiley.

Gilbert, M. (1997) 'Group Wrongs and Guilt Feelings', *Journal of Ethics*, 1: 65–84.

Gilbert, M. (2000) *Sociality and Responsibility*, Lanham, MD: Rowman and Littlefield.

Gilbert, M. (2006) 'Who's to Blame? Collective Moral Responsibility and Its Implications for Group Members', *Midwest Studies in Philosophy*, 30: 94–114.

Harbin, A. (2014) 'Collective Responsibility and Collective Feeling', *Dialogue*, 53: 31–42.

Held, V. (1986) 'Corporations, persons, and responsibility', in H. Curtler (ed.) *Shame, Responsibility, and the Corporation*, New York: Haven.

Isaacs, T. (2011) *Moral Responsibility in Collective Contexts*, Oxford: Oxford University Press.

Lacey, N. (2001a) 'Responsibility and Modernity in Criminal Law', *Journal of Political Philosophy*, 9: 249–276.

Lacey, N. (2001b) 'In search of the Responsible Subject: History, philosophy and criminal law theory', *Modern Law Review*, 64: 350–371.

Llewellyn, J. J. (2004) 'Doing justice in South Africa: restorative justice and reparations', in C. Villa-Vicencio and E. Doxtader (eds) *Repairing the Unforgivable: Reparations and reconstruction in South Africa*, Claremont, South Africa: David Philip Publishers/ New Africa Books.

Llewellyn, J. J. (2005) 'Restorative justice in transitions and beyond: the justice potential of truth telling mechanisms for post-peace accord societies', in T. Borer (ed.) *Telling the Truths: Truth telling and peacebuilding in post-conflict societies.* Notre Dame, IN: University of Notre Dame Press.

Llewellyn, J. J. (2007) 'Truth and Reconciliation Commissions: restorative justice in response to abuse and violence', in G. Johnstone and D. van Ness (eds) *Handbook of Restorative Justice*, Collumpton, UK: Willan Publishing.

Llewellyn, J. J. (2008) 'Bridging the gap between truth and reconciliation: restorative justice and the Indian residential school Truth and Reconciliation Commission', in M. Brant-Castellano, L. Archibald and M. DeGagne (eds) *From Truth to Reconciliation: Transforming the legacy of residential schools.* Ottawa: Aboriginal Healing Foundation.

Llewellyn, J. J. (2011) 'Restorative justice: thinking relationally about justice', in J. Downie and J. J. Llewellyn (2011) *Being Relational: Reflections on relational theory and health law and policy*, Vancouver: UBC Press.

Llewellyn, J. J. and Howse, R. (1998) *Restorative Justice – A Conceptual Framework*, Ottawa: Law Commission of Canada.

Llewellyn, J. J. and Howse, R. (1999) 'Institutions for Restorative Justice: The South African Truth and Reconciliation Commission', *University of Toronto Law Journal*, 49: 355–388.

Llewellyn, J. J. and Philpott, D. (2014) 'Restorative justice and reconciliation: twin frameworks for peacebuilding', in J. Llewellyn and D. Philpott (eds) *Restorative Justice, Reconciliation and Peacebuilding*, Oxford: Oxford University Press.

Mackenzie, C. and Stoljar, N. (2000) *Relational Autonomy: Feminist perspectives on autonomy, agency, and the social self*, New York: Oxford University Press.

Mandate for Canadian Truth and Reconciliation Commission, *Residential Schools Settlement Schedule N* available online at: www.trc.ca/websites/trcinstitution/File/pdfs/SCHEDULE_N_EN.pdf.

Marshall, T. (1999) *Restorative Justice: An overview*, London: Home Office Research.

May, L. (1987) *The Morality of Groups*, Notre Dame, IN: University of Notre Dame Press.

May, L. (1992) *Sharing Responsibility*, Chicago: University of Chicago Press.

May, L. and Hoffman, S. (1991). *Collective Responsibility: Five decades of debate in theoretical and applied ethics*, Lanham, MD: Rowman and Littlefield.

McCold, P. (1996) 'Restorative justice and the role of community', in B. Galaway and J. Hudson (eds) *Restorative Justice: International perspectives*, Monsey, NY: Criminal Justice Press.

Narveson, J. (2002) 'Collective Responsibility', *Journal of Ethics*, 6: 179–198.

Nedelsky, J. (2011) 'The reciprocal relation of judgement and autonomy: walking in another's shoes and which shoes to walk in', in J. Downie and J. Llewellyn (eds) *Being Relational: Reflections on relational theory and health law and policy*, Vancouver: UBC Press.

Raikka, J. (1997) 'On Dissociating Oneself from Collective Responsibility', *Social Theory and Practice*, 23: 1–9.

Sadler, B. J. (2007) 'Collective Responsibility, Universalizability, and Social Practices', *Journal of Social Philosophy*, 38(3): 486–503.

Smiley, M. (1992) *Moral Responsibility and the Boundaries of Community*, Chicago: University of Chicago Press.

Smiley, M. (2010) 'From Moral Agency to Collective Wrongs: Re-thinking collective moral responsibility', *Journal of Law and Policy*, 1: 171–202.

South African Promotion of National Unity and Reconciliation Act 34 of 1995, available online at: www.justice.gov.za/legislation/acts/1995-034.pdf.

Todorov, T. (1996) *Facing the Extreme: Moral life in the concentration camps*, translated by A. Denner and A. Pollack, New York: Henry Holt.

Truth and Reconciliation Commission of South Africa Report (1998), Cape Town: Juta Press.

Tuomela, R. (1995) *The Importance of Us: A philosophical study of basic social notions*, Palo Alto, CA: Stanford University Press.

Umbreit, M. S. and Armour, M. P. (2011) 'Restorative Justice and Dialogue: Impact, opportunities, and challenges in the global community', *Washington University Journal of Law and Policy*, 36: 65–88.

Van Ness, D. and Heetderks Strong, K. (2006) *Restoring Justice: An introduction to restorative justice*, Cincinnati, OH: Anderson Publishing.

Young, I. (2010) *Responsibility for Justice*, Oxford: Oxford University Press.

Zehr, H. (1990) *Changing Lenses: A new focus for crime and justice*, Scottdale, PA: Herald Press.

9 Harmonising global criminal justice for peacebuilding

Mark Findlay

Introduction

In keeping with this collection's central analytical concerns, there can be no effective discussion of restorative justice in conflict zones without an appreciation of what is meant by restoration for victims and, more importantly, what is meant by justice for them. In reality, while transitional justice has become prominent in the patterned niches of global conflict resolution, it has failed to confront justice in transition from the formal to the alternative frames. That transition to a more holistic justice offering is now a more viable possibility with the demise of retribution, and a challenge for justice scholars and professionals to take up.

As John Braithwaite's chapter in this collection identifies, when global conflict resolution is the objective, transitional justice focuses on restoration, adopting what loosely could be considered as indigenous justice forms, adapting their peacebuilding capacities in more stable and less conflict ridden contexts. At the same time he wonders about the nature of transition. Despite the varying views concerning the role of transitional justice in conflict resolution, one theme is constant: that adversarial/retributive and introduced justice forms, institutionalised as they so often are in the cement of post-colonial governance and paternalism, represent part of what requires an alternative paradigm. This sometimes simplistic evaluation ignores that the legitimacy of international criminal justice, and its capacity to advance victim interests through more transparent and accountable global governance, requires engagement with formal justice frames.

If transnational and global conflict are to receive the assistance of restorative justice towards peacemaking then its embedding within more formalised international criminal justice (ICJ) must not be passed over through a general aversion to the prosecutorial model. The preamble to the *Rome Statute*, the foundation instrument for the International Criminal Court (ICC) identifies a clear victim focus for the justice it shall promote:

> Mindful that during this century millions of children, women and men have been victims of unimaginable atrocities that deeply shock the conscience of humanity.

The preamble also talks of a justice focus which is for 'all people ... united by common bonds'. It recognises that the crimes to be prosecuted under the statute threaten the 'peace, security and wellbeing of the world'.

The Statute talks of a preventive purpose being the end to impunity. In its constituting vision, the *Rome Statute* demands a broader scope for the international criminal trial than solely prosecuting and punishing. A more expansive role for the court is not without controversy (Damaska 2008). Conventional criminal justice in its trial manifestation is designed to determine guilt or innocence, and to apportion punishment. Besides any aspiration to reform the offender, there are no higher order claims made for peace and security. Even though the ICC appears to work in an adversarial model of retributive justice, it is uniquely influenced by restorative justice methods, particularly as they relate to victim participation (Findlay 2013a). Victims are given a voice with independent representation at all stages of the trial process and their interests are recognised as not always according with the prosecution. After trial there is financial provision for victim reparations. Unfortunately the restorative and transitional justice camps largely ignore this unique phenomenon in an attempt to distinguish two justice paradigms (Zehr 2002).

For the purpose of argument it is accepted that justice can bring peace (even though that may be a big ask) (Llewellyn and Philpott 2014). Following on from the realisation that restorative justice is not absent from formal international criminal justice processes, the second string of my theoretical assertion is that pluralist justice delivery modes (indigenous, restorative, retributive and those which are responsibility focused and communitarian), working from a more holistic notion of justice, have the capacity to improve the conflict resolution capacity of justice interventions. With the demise of retribution as the justification for prosecutorial models, the restorative justice dimensions of international criminal justice can come to the fore more painlessly. Obviously if the strictures of retribution and their dependence on individualised liability are diminished then communitarian and responsibility-focused justice directions will not be subordinated or excluded in the trial process and beyond. The transformation and synthesis scholarship directed to international criminal justice has argued that retributive and restorative justice need to develop a supportive justice capacity and that the dominance of retributive justice is one impediment which lawyers claim to deny the possibility and appropriateness of this eventuality (Findlay 2013c). Accepting that transformation and synthesis will produce a more inclusive, accessible and integrated justice form (as is argued in much of my earlier work), it is fair to assume that a pluralist justice model which is more likely to eventuate beyond the confines of a liability model at the global level may provide more effective peacebuilding and conflict resolution outcomes in transitional settings.

Before reaching this analytical conjecture, it is necessary to reiterate how justice harmonisation is possible. My earlier writings have done this at length (Findlay and Henham 2005, 2010). The novel argument in this chapter identifies the demise of retribution as a trigger for harmonisation. More particularly, it contends that, whether restorative or otherwise, justice models need a compatible theorising of *justice* which recognises peacemaking if harmonisation is to be achieved. Despite the overwhelming evidence that legitimate victim interests emerging from serious conflict include a retributive concern (Kiza and Rohne 2011), retribution as the centre-piece of formal justice modes has, it is argued, distracted the development of compatible justice theorising when applied to global conflict. The chapter reveals that, at the domestic level, and arguably in the international arena, retribution as the prevailing principle of punishment has had its day.

On the other side, restorative and transitional justice advocates can be criticised for either unclear or uncompromising justice theorising that has been as much oppositional to retribution as it has been inclusive of peacemaking from whatever justice direction. Therefore, transition and restoration need to engage with the possibility of harmonious justice theorising which can maximise the influence of different justice paradigms when called upon to play a part in conflict resolution. On this theme, the chapter applies the notion of transition to pluralist justice inclusion, at least in a formative direction. Finally, in returning to the contention that justice can make peace and minimise conflict, it is instructive to talk about a governance (post-conflict) model of justice that would maintain a peace legitimised through the satisfaction of credible victim interests (Findlay 2014, chapter 6). Before briefly touching on the restorative justice dimensions of formal international criminal justice, it is useful to pause and reflect on concepts of transition which underpin not only the nature of conflict which justice might be required to address, but also the forces at work on justice paradigms available to peacemaking.

Transition

It is not radical to suggest the relationship between transitional justice and the rationales for trial-based justice. In the context of post-electoral violence in Kenya in 2008 and 2013, Corradetti (2015a) identifies a role for ICC-stimulated deterrence influences in *post bellum* efforts to restore both peace and justice. The argument asserts that transitional justice through conflict deterrence introduces and perhaps problematises in an irreconcilable manner the need to renovate polity in order to dissuade the recurrence of conflict. In so doing, Corradetti continues, it is not necessary to sacrifice internally articulated distinctions between proactive transformative action and more reactive and narrowly defined prosecutorial directions. The challenge is that, in entertaining a bifurcated response to conflict in which transformative and retributive policy action can achieve deterrent functions, the wider goals of transitional justice will need to be reconciled through balancing these two approaches:

> transitional justice processes face potential failures not only when confronted with cases of forward-looking transformative policies conducted independently from considerations of impunity, but also when the latter

policies are conducted outside an overall socially-transformative frame-work.... The identification of a third major function that transitional justice is asked to satisfy [to restore a minimal threshold of peace and justice in conflicted societies] ... would provide an orienting principle for the balancing of such goals.

(Corradetti 2015b, editorial comment added)

In the spirit of justice synthesis, this chapter suggests two analytical considerations that are strangely absent in the transitional justice literature:

- within the international jurisdiction, adversarial justice is in radical transition away from its retributive traditions; and
- transformed adversarial justice with a more specific and potent restorative engagement can have a positive influence in managing post-conflict governance, alongside what are unhelpfully designated as alternative justice forms.

A vibrant and vital measure of trial transformation is victim access, integration and inclusivity. This unique shift in trial dynamics is not only about broadening the active recognition of stakeholders. It is an essential recognition that victim interests go beyond the prosecutorial mission of conviction and punishment. If the victim is given voice in pre-trial determinations, trial narrative and post-trial reparations, restorative themes developing responsibility on top of liability are made possible.

Recognising that opening up the trial process to more than prosecutorial and defence contestation will expose judicial decision-making to a richer range of interests and potential outcomes, the peacebuilding aims of formalised international criminal justice are more viable as both trial dialogue and direction. An example of this is the manner in which the ad hoc tribunals have dealt with submissions that rape should provide evidence of a crime against humanity, challenging a more expansive in-trial and post-trial response. Even at the level of procedure, the ability of judges to explore the horror of rape in war has required trial narrative and evidence pathways to enter the realm of deep victim experience (Haffajee 2006).

Adversarial justice transition internationally is inevitable. One only needs to examine the broadest aims of the *Rome Statute* and wonder at the legalist attack against them (Damaska 2008) to confirm the startling dimensions of this transition and the apprehensions it has stirred up among conventional trial lawyers. The drafters of the *Rome Statute* knew that victims in particular wanted institutional justice at the international level, and the punishment it portents, but much more. This could be achieved by some uncomfortable plastic surgery on the trial process, or more permanently through requiring its gradual and permanent transformation. The latter eventuality is fortunately underway through the courts adapting evidence to wider story-telling, by allowing a wider range of voices and experiences to influence trial decision-making, and by employing (particularly) pre-trial deliberations and a more mediated approach to engaging matters at issue.

A closer examination of any transitional justice environment (particularly post-colonial) reveals there are modes of justice (state-centred, restorative, indigenous) that have failed to contribute in a collaborative way to conflict resolution. In particular, the role of justice as an agent of conflict resolution in disaggregated or dysfunctional state settings, especially at the intersection of justice and conflict in transitional governance frames, requires addressing much more than one justice mode, in a pragmatic search for holistic justice.

Despite some notable advances in restorative conflict resolution on a large scale, so often for instance claimed of the South African truth and reconciliation experiment, it is a failed exercise to project restorative justice alone into the realm of peacemaking against expansive conflict. Even advocates of its potential would never be comfortable with that expectation (Hansen 2011). Through advancing pluralist justice intervention, with an intersected and holistic justice/peace purpose, it is necessary to 'transform' the place of restorative justice to empower (and be empowered by) other justice forms if it is to succeed in cross fertilising the justice/ peacemaking link. This future for restorative justice in mass conflict resolution is similar, in some respects, to the challenge for public international law in moving from protect to prevent responsibilities. Pluralist justice in its restorative mode will find its greatest impact when evidencing both backward and forward-looking conflict resolution potentials (such as truth telling followed on by positive restitution).

As a foundation for such practical policy intervention, holistic justice theorising needs to be engaged and expanded rather than forcing uncomfortable justice transplants or overburdened indigenous justice expectations. If this theorising is for a peacemaking purpose, then advocates must empirically and convincingly establish that justice has a place in conflict resolution (and that is far from settled as the voluminous debate over peace and justice disjunctions demonstrates). Next on the analytical agenda, a notion of 'justice' that informs whatever model you prefer – restorative or otherwise – has to be settled in a harmonious rather than some dichotomous transformation.

A broader interpretation of transitional justice in a holistic mission needs to be victim-centred in order for it to maximise its contribution to post-conflict resolution and governance. If this harmonised concept of justice can be imbued with and inspired by a victim constituency at the international conflict level, institutionalised justice should not stand merely in counterpoint to the transition of other less formal and less law-centric justice forms. As the following section highlights, the development of international criminal justice is witnessing the infiltration of formal justice delivery with restorative imperatives and processes (Findlay and Henham 2005, part 3).

The victims focus/theme for overall conflict resolution through justice delivery projects the difficulties with achieving legitimate outcomes for a victim constituency (Kiza and Rohne 2011). The delivery of international criminal justice, particularly but not exclusively in its more formal paradigms, still suffers from an under-developed *concept of justice* compatible with this task. A major impediment to this project is the divide between formal, trial-based justice models and the restorative and transitional paradigms.

This chapter is less concerned with unhelpful dualities beyond highlighting how they retard achieving a genuine victim constituency rather than advance it. The chapter takes a more fundamental look at that divide and questions whether the retributive/restorative justice directions need to be distinguished at all in order to achieve a truly victim-centred approach to humanity as the international criminal justice constituency. Victims certainly do not see it as an either/or choice (Kiza and Rohne 2011). With a clearer and more common conceptualisation of justice (certainly in the restorative aims enunciated in the *Rome Statute*, discussed below) we have a much greater chance of using international criminal justice as a global governance influence, away from securitisation and towards peacemaking.

Restorative international criminal justice – the victims' rights perspective

Article 1 of the UN Charter reminds us of the conflict deterrence and long-term violence preventive functions of the UN mission:

> To maintain international peace and security, and to that end: to take effective collective measures for the prevention and removal of threats to the peace, and for the suppression of acts of aggression or other breaches of the peace, and to bring about by peaceful means, and in conformity with the principles of justice and international law, adjustment or settlement of international disputes or situations which might lead to a breach of the peace.

Formal legality is assumed, therefore, to provide a counterpoint to establishing out of conflict 'conditions of stability and well-being' (UN Charter, Art 55). That said:

> transitional justice measures do not simply absolve to a prosecutorial function but provide, rather, internally legal and non-legal resources for the reconstruction of minimal conditions of social cooperation. Accordingly, traditional conceptions of the *post bellum* become problematic when applied to the understanding of contemporary humanitarian warfare particularly when they show lack of understanding of the interconnection with other warfare domains.
>
> (Corradetti 2015b)

The need for interconnection is not restricted to the understanding of different conflict forms. Rather, law-based and non-law-focused justice delivery offer a more holistic approach when justice resolutions are directed to mass conflict settings. For the purposes of distilling restorative potentials in formal ICJ, this chapter conceives restorative justice as victim-focused conflict resolution and victim–community peacebuilding. In formal ICJ paradigms, restorative justice influences are clearly victim-centred and *peacebuilding* driven. They also exhibit a humanitarian morality. Specifically restorative justice and the ICC converge in:

- a variety of victim participation opportunities within the justice process;
- aims which express peace and conflict minimisation as their primary outcomes;
- procedures governed by concerns that justice service delivery will not challenge peace; and
- the compensation fund for community rebuilding after justice has been dispensed.

These restorative dimensions are clearly designed to satisfy legitimate victim interests, beyond retribution and punishment.

Steven Roach (2009) posits that a negative global responsibility needs to be distinguished from a positive global responsibility when it comes to a 'shared open-ended duty to promote the universal morality of (formal international criminal justice)'. In substantiation of the assertion that institutions and processes of justice should contain a moral dimension, he comments on the ICC's evolving role in the developing institutional network of global justice, the court's expansive positive global responsibility to promote universal norms and morality, and the cosmopolitan principles of fairness and equality (Roach 2009: 2–3). International courts and tribunals, including the ICC, have interpreted their roles and functions in an expansive sense to include:

- operating a historical record of conflicts and crimes
- helping to end contemporary violent conflicts
- facilitating peace initiatives and providing opportunities to hear the victim voice.

(For various interpretations of the goals of International Criminal Courts, see Bass 2000.)

The rules and procedures for the ICC demonstrate a wide consideration of justice beyond trials and punishment. The *Rome Statute*, for example, requires the prosecutor to consider whether there are 'substantial reasons to believe that an investigation would serve the interests of justice' (*Rome Statute* Art 53). This requirement has been interpreted as whether a prosecution would negatively affect the social and political environment of the jurisdiction in question, such as related ongoing peace processes and non-judicial conflict resolution (Cote 2005). In this sense there are multiple notions, narratives and nominees of justice embedded in the legislature and procedures of international criminal justice institutions. On a larger front, take the notion of fairness which is to be exhibited:

> For the international criminal trial, even simple procedural fairness is not couched alone in the protections of the rights of the accused. The sometimes-competing interests of victims and their expression in the trial will also be argued as a measure of fairness in balance.
>
> (Findlay 2013c: 72)

Some commentators argue that the justice core of ICJ is located in 'the imminent rise of human rights sanctioned by international criminal tribunals as the emerging paradigm of international relations and law' (Mégret 2002: 1266). If one limits the focus primarily to trial-based ICJ, it becomes clear that the development of the new place of humanitarian rights in international relations was critical in founding the post-Second World War crimes tribunals. Out of this coalescence emerges the conviction that a human rights foundation should be an essential feature of contemporary formal ICJ.[1] Even expanding out our focus on ICJ to include the national jurisdictions and management of international criminal liability demonstrates the impact of human rights discourse and commitments, as evidenced by widespread domestic legislative ratification and enactment of human rights principles from international conventions. This is particularly important if it is agreed that the practical operational activity of formal ICJ will remain, in the immediate future, limited and selective, and therefore rights protection against even the most widespread global crimes vests in the responsibility of national courts or in regional cooperation. In this way the state and the globe are to give effect to the conflict resolution potential of justice, in part through determining *liability*, complemented by the restorative aim that *responsibility* precedes reconciliation. One of the central criticisms of public law-based justice delivery is its over-emphasis on individual liability and its apparent ignorance of responsibility considerations at the heart of private law damages determinations, and of restorative intervention based on offender contrition. Another side to this argument is that through the possible merging of responsibility/liability modes justice can better satisfy legitimate victim expectations (Findlay 2013c, chapter 6).

Directly following the humanitarian horrors of the Second World War, there emerged a new and fresh commitment to formalising basic human rights principles at an international level. The Genocide Convention (1948a) and the Universal Declaration on Human Rights (1948b) were both adopted in 1948 by the United Nations General Assembly in a climate of renewed humanitarianism and peacekeeping. The update and expansion of the Geneva Conventions in 1949 show how international laws had a significant influence on the development of international humanitarian law. The Geneva Conventions, especially through the rights protections of prisoners and those directly affected by military conflict, have had a rich influence on the development of a wider, non-military human rights framework internationally, which certainly influences the contemporary era of ICJ.

The growing importance of global human rights as a measure of civilised national and international relations has opened up opportunities for increasing the potency of international organisations and non-governmental organisations in global governance. It is these organisations, perhaps more than nation state agencies, that have taken on the critical burden of the 'honest broker' in the monitoring of state compliance with international human rights commitments.

Further, the creation of post-Second World War crime tribunals represented the first attempts to direct the remit of international humanitarian law towards individual rather than state interests, by incorporating rights violation within criminalisation and picking up their consequences in criminal sanctioning. Behaviours that offend the human rights of individuals were criminalised, and for the first time individuals were prosecuted for international crimes. In this sense, the creation of international criminal tribunals, in particular the ICC, can be seen as the institutional culmination of the belief that 'because individuals live under the international legal system that must necessarily have rights and obligations flowing from it' (Findlay 2013c), founding a clear connection between ICJ and human rights.

The emerging body of criminal procedure adopted in international criminal courts also displays the influence of human rights, not just through the conventional due process protections favouring accused persons (Amann 2000). However, as with any international human rights legislation or institutions, there are complex challenges to enforcing ICJ rights in many situations of conflict and resistance. That said, the restorative possibilities now contained in formalised ICJ institutions and processes, such as independent victim representation, and compensation as well as punishment, mean that a drift away from a retributive focus might be viewed as more compatible with both human rights and conflict resolution from the victim perspective. Representation leads to victim inclusion in justice resolutions and compensation/restitution offers concrete outcomes for both retributive and restorative interventions.

Retribution on the rocks?

The correlations between punishment styles and social and economic epochs have been known for some time in criminology and socio-legal studies. Rusche and Kircheimer (in the era of political and material uncertainty between the world wars) posited the direct relationship between the form of punishment and wage labour: 'Every system of production tends to discover punishments which correspond with its productive relationships' (1939: 5).

In *Crime Control as Industry*, Nils Christie (1993) drew the connection between Western modernity and the crime control market in which warehouse imprisonment features as an inevitable logic. Melossi and Pavarini in *The Prison and the Factory* (1981) continue the examination of materialist synergies between penal systems and capitalist societies when they advance the Marxist premise that 'prisoners must be workers, and workers must be prisoners' (Melossi and Pavarini, 1981: 188). Foucault in his definitive work *Discipline and Punish: The Birth of the Prison* (1979) observes the transition from a punishment focus on docile and condemned bodies to the institutional and carceral control of the mind. Michael Ignatieff in *A Just Measure of Pain* (1978) charts the ways in which the middle and upper classes of industrialised England in the early 1800s used the penitentiary to control the poor. Even what were represented as philanthropic reforms to the reign of terror in punishment could be considered through imprisonment to be a consolidation of state power, establishing moral boundaries of authority and encircling industrial order. David Garland in *Punishment and Modern Society* (1990) argues that:

Where once penal institutions appeared to offer a self-evident rationale, in the late 20th century they increasingly come to seem less obviously appropriate. Their 'fit' with the social world and their grounding within the natural order of things begin to appear less and less convincing.

(Garland 1990: 277)

It is with these prophetic observations, now well established in 'over-prisoned' modern societies where post-global financial meltdown the economic more than social costs of excessive imprisonment are hastening the flight from institutional punishment, that the operational benefits of retributive punishment are no longer presumed. Some caution, however, that replacing prison walls with intensive community supervision and communitarian exclusion will ghettoise the social and economic foundations of racial and class exclusion through criminalisation (Rodger 2008).

It is not difficult to chart the rise and fall of retribution as the driver for criminal sanctioning and penality concurrent with the growth in individualist liberalism and with neo-liberal economics. To do so one could:

- look at the relationship between prevailing retributive principles of punishment such as individual autonomy (emblematic in record high imprisonment rates) and the economic 'boom times'; and
- speculate on the manner in which retribution and imprisonment were assumed to be socially, economically and politically compatible with the boom times, dependent as they are conceived to be on free will rationalism, and speculate on the demise of retribution and excessive imprisonment, in light of cost/benefit questions, as boom times turn to bust.

The boom/retribution nexus is much more than the product of neo-conservative political social ordering. To appreciate the economic and social location of punishment 'fads', a critical examination of points of transition tends to reveal much about this essential contextualisation of punishment principle and manifestation. If the analysis is then taken beyond considerations of national economy and nation state securitisation, and translated into ICJ and global governance concerns (Findlay 2008), where individualised rights and responsibilities are authorised in determinations of liability and denials of impunity, retribution predictably might be seen as equally (and rationally) dominant. However, for different reasons other than economic repositioning and social disillusionment, it is speculated that legitimate victim interests are tending at the global level to modify the influence of retribution over conceptualising ICJ. Victims want more than offender imprisonment, and right from the investigation stage formal ICJ is considering deterrent possibilities through attacking impunity, and considering peacebuilding outcomes for conflict resolution through a prosecutorial model. This modification, in turn, offers a broadened possibility for ICJ to ensure more *just* frames of global governance, with clear peacemaking rather than securitisation emphases.[2]

Putting forward this view is not to deny the rejuvenation of interest among victim communities in retribution along with restoration. It is more a question of balance and benefit. As the eventual disillusionment with truth and reconciliation outcomes in South Africa have revealed, denial of conventional 'just deserts' punishment frames for victims, who feel that little, after restorative justice, has changed, will undermine the wider legitimacy of both justice and truth (van der Merwe and Chapman 2008).

At the national level, it should be remembered that the most recent age of retribution grew out of the wreckage of rehabilitation and the medicalisation of punishment forms. In the 1960s, the movement was towards deinstitutionalisation (Schur 1973; Scull 1977), and surviving custodial facilities were envisaged with a treatment and not a retributive purpose. But, as the crime-control consequences of rehabilitation were called into question with a return to retribution, the same 'cost–benefit' language was not required of a resurgent prison with retributive purposes. The move from a 'results-oriented' critique of punishment modes to a more doctrinal commitment to the protective and responsibilising possibilities of retribution was compatible with the emerging political and economic context of neo-liberal individualism, autonomy and rational choice self-governance.

The interesting constant in the rise and fall of retribution as a touchstone of justice is individualist autonomy. A very similar rights and responsibility context prevails around the development of the current phase of ICJ (Findlay 2013c). In the international setting, much more than has been the case in domestic criminal justice jurisdictions, the countervailing 'individualist' pressure revealed through the reflection of legitimate victim interests has offered a new and critical constituency for global justice (Findlay 2013c).

Autonomy and responsibility as critical for conflict resolution

Another motivation behind the initial significance of retribution as a punishment model for ICJ has been the commitment in its justice aims to protect and advance the rights of victims. Interestingly, however, the seeds for diminishing the growth of retribution as the dominant principle for ICJ may also lie in the contestation of legitimate victim interests beyond retribution.

The compatibilist philosophers are sometimes too quick to dismiss the link between free will/determinism and political philosophy, and this holds for international governance paradigms as well. However, if determinism is incompatible with the deontological ethics which determine critical global positioning such as location within a *global community*, then it also would be incompatible with having rights as a consequence of such inclusion and thus incompatible with the essential individualism which governance paradigms such as ICJ are dedicated to protecting.[3]

In *Punishment, Communication and Community*, Duff (2003: 36) states that: 'liberal values fuelled the moral reaction against consequentialism in the 1970s'. Duff may be sympathetic to the view that any decline in the liberal value of individualism might equally lead to a retributive bust. According to Duff, the idea of 'autonomy' is central to liberalism and it was the idea of a *rights bearing* individual that leads to concerns about consequentialist punishment. That said, the reaction against indeterminate rehabilitative and reformist motivations for punishment in the medicalisation and treatment eras fuelled a vigorous re-engagement with 'just-deserts' punishment models, which Simon (2014) suggests have been distorted to justify the mass incarceration frenzies of past decades.

Norrie (1991: 40) says that 'the concept of free will, as the basis for the idea of individual responsibility, is a development of the ideology of abstract individualism in which a central element is the idea of the free individual'. Elsewhere he appears to espouse free will scepticism, certainly regarding compatibilism, and he also appears sceptical of libertarian free will (Norrie 1991: 143–153) and so presumably he sees free will solely as an ideological construct. Norrie (1991) argues that a commitment to free will is part of an individualistic ideology and Honderich (1982) mounts an argument that individualism needs to be justified by desert which in turn presupposes the ability to do otherwise, an aspect of freedom of the will. However, some might say *autonomy*, rather than freedom of the will, is all that an individualistic ideology needs. Norrie (1991) distinguishes between subjective individualism that generated more offender-focused punishment rationales and the universalism on which rational choice is grounded:

> the dominant intellectual structures of our social, political and legal world are not necessarily immanent in human existence but are the politically achieved artefacts of particular society. It is this historical and political structuring of law's architectonic of judgement … that ultimately guarantees its strength and longevity.
>
> (Norrie 2005: 73)

The unique interest in individualised liability, which is also a distinguishing feature of the present stage of ICJ, might be viewed as a reaction to the 'boom/ bust' cycles which pre- and post-date major international military conflict. In addition, a critical characteristic of formal ICJ, at least, is the commitment to deterrence which the threat of prosecution and punishment is deeply assumed to proffer (Cronin-Furman 2013). Even so, individualist liability is what gives formal ICJ its uniqueness within public international law traditions. 'Liability itself is based on the attribution of a criminal offence to a particular individual' (Bantekas and Nash 2001: 15).

Acts that constitute international crimes are deemed to be committed by individuals. However, these acts are also often under the direction of state or military organisations; for instance, the genocide against Jewish people was a systematic government policy of the German Nazi party. In addition, global crimes may be the consequence of:

- collective and group behaviour;
- behaviour encouraged and supported by other individuals or collective entities;
- behaviour ordered or governed by superiors; and

• consequential behaviour, which may have been within the contemplation of other members of a group, if not the substance of their specific agreement.

The question of who should be liable for international crimes goes to the heart of the objective of international criminal trials which seek to determine 'the attribution and calibration of individual responsibility for mass atrocities' (Danner and Martinez 2005: 79). How ICJ determines, allocates and attributes liability is also critical to its legitimacy. Of this, Richard Goldstone, South African constitutional court judge and the first chief prosecutor of the ICTY and ICTR, said: 'With regard to the seriousness of the crimes, the most guilty are those who ordered them' (Goldstone 1995: 7).

Hierarchical command structures such as the military can protect superiors from criminal responsibility, by arguments about the absence of knowledge or direct participation, and the court's reluctance to entertain defences of superior orders. Conviction of only those lower in command structures undermines the effectiveness of international criminal law to achieve justice when deterrence of those most morally responsible is its motivation. Yet, on the other hand, criminal law doctrines of joint criminal enterprise and command responsibility run the risk of supporting convictions that criminalise by association rather than by participation. This is particularly so if actual knowledge is replaced by constructive knowledge, or if merely the contemplation of consequences is seen to satisfy the necessities of agreement. An overly expansive approach to these doctrines also contradicts the ICC's adherence to criminal law principles resting on subjective liability, and the court's legitimacy as a legal rather than solely political forum where the culpability for criminal acts is the measure of liability for punishment, rather than broader chains of responsibility or contribution.

An essential challenge in ICJ is the tension between individual criminal liability and collective moral culpability. It should be remembered that, in its peacekeeping and conflict resolution aims, ICJ is accountable to a broader measure of legitimacy than that of narrow individual liability to satisfy subjective legal principles. How international criminal law in future treats collective responsibility for international crimes will define what aims it emphasises, and how it reflects the concerns of what the courts conceive of as their primary constituency and their purpose. It is argued that existing international criminal law fails to determine collective liability beyond the realm of distorted legal fictions, and therefore is unable to fully discharge its responsibility to the satisfaction of legitimate victim interests where perpetration and victimisation were collective (Findlay 2009). This failure, it is suggested, contributes to international criminal trial justice reflecting a more retributive rather than a restorative or victim-centred approach. This argument lies on the assumption that victims of collective perpetration are not satisfied by 'scapegoat' prosecutions.

There is some capacity under the *ICC Statute* to prosecute persons other than the individual directly committing a particular crime. Rather than embracing responsibility through the notions of vicarious and corporate liability, the courts have considered collective responsibility in the debate over the nature of joint criminal enterprise, common purpose and accessorial liability (Findlay 2011b). Even so, because of the necessities required through constructive agreement, the joint criminal enterprise pathway to collective liability does not consider aggravation or proportional contribution. The *ICC Statute* provides that a person may be criminally liable if that person:

- *orders* the commission of a crime (Art. 25(3)(b) ICCSt.);
- *aids, abets or assists* the commission of a crime (Art. 25(3)(c) ICCSt.);
- contributes to the commission of a crime by a group *acting with a common purpose*, involving the intention to further the criminal activity of the group or with the knowledge that the group intends to commit the crime (Art. 25(3)(d) ICCSt.)
- directly and publicly *incites* others to commit genocide (Art. 25(3)(e) ICCSt.); and, in some circumstances,
- *commits substantial acts towards* the execution of a crime (Art. 25(3)(f) ICCSt.).

It is my view that the challenges to incorporate collective criminal liability into a more realistic appreciation of perpetration and victimisation at the international level will be a test of the capacity of ICJ to grow into a relevant and responsive global justice paradigm. This could be achieved through a two-pronged approach:

- creative applications of collective liability used in domestic jurisdictions through complementarity; and
- the development of new iterations of the natural person acting in consort to establish both proportional individual and shared liability.

More fundamental than this, however, is for ICJ to recognise the limitations inherent in an individualised liability model. The tensions inherent in this approach are apparent even from the simplest consideration of the crimes over which the ICC has jurisdiction: genocide, crimes against humanity, war crimes and crimes of aggression. These are phenomena emerging from complex collective conflicts. They are neither committed by an individual perpetrator, nor do they victimise an individual. That said, victims are people as well as communities, and perpetrators, whether they are presidents or paramilitaries, carry individual responsibilities for their actions. While the *end to impunity* is in the ICC sense prosecuted against individuals for acts against people and their communities, its intended impact is to achieve general as much as specific deterrence. In this sense, the collectivisation of responsibility for insurgent, transnational and global conflict is about more than legal niceties within the liability project.

It is interesting that the individual/collective clash also has resonance in restorative justice (also see Harbin and Llewellyn, this volume). In domestic settings at least, and in the general truth and reconciliation model, offenders are required to admit individual responsibility for victimisation before restoration efforts are engaged. The autonomy of the individual in recognising guilt and internalising shame is essential. So whether it is a liability or responsibility model, justice starts with an offender and a victim. In major conflict resolution models, the influence of justice cannot end there. Returning to what victims want, individualised liability is high on the list (Kiza and Rohne 2011), but it is rare that the singular removal of a perpetrator out of a conflict compendium will bring peace. In this regard, theorising justice as a peacebuilding technology should build, where appropriate, from individualised liability determinants and responsibility confessions on to the creative incorporation of aggregated responsibility. How justices address the relationships of responsibility which produce mass victimisation and expansive and ongoing conflict will be the eventual test of its governance potential (Findlay 2008).

Justice from a victim rights perspective

As mentioned earlier, in the preamble to the *Rome Statute*, it is affirmed that the 'most serious crimes must not go unpunished'. This is a clear reference to retributive justice in a strict sense, as it alludes to the principle that crime demands punishment (Blumenson 2006: 826). This retributive underpinning of justice does not enquire into the aggregate social benefit that would be brought about by the punishment. Another part of the preamble, however, makes reference to the parties' desire to 'put an end to impunity' and 'contribute to the prevention of such crimes'. These words bring to mind an image of justice as performing peacekeeping functions with the deterrence of the future commission of war crimes and gross violations of human rights. Retributive conceptions of ICJ, such as this, confirm justice as punishment, punishment bringing with it deterrence.

Given that the ICC Prosecutor has to consider whether an investigation or prosecution is in 'the interests of justice' (Art. 53 ICCSt.), the scope of justice implied here goes beyond the punishment of crime, while envisaging the possibility of encompassing forces that do not essentially advance retributive justice. These may include peacekeeping, or the justice themes of reconciliation, restitution, and restoration. 'Justice' in ICJ incorporates certain due process rights (Art. 22–24 ICCSt, Art. 55 ICCSt.), which ensure that the international criminal trial is built upon evidence and procedural legality. Through these due process rights accorded to the accused person, as against the state, the protection of the individual rights is prioritised against a rule of power.

Recognising the diverse conceptions of justice depending on whose rights and protections are considered paramount, it is challenging to find unequivocal normative guidance for the question of what should be uniquely distinguish 'justice' in ICJ. Can a normative foundation be settled that respects, satisfies and incorporates the diversity of views regarding whose interests most require protection at the international level? Is justice relativity a pathway to understanding or confusing the justice component of ICJ?

Preferring one principle to legitimate the process requirements of 'justice' in ICJ means that a monocultural/monolithic normative core would be imposed on the constituent Member States of the ICC, particularly those with different justice conceptualisations. A resistance to such autocracy might be behind a reluctance to stipulate in legislation the parameters of *justice in ICJ.* At the same time, the problems identified with the relative conceptualisation of justice are exacerbated when, in hegemonic international relations, power and domination overbear the contest for justice. This is the situation procedurally where Anglo-American and European justice traditions dominate how ICJ is formally actioned. In this procedural bias is evinced the deliberate exclusion of particular communities' views, if not about justice, then about how it should be manifested.

When it comes to the normative foundation of justice, which has the potential to be culturally inclusive without being inconclusively relative, principles should emerge that are sufficiently broad to embrace and bond the diversity of cultures through a consistency which is based on *meaningful outcomes* rather than some strained effort at procedural harmonisation. The emphasis in developing international criminal law as a procedural discourse, removed from essential conditions of principle, has made both the convincing determination of constituency and the problematic conceptualisation of legitimate victim interests major impediments to a grounded discussion of justice and its service delivery at the international level.

More than this, a credible and actionable normative foundation for ICJ must, from its pluralist form, reach out to the constituent states and local populations, and thereby contribute to building on a functional domestic capacity for justice, empowered through a strong belief in outcomes for ICJ which reflect central stakeholder concerns.

Deciding on a capacious and encompassing conception of justice, with a broad and constant normative space tolerant of more self-enclosed notions in constituent states, is the first step in taking *justice* in ICJ closer to the purpose of satisfying legitimate victim interests. Such an outcome-directed approach to justice avoids exclusive and alienating definitional debates and better accords with the purpose-directed aims of institutions such as the ICC.

Having considered that the trajectory of a rights-based perspective on ICJ moved away from narrow retributivist concerns, the analysis can interrogate the relationship between the principles behind ICJ, the peacebuilding services delivered under the influence of such principles, and the manner in which justice service-delivery infuses wider governance projects with *justice in principle and practice.* This project necessitates a brief reflection on the manner in which an appropriately constituted justice 'frame' (more than retribution alone) can contribute effectively to global governance with peace above security as its motivation.

Justice, morality and governance – synthesising justice and governance

One way of looking at the assertion of a relationship between ICJ and global governance, which will be enriched by the development of global justice away from a particularist retributive focus and more towards the holistic satisfaction of victim's rights and legitimate (achievable) peacebuilding outcomes, is through the medium of cosmopolitanism. For the purposes of this analysis, cosmopolitan thinking is viewed as a method for realising the *Enlightenment Project.* In our case it is two projects:

- accessible, inclusive and integrated global justice; and in turn
- principled global governance.

In the current application, cosmopolitanism argues for the basis of global justice and global governance, both in terms of sentiment and reason. Similar to the new normative frame for global justice suggested above, the sentiment is *communitarian good.*[4] The reason is for the advancement of humanity as the critical *justice* constituency when it comes to mass conflict resolution.[5]

However, cosmopolitan imaginings of global justice and global governance and their relationship with each other do not stop at theory or model. Tensions naturally emerge in justice and governance, arising from the application of ICJ to contexts of governance, producing new forms of localism which are open to the world. The localism of justice ideology when transferred to the global is either confined to procedural integrity or to rights discourse. If a more holistic form and function of global justice are achieved, it is argued that global governance will become compelling in the everyday lives of those who are touched by both. A reason for this is the conviction that ICJ has the capacity, compatible with the aim of the end to impunity, to require accountability of governance personalities and platforms. If ICJ better reflects peoples' personal identities, then the orderliness offered through ICJ is more likely to root global governance in the needs of human beings and not in some rootless concept of humanity. In this sense, cosmopolitanism is politics which, through the rituals of control paradigms such as ICJ, can create and reinforce human identity and integrate these creations into communities of justice.[6]

How is this institutionalised? Let us take the governance capacity of the ICC, for example. In recent cosmopolitan thinking, the ICC has been represented as a 'moral' court, imbuing its influence over global governance with authority through truth-based judicial decision-making. However, as with our critical advocacy for trial transformation, the proof of the court's morality must be tested against the words and actions of individuals who provide the testimony on which the claims for truthful authority are based.

The assertion that the ICC is a 'moral court' requires theoretical location. In his chapter 'Four cosmopolitan projects: the International Criminal Court in context', Antonio Franceschet (2009) develops a conceptual typology of four distinct cosmopolitan political projects that have influenced international law: control, order, governance and citizenship. Each of these provides potency when pluralist justice intervention focuses on conflict resolution. Let us chart this briefly, employing liability and responsibility intersections offered through the harmonisation of adversarial and restorative justice:

- *Control* – the end to impunity by making the individual liable, and the generalisation of responsibility through incorporating communities into the restoration of the offender, are both designed with specific conflict-control capacities.

- *Order* – the individual deterrence direction of liability determinations is said to create a power reordering between the victim, the offender and the state. The incorporation of communities of victims in responsibilising collectives of offenders is directed at the restoration of fundamental communitarian bonding for social order.
- *Governance* – the role of the state/global state in representing community interests through the prosecution of individualised liability is justified as good governance. In the current ICJ thinking, however, there is a clear recognition that the interests of the global state and of victim communities may crucially diverge. To achieve positive governance outcomes then communitarian justice relationships may be required to replace global state sponsorship and representationalism.
- *Citizenship* – this controversial status is an essential challenge for achieving peacebuilding and conflict resolution beyond nation states, or even within nation states that are fragmented and de-legitimated through conflict. Exclusioninst citizenship paradigms cause conflict. Euphemisms about a *global community* do not provide an alternative platform to create the communitarian context essential for restorative justice. The answer may lie in a retheorising of justice with a humanitarian constituency, wherein *inclusive citizenship* offers fundamental protections for rights and dignity.

Cosmopolitans have supported the reform of world politics in ways that emphasise or privilege one or more of the following objectives: control for the sake of rights enforcement; order for the sake of international peace and security; governance for the sake of democratic reform; and citizenship for the sake of a common humanity. Although each of these projects supports the cosmopolitanisation of international law, they do so in different ways (Franceschet 2009).

Against the background of cosmopolitan morality, the idea of the ICC as a moral court could be envisaged through creating a cosmopolitanised public and political space that reinforces moral interdependencies (Levy and Sznaider 2004, p. 143). Justice as a moral endeavour will always have problems over truth-telling and its impact. Whether a judge discounts a witness who changes her story through fear of reprisals, or a truth and reconciliation panel baulks at incompatible histories of the same conflict, truth-telling as the foundation for conflict resolution is what justice has to reconcile. It is this moral function which is asserted as a core variable in the capacity of justice to restore peace. Justice, therefore, becomes a context as much as a process wherein peace can be moulded against contested stories, and community safety can be restored as histories are negotiated.

Fundamentally, justice, where it identifies the guilty on the way to an acceptance of responsibility and an inclusion of communities in victim restoration, should be pluralist and interactive. That said, there can be no walking away from the challenge to establish a holistic concept of justice, recognised by and compatible with the different justice paradigms which employ a peacebuilding capacity. Removing formalised ICJ, and the international criminal law which underpins its functions, from retributive purposes, offers a peacebuilding and conflict resolution capacity which is forward looking. It is argued that this is not only compatible with, but complementary to, the forward-looking dimensions of transitional justice (such as humanitarian intervention) (Teitel 2000).

How can the transformational momentum in formalised international criminal justice be maintained? The chapter has suggested that the demise of retribution as a driver for domestic adversarial justice traditions will offer a unique stimulus for this transition internationally. The argument asserts that the cornerstone of adversarial justice, individual liability, is an impediment for engagement with more communitarian transitional delivery and needs to give recognition to broader victim concerns for the consequences of collective responsibility. Individualism is seen by international lawyers as a definitive characteristic of trial justice, yet the nature of global crime and its victimisation call into question whether truly restorative outcomes can be achieved without more collective responsibility being recognised. The legitimacy of transitional (and adversarial justice internationally) depends on the satisfaction of victim interest. As a crucial restorative justice backdrop, the chapter asks whether a blind adherence to individualised rights commitment can be compatible with transitional intent and the more effective achievement of conflict resolution in global insurgencies.

Put simply, the chapter argues for replacing the unproductive debate about the normative components of justice (legalist and beyond) in preference for a very general determination of *justice outcomes* consistent with a new justice constituency that has focus and form; *justice in ICJ* when applied to mass conflict resolution needs to produce good conditions, circumstances and results for victims and their communities.[7]

Notes

1 This is developed further in the critical consideration of rights, justice and order in the context of a torture case-study in Findlay 2012.
2 For a fuller development of this argument see Findlay 2013a, chapter 10.
3 For a detailed critique of the construction of global community and the rights advantages which follow or are denied, see Findlay 2013b, 2013c.
4 Elaborated in detail as a new normative framework for justice, see Findlay (2011a).
5 This deeply problematic foundation is critiqued in detail concerning morality and procedural actuality, in Findlay and Ngane (2012).
6 For an elaboration of this concept see the relevant sections of Findlay and Henham (2005, 2010).
7 For a very formative discussion of this progress, see Findlay, 2013c, chapter 5.

References

Amann, D. (2000) 'Harmonic Convergence? Constitutional Criminal Procedure in an International Context', *Indiana Law Journal*, 75 (3): 810–873.
Bantekas, I. and Nash, S. (2001) *International Criminal Law*, London: Routledge-Cavendish.
Blumenson, E. (2006) 'The Challenge of a Global Standard of Justice: Peace, pluralism

and punishment at the International Criminal Court', *Columbia Journal of Transnational Law*, 44: 797–867.

Christie, N. (1993) *Crime Control as Industry: Towards gulags, Western style*, London: Routledge.

Corradetti, C. (2015a) 'The Priority of Conflict Deterrence and the Role of the International Criminal Court in Kenya's Post-Electoral Violence 2007–2008 and 2013', *Human Rights Review*, 16: 257–272.

Corradetti, C. (2015b) 'Transitional Justice: *Jus Post Bellum* and the priority of conflict deterrence: assessing Kenya's post-electoral violence 2008–2013'. Available at SSRN: http://ssrn.com/abstract=2576471 or http://dx.doi.org/10.2139/ssrn.2576471.

Cote, L. (2005) 'Reflections on the Exercise of Prosecutorial Discretion in International Criminal Law', *Journal of International Criminal Justice* 3(1): 162–186.

Cronin-Furman, K. (2013) 'Managing Expectations: International criminal trials and prospects for deterrence of mass atrocities', *International Journal of Transitional Justice*, 7(1): 10–25.

Damasksa, M. (2008) 'What's the Point of International Criminal Justice?', *Chicago-Kent Law Review*, 83: 329–368.

Danner, A. and Martinez, J. (2005) 'Guilty Associations: Joint criminal enterprise, command responsibility, and the development of International Criminal Law', *California Law Review* 93(1): 75–169.

Drumbl, M. (2005) 'Collective Violence and Individual Punishment: The criminality of mass atrocity', *Northwestern University Law Review*, 99(2): 539–610.

Franceschet A. (2009) 'Four cosmopolitan projects: the International Criminal Court in context', in S. Roach (ed.) *Governance, Order, and the International Criminal Court*, Oxford: Oxford University Press.

Findlay, M. (2008) *Governing through Globalised Crime: Futures for international criminal justice*, Collumpton, UK: Willan Publishing.

Findlay, M. (2009) 'Activating a Victim Constituency in International Criminal Justice', *International Journal of Transitional Justice*, 3: 183–206.

Findlay, M. (2011a) 'Introduction', in R. Henham and M. Findlay (eds) *Exploring the Boundaries of International Criminal Justice*, Farnham, UK: Ashgate Publishing.

Findlay, M. (2011b) 'Collective responsibility for global crime: limitations with the liability paradigm', in R. Henham and M. Findlay (eds) *Exploring the Boundaries of International Criminal Justice*, Farnham, UK: Ashgate Publishing.

Findlay, M. (2012) 'Paradox in Preventing and Promoting Torture: Marginalising "harm" for the sake of global ordering. Reflections on a decade of risk/security globalisation', *The International Journal of Human Rights* 16(7): 1040–1058.

Findlay, M. (2013a) *Contemporary Challenges in Regulating Global Crises*, Basingstoke, UK: Palgrave Macmillan.

Findlay, M. (2013b) *International and Comparative Criminal Justice: A critical introduction*, Abingdon, Oxon: Routledge.

Findlay, M. (2013c) 'Enunciating Genocide: Crime, rights and the impact of judicial intervention', *International Criminal Law Review*, 13: 297–317.

Findlay, M. (2014) *International and Comparative Criminal Justice: A critical introduction*, London: Routledge.

Findlay, M. and Henham, R. (2005) *Transforming International Criminal Justice: Retributive and restorative justice in the trial process*, Collumpton, UK: Willan Publishing.

Findlay, M. and Henham, R. (2010) *Beyond Punishment: Achieving international criminal justice*, Basingstoke, UK: Palgrave Macmillan.

Findlay, M. and Ngane S. (2012) 'Sham of the Moral Court: Testimony sold as the spoils of war', *Global Journal of Comparative Law*, 1: 73–101.

Foucault, M. (1979) *Discipline and Punish: The birth of the prison*, New York: Vintage Books.

Garland, D. (1990) *Punishment and the Modern Society: A study in social theory*, Oxford: Clarendon Press.

Goldstone, R. (1995) 'The International Tribunal for the Former Yugoslavia: A case study in Security Council action', *Duke Journal of Comparative & International Law*, 6(1): 5–10.

Haffajee, R. (2006) 'Prosecuting Crimes of Rape and Sexual Violence in the ICTR: The application of joint criminal enterprise theory', *Harvard Journal of Law and Gender*, 29: 201–221.

Hansen, T. (2011) 'Transitional Justice: Towards a differentiated theory', *Oregon Review of International Law*, 13(1): 1–46.

Honderich, T. (1982) 'The Argument for Anomalous Monism', *Analysis*, 42: 59–64.

Ignatieff, M. (1978) *A Just Measure of Pain: The penitentiary in the Industrial Revolution, 1750–1850*, New York: Pantheon Books.

Kiza, E. and Rohne, H. (2011) 'Victim expectations towards justice in post-conflict societies: a bottom-up perspective', in R. Henham and M. Findlay (eds) *Exploring the Boundaries of International Criminal Justice*, Aldershot, UK: Ashgate.

Levy, D. and Sznaider, N. (2004) 'The Institutionalization of Cosmopolitan Morality: The Holocaust and human rights', *Journal of Human Rights*, 3(2): 143–157.

Llewellyn, J. and Philpott, D. (2014) *Restorative Justice, Reconciliation and Peace Building*, Oxford: Oxford University Press.

Mégret, F. (2002) 'The Politics of International Criminal Justice', *European Journal of International Law*, 13(5): 1261–1284.

Melossi, D. and Pavarini, M. (1981) *The Prison and the Factory: Origins of the penitentiary system*, London: Macmillan.

Norrie, A. (1991) *Law, Ideology and Punishment: Retrieval and critique of the liberal idea of criminal justice*, Dordrecht: Kluwer Academic Publishers.

Norrie, A. (2005) *Law and the Beautiful Soul*, Abingdon, UK: Routledge.

Roach, S. (2009) *Governance, Order, and the International Criminal Court*, Oxford: Oxford University Press.

Rodger, J. (2008) *Criminalising Social Policy: Anti-social behaviour and welfare in a decivilised society*, Abingdon, UK: Routledge.

Rusche, G. and Kircheimer, O. (1939) *Punishment and Social Structure*, New York: Columbia University Press.

Schur, E. (1973) *Radical Non-intervention: Rethinking the deviancy problem*, Eaglewood Cliffs, NJ: Prentice-Hall.

Scull, A. (1977) *Decarceration, Community Treatment and the Deviant: A radical view*, Eaglewood Cliffs, NJ: Prentice-Hall.

Simon, J. (2014) *Mass Incarceration on Trial: A remarkable court decision and the future of prisons in America*, New York: The New Press.

Teitel, R. (2000) *Transitional Justice*, Oxford: Oxford University Press.

UN Convention on the Prevention and Punishment of the Crime of Genocide, GA Res. 260(II), 9 December 1948a.

UN General Assembly Res. 217A (III), 10 December 1948b.

van der Merwe, H. and Chapman, A. (2008) *Truth and Reconciliation in South Africa: Did the TRC deliver?*, Philadelphia: University of Pennsylvania Press.

Zehr, H. (2002) *The Little Book of Restorative Justice*, Intercourse, PA: Good Books.

10   Learning to scale up restorative justice

John Braithwaite

Introduction

A limitation of transitional justice with limited years of existence is that many of the worst victims are afraid to come forward, not ready to do so, or too busy rebuilding burnt homes and caring for burnt loved ones during those few years. One option is a permanent Truth Commission that keeps its doors open to victim testimony in perpetuity. Even well-funded truth commissions such as that of Timor-Leste provide the opportunity for some form of restorative justice to only a tiny proportion of the victims who would like it. In the case of Timor-Leste, many individual victims and many villages were asking for the Community Reconciliation Program to come to their village at the time that program ended with the closing of the doors of the Timor-Leste Commission (see discussion below).

The transience of transitional justice is compounded by the failure to invest in management improvement of transitional justice institutions. Transitional justice learns little. It does not monitor continuous improvement in the proportion of victims who are getting a form of justice they value. Transitional justice does not improve in iterated processes of fail fast, learn fast, adapt fast. Instead it fails fast, learns little, claims fast the closure that 'something has been done'. This chapter proposes a remedy to this limitation in the form of a permanent Truth and Reconciliation Commission that keeps its doors open to victim testimony in perpetuity. It is argued that dealing with the harms that have been caused during an extended period of conflict and/or oppression in a manner that does not set time frames might result in a transformation of transitional justice that is more victim focused.

Learning through monitoring

A problem with transitional justice is that it is transitional. In a different way, this is also a theme of Chris Cunneen's contribution to this volume. Particularly in developing countries that suffer wars, but not only there, a core failing of all manner of development and peacebuilding programs is short-termism. Donors like to be seen to be doing something new and innovative. It is less attractive to pour more support into preventing the shutdown of something that has been performing well. This is sad because we know that few initiatives to support poor people post-conflict work well at first. A long process of local learning and local adaptation is normally required to make a difference. The learning through monitoring approach to transformation that we have reason to think can work (Doff and Sable 1998) is not the norm. Instead donor funding tends to drop in templated programs from somewhere else (that are therefore not locally attuned) and then shut them down after evidence of disappointing results. This happens before the Silicon Valley mantra of 'fail fast, learn fast, adapt fast' has had time to work through a sequence of failures that promote growth.

We must be wary of 'restorative justice' becoming one of those dropped-in templates that feeds this frenzy of non-learning. That is one reason why it may be preferable to ask which traditions of doing justice locally already have a track record of learning through monitoring within the cultures of that place (Braithwaite 2014). I am yet to encounter a developing country context where practices with considerable restorative character do not already exist. Perhaps there are developing countries that do not have any justice tradition that is a better fit to definitions of restorative justice than some of what passes for it in developed economies; it is just that I have not encountered such a poor country. If that justice institution grounded in local learning is called *Gacaca*, then it is better to discuss it, support it, adapt it through further learning as *Gacaca* rather than as a program that donors call restorative justice, simply because it has restorative qualities (at least in some contexts in the case of Rwanda's *Gacaca*).

Pathologies of short-termism are everywhere to be found in transitional justice programs that have disappointed their advocates. For many commentators (Braithwaite *et al.* 2012; Kent 2004; Stanley 2009), the prosecutorial Serious Crimes Process of transitional justice in Timor-Leste was a disappointment, but the Community Reconciliation Process was one that showed great promise. Timorese did not describe the Community Reconciliation Process as 'restorative justice'. It leaned heavily on indigenous *lisan* traditions of justice. It was making mistakes, but was learning from them. Sadly, it closed down in circumstances where many communities were clamouring for the Community Reconciliation Process to come to their village to support its victims and reconcile its returning perpetrators. This was about CAVR (the Timor-Leste Commission for Reception, Truth and Reconciliation) being funded by donors for only a finite number of years. CAVR was one of the better-funded truth commissions the world has seen and it benefitted from some wonderful leadership.[1] Hence, its failure to leave behind a sustainable Community Reconciliation Process goes to the limitation of the very idea of transitional justice.

Not all abrupt terminations of learning through monitoring are a result of transitional institutions being required to close their doors after a few years because they are conceptualised as transitional. The National Peace Council (and its predecessor, the Peace Monitoring Council), which operated in Solomon Islands from 2000 to 2006, like CAVR, had inspiring strengths and indigenous leaders whose network of 80 local mediators initiated a galaxy of local reconciliation and peacebuilding initiatives largely crafted at the village level. An example was spreading its 'Weapons Free Village Program'. The Council nurtured dispersed peacemaking networks in the villages, encouraging traditional leaders to mediate conflicts (including all-important land disputes) locally, to support the local rebuilding of the legitimacy of the Solomon Islands police, to watch for weapons, to provide an early warning of rekindling hot-spots and to involve schoolteachers and churches in peace education and assisting children recovering from trauma. In other words, a strength of the National Peace Council was that it was participatory, indigenously led and under the thumb of neither the government nor the international peace operation. Those from Honiara and Australia who killed it off had an agenda of more centralised control of, and spin about, the peace process from the capital (Braithwaite *et al.* 2010b: 40–43).

The Australian-led peacekeeping operation was prone to take credit for the successful surrender of weapons as part of the Solomon Islands peace. The fact is that most weapons were handed to the National Peace Council, working with church leaders, before peacekeepers arrived in 2003! Australian funding for the National Peace Council was cut, partly because the Howard government (and the Rudd government at first) was more interested in a prosecutorial approach to transitional justice than a restorative one. But the more fundamental reason the National Peace Council was cut down was that a new Solomon Islands government saw it as an initiative of their predecessors with Commissioners whose political past was not to their liking. The fact that the National Peace Council was succeeding and learning through monitoring therefore increased the political appeal of discrediting and closing it.

Transforming transitional justice

Kerry Clamp's final chapter of this volume is about a transformative vision for restorative justice as a response to mass victimisation. It follows from this chapter so far that one way for transitional justice to become more transformative is for it to become less transitional. In her recent writing, Clamp (2014: 46, 122–123) has also questioned quick closure as a transitional justice objective. Rather, Clamp is attracted to the Nils Christie ideal that it is often better to own and live within a conflict rather than to 'solve' it. The conflict between restorative and prosecutorial justice itself is a good example of one that is best not 'resolved', but continually contested by advocates with different visions of justice.

Nickson and Braithwaite (2013) have made a case for permanent truth and reconciliation commissions that broaden, deepen and lengthen their conception of justice. Restorative justice learnings are the path we see for deepening justice through participatory ownership of it by neglected stakeholders, particularly victims, but not only victims. The way restorative justice can deepen the meaning of justice is by being responsive to the centrality of [affected] communities as stakeholders in justice work. Justice can be broadened so that it includes reparations of diverse kinds that encompass 'symbolic reparation', sometimes with a tangible quality such as returning bones, as well as 'material reparation', 'justice as a better future' (Shearing and Froestad 2007), apology, memorialisation and much more. Lengthening justice means making transitional justice permanent! This means truth and reconciliation commissions or an archipelago of local and national peace committees as permanent institutions.

Empirically, Ray Nickson's (2013) Ph.D. research was about an expectations gap with transitional justice that he found to be widespread. For example, local villagers speak of their despair, a decade on, when they go to a market and encounter a man still wearing their son's watch on the arm that murdered him. In contexts such as Cambodia and the former Yugoslavia that Nickson studied, and with the 33 wars for which I have done fieldwork so far in *Peacebuilding Compared*, it is exceptionally rare for prosecutorial transitional justice to get down to low-level murders or rapes of single people by officers of low or middling rank. So, in terms of the theme of this book, the problematic is not only about transitional justice being too transitional, but overly concentrated on mass national atrocity, neglectful of local and personal atrocity. Broadening and lengthening justice means that, even if it continues to be the case that the mother who sees that watch on that arm cannot get her day in court, she might get access to a (deeper) form of justice that is restorative. A lot of that kind of deeper justice was done by Timor's Community Reconciliation Process 'on the mat' in the village where victims could insist that at least this man could stop using their son's watch and indeed return it to them. By broadening the conception of justice to encompass participatory empowerment of a demand that a watch be returned, or affirmation of a family request that a village tap be named in honour of a disappeared family member,[2] many more survivors can get some kind of justice. Not a full measure of justice, but a spoonful of justice that has meaning for them.

One problem with the truth and reconciliation commission that runs for just three years is that most of the most damaged victims, especially children but also adults traumatised by rape, will not be ready to disclose things in front of others that they have never before spoken of to anyone. Timing is the essence of justice that restores. This is not just a challenge of whether survivors are ready yet. It is also a problem of victims being ready right now and the justice institution not yet being in place to hear them. An Australian Aboriginal friend of mine recently agreed to testify before the Royal Commission on Child Sexual Abuse. It was her first time telling details of her abuse as a child of the 'stolen generation' who was taken from her parents and institutionalised. She was unable to do anything else in her life as she prepared for the testimony. She was ready to take the big step. Her testimony date was deferred for weeks, then deferred again. Her emotional well-being plummeted shockingly during this period and again after the testimony, though on balance she felt the experience was beneficial for her once she had climbed the mountain of giving it. Most victims of the most terrible atrocities, I speculate, come to a state of readiness for testimony either too early or too late for when a transitory transitional justice institution has its doors open to them. That is something we must fix.

Most of the world's anti-corruption commissions are permanent standing commissions (for good reason). Why cannot truth and reconciliation commissions be permanent? Cost is a reason of course. The cost challenge is not as huge as it seems. One of the few ways developing countries export some services to rich countries is through tourism. The challenge for their national capital, if not their wilderness areas, is that it lacks tourist attractions. In countries that have a history of mass atrocity, the evidence is very clear now that one of the best tourism sites one can build memorialises mass atrocity (Lennon and Foley 2002; Causevic and Lynch 2011). Even when we tourists go to cities that are wealthy and bristling with alternative attractions, usually if we go to Berlin or Cape Town we go to the Holocaust Museum and to Robben Island.

For developing countries, this means westerners can be asked to pay an entrance fee that funds the local staff of a museum that maintains all of the evidentiary artifacts and all the stories of the victims who came forward to the Truth and Reconciliation Commission. And they contribute to the national economy by staying in hotels and dining at restaurants near the museum. The idea of a permanent commission is that, after all the victims and all the perpetrators have died, the commission will remain as little more than a museum, an institution of national collective memory and education of the next generation. One would hope for a museum with rich community outreach to schools and across the generations, as well as one that attracts tourists.

Perhaps the deeper objection than cost is touched upon in Wendy Lambourne's chapter. This is that broad, deep and long justice in respect of mass atrocity is 'too messy'. Political leaders and donors alike tend to prefer institutionalised 'closure', tied up and tidy, transition done. That is why they also too often push for a post-conflict election and withdrawal of peacekeepers that entrenches a new tyranny before the institutions have been put in place to guard against an electorally endorsed tyranny. Just as premature closure through an election can make democracy a cause of war rather than a cause of peace (Collier 2009), so I worry that temporally truncated reconciliation can make transitional justice a cause of war rather than a cause of peace.

Yes, many individual victims do crave closure. Perpetrators certainly crave the kind of closure that lifts a future threat of investigation and prosecution from their heads. Closure can be socially and emotionally a good thing. But, in other contexts, closure is the last thing stakeholders want. Consider again Chris Cunneen's chapter. Do Australian Aboriginal people want a commission to come along, give them closure in a transitional moment when injustices such as theft of their land, stripping their identity, is healed, and an institution of reconciliation that is wound up with white and black Australians then enjoying closure? It is good and fine for individuals to decide that what they want in relation to their abuse is personal closure. Institutionalisation that dictates closure for a society that persists with deep structures of injustice is quite another matter. Dictating what is best for all individuals, with their great diversity of needs, through institutionalised closure is quite another matter. In Lambourne's terms, there is a need to defend the idea that the most productive forms of justice are likely to be radically plural and therefore messy. Closure here, opening up wounds there, for a project of disinfecting them in the *longue durée*.

In his chapter, Jonathan Doak rightly worries about the risk of 'victor's justice' in transitions. Most transitional justice is victor's justice. At the Tokyo War Crimes trials, Japanese political and military leaders were convicted of terrible war crimes. But were any of them as terrible as dropping atomic bombs on civilians, or the firebombing of Tokyo for that matter? Yet there are ways that tables of victor's justice have turned. In the decades after the Second World War, Japan became a more dominant world economic power than it ever was before the war. Its Prime Minister Shinzo Abe and much of his right-wing political constituency use that position of formidable global economic power to assert a kind of war crime denial. This has extended to political pressure from Abe's supporters even to close a memorial to Korean slave labourers who perished in terrible conditions in Japan during the Second World War.

Because the victor's justice of the Pacific war crime trials was of such poor quality, a poor transitional platform was laid for the *longue durée* of reconciliation in the Asian theatre. My father was one of the six survivors of a war crime that took 2,400 lives – the Sandakan death march. At least one of the Japanese officers who hung for that mass atrocity was innocent because one or more survivors fabricated testimony against him, as one confessed on his death bed. The haphazard injustice and humiliation of war-time leaders at the gallows leaves some contemporary Japanese political leaders with a distaste for adding to this discomfort by appropriate justice for elderly sex slaves of their wartime military, victims of the rape of Nanjing, and many more. Had a permanent truth and reconciliation commission been established, instead of the kind of selective and shabby prosecutions that were done, the *longue durée* of reconciliation with Japan's neighbours might today be in better shape. The challenge would be to put that permanent commission beyond the reach of the anti-reconciliation political power of the likes of a Prime Minister Abe. To this challenge we turn in the next section.

Architectures of permanence

A further strength of the Timor-Leste CAVR was that it became part of the country's separation of powers (Braithwaite *et al.* 2012: 214–250). The seemingly all-powerful Prime Minister of Timor-Leste Xanana Gusmao believed in closure once his government had achieved some quite productive reconciliation with the government of Indonesia. He stalled publication of the CAVR report and sought to silence the Commission in various ways. He failed in the sense that ultimately the Commission won enough support from the parliament and donors to disseminate the report very widely.

As is usual after terrible protracted conflicts, whichever faction prevails to capture the successor state has skeletons in its closet. From Sri Lanka to Solomon Islands to Nepal, so many commitments to truth and reconciliation commissions in peace processes have been delayed and suppressed by executive governments (often with support from parliamentary opposition leaders who also have skeletons in their closets). Institutional breakthroughs are needed in our thinking about how to lock in the political independence of truth and reconciliation commissions within the separation of powers.

The problem of the independence of truth commissions falling to the domination of executive governments is just one example of the whole range of accountability institutions that are repeatedly dominated and compromised by the executive branch of the state. These include ombudsmen, audit offices, anti-corruption commissions and independent regulatory commissions, especially in sensitive areas such as the media and financial regulation.

In Western democracies and many other societies, domination of the judicial branch by the executive is not as profound, partly because, like the legislative branch, the judicial branch benefits from a long tradition of independence advocacy that dates from Montesquieu (1977) and earlier. More importantly, the independence of the judicial branch is backed by a wealthy and powerful fraction of the ruling class with a class interest in defending that independence – judges themselves, prosecutors, lawyers in private practice, law societies and other professional associations, professors in law schools. An office such as that of the Ombudsman benefits neither from a deeply embedded historical commitment to independence nor from the backing of a politically powerful profession. Nor does a restoratively oriented truth and reconciliation commission enjoy either of those bulwarks. Indeed restorative transitional justice regularly comes under attack from that legal faction of the ruling class who mostly succeed in ensuring that more of the budgets for transitional justice go into the pockets of lawyers than to rebuilding lives of victims.

While Western constitutionalism is rather sewn up by legalists, the Chinese contestation between the legalist and Confucian traditions, or about how to create a hybrid of them, as President Xi Jinping claims to be doing, is a more uncertain historical contest. Restorative justice is very much in the mix with what is being discussed as an option for the future in China. Who could predict if all this will become a step forward or a step backwards for freedom as non-domination?

What is rather more settled and interesting is how Taiwan's (the Republic of China's) Constitution has developed. This framework also applied to mainland China until the Maoists drove the Kuomintang from power. The Taiwan Constitution has five branches of governance ('Yuan') grounded in Sun Yat Sen's principles of republican governance (still revered in the Peoples' Republic). Three of the Taiwan Yuan are branches that all Westphalian states have inherited from the Montesquieu tradition – an executive, a judiciary and a legislature. A fourth is an examinations branch based on the Confucian ideal of protecting all other branches from cronyism by an Examinations Yuan that is independent of other branches of governance. The Examinations Yuan decides who will get jobs in other branches on the basis of beating their competitors in exams. Not such a bad idea for countries with histories of family dynasties running the state or of a legal profession recruited from bestowing articled clerkships upon young men who attended an elite private school or the same school as one of the partners of a law firm.

The fifth branch is the one of particular interest to this analysis. This is the Control Yuan. Its job is the regulation of the state, meta governance, the governance of governance (Sorensen 2006) or meta regulation (Parker 2002). The idea of a Control Yuan has a pre-republican history, starting with the office of the Censor (御史; *yù shǐ*) under the Qin and Han dynasties. Later, the Sui and Tang dynasties established the office of the *tái* (臺) who supervised the conduct of civil servants and military officers. Sun Yat Sen's original thinking on the separation of powers had a sixth branch, the Auditing Yuan. However, in 1931 the Auditing Yuan was subsumed as the Ministry of Audit into the Control Yuan, an architecture that remains in Taiwan today.

In addition to supervising what would be called the Auditor-General function in the West, the Control Yuan also deals with impeachment of Ministers, members of parliament, officers of the Examinations Yuan, prosecutors and judges. It supervises the integrity and independence of the other four branches. The Control Yuan Committee on Anti-Corruption is central to this function. There is also a Control Yuan Committee on Human Rights with functions similar to Western human rights commissions. There is a Standing Committee on Judicial Affairs and Prison Administration that performs the functions of judicial self-regulation in the West and the prison ombudsman and prison inspectorate functions that exist in some Western jurisdictions. The Control Yuan also has an oversight Standing Committee for National Defence and Intelligence Affairs. Another Control Yuan standing committee has oversight of procurement by all branches of governance.

Most interesting from a reconciliation perspective, it has a standing committee concerned with ethnic minority affairs. Like white-settler colonies, Taiwan has an indigenous minority who were the original owners of the land before the historically recent Han Chinese invasion. As in white-settler societies such as the United States, Canada, Australia and New Zealand, the judicial branch has a history of defending their ruling class interests by finding that white settlers have legal title over the stolen land. Of course the Control Yuan membership has the same class interest. Yet it does seem a visionary idea in principle to have a branch of governance within a branch that is independent of the judiciary with heavy indigenous representation and with the job of holding the other branches to account in terms of indigenous rights and indigenous reconciliation. One reason it merits consideration in principle is that it is a permanent institution that therefore has the potential to reconcile open wounds of the *longue durée*. This virtue is that it is an institution that can be adapted when it fails, but that will not be shut down at the whim of executive governments, as has happened repeatedly to indigenous rights and reconciliation institutions in Australia, for example.

Thailand is the only country I know to have emulated the Taiwan architecture of a Control Branch or Integrity Branch of governance. The 1997 'People's Constitution' was a radical document in terms of public participation and rights accountability. It was dismantled by the 2006 military coup and the 2007 Constitution promulgated by the Council for National Security, which made it a crime to criticise the draft constitution (Sapsomboon and Khundee 2007). Members of the fourth branch, the inspection branch of the 1997 Thai Constitution, oversaw impeachment in the other three branches, the election commission, the human rights commission, ombudsman, audit and anti-corruption functions as in the Taiwan Control Yuan. The 1997 Thai Constitution involved the further innovation of that fourth branch being elected from candidates who were not members of political parties and for one term only (as a check against progressive capture by parties that dominate the executive and legislature and stack the judiciary).

There is something attractive about this Sun Yat Sen architecture of a fourth accountability branch of governance comprising many branches. In terms of the issues of this book, for societies where settlers have forced indigenous landowners off their country, there is appeal in one of those branches being elected from indigenous peoples for oversight of the other branches in terms of the *longue durée* of reconciliation of histories of indigenous dispossession and mass atrocity, disproportionate contemporary imprisonment and deaths in custody and indigenous rights more broadly. The next section argues that one potentiality of such an architecture in contrast to extant Western constitutional architectures is that they might incubate the application of modern management techniques of continuous improvement to monitor the scaling up of restorative justice and other forms of social justice to eventually benefit all indigenous victims of injustice, rather than a token few.

For societies that have suffered from civil war, actual genocide, 'creeping genocide' or politicide, there is appeal in establishing a permanent truth and reconciliation commission as a branch within a permanent independent accountability branch. That would give it the backbone to stand up to political parties, to clean out Nazi judiciaries, Soviet carceral archipelagos or Apartheid policing, to stand up to a Ku Klux Klan and to state judiciaries that fail to act against them and to stand up to abuses of power of more subtle kinds.

Freeing transitional justice from the legal shackles that go with institutions such as the International Criminal Court or Royal Commissions to investigate past mass victimisation in Australia, means that reconciliation strategies more grounded in civil society become possible. One of the problems of the South African Truth and Reconciliation Commission is that many victims who offered to testify were not selected for public hearings. Others felt they lived in rural areas that were too remote to get themselves to sites of testimony. Others were not ready at that time. And there were many other reasons that the South African Commission touched in a personal way the circumstances of only a tiny fraction of victims of Apartheid.

One of the creative programs of South African civil society's Institute for Justice and Reconciliation to respond to these limitations has been to engage schools by encouraging their students to create videos of the testimony of their loved ones. A granddaughter might approach a victim who did not want to testify before Archbishop Tutu to enable the collective memory of the family concerning her suffering under Apartheid. The granddaughter's appeal might be to encourage the grandmother simply to do for her granddaughter what she would not do for Archbishop Tutu if she now felt ready and strong enough to do that much. One possibility from such family reconciliation initiatives (children-up rather than judiciary-down or Commission-down) is that a person who did not wish to disclose the atrocity she suffered as a younger person discovers with her granddaughter in old age that she benefits from telling the story. So much so in some cases that perhaps she might change her mind about the permanent truth and reconciliation commission and then lodge her video on their archive for the collective memory and history of the nation, as well as for the collective memory of future generations of her family. One possibility is that this kind of initiative could be catalysed in civil society by a commission that was in the business of reconciliation for the *longue durée*.

An Interim (transitional) Truth and Reconciliation Commission could be considered to gather testimony for an Interim Report and build consensus toward a mandate for the Permanent Commission which might be constitutionally entrenched. Under this vision, the Permanent Commission could become an integral part of the separation of powers, an extra check and balance in the polity. Hence, if the Interim Commission in a case such as post-apartheid South Africa decided that justice as a better future (Shearing and Foestad 2007) was fundamental to transitional justice, it might recommend to the drafters of the new constitution that the Permanent Commission be mandated to produce five-yearly comprehensive reports evaluating the successes and failures of national institutions in reducing racial inequality, eliminating poverty, and creating educational equality and less brutal security forces.

When I interviewed one of the leading lights of the South African Truth and Reconciliation for Peacebuilding Compared, he said (anonymously according to my ANU Ethics protocol) that perhaps a better idea than making the Truth and Reconciliation Commission a permanent institution would have been to make the South African architecture of local and provincial Peace Committees permanent. He argued that these were effective in preventive peacemaking (for example, by steering routes of funeral marches from rival parties away from each other) as well as for local truth and reconciliation. The Peace Committees were established under the 1991 National Peace Accord. They were shut down in 1994 by the African National Congress precisely because they were a competing check and balance and a bottom-up source of peacebuilding competing with the ruling party's top-down authority.

Bottom-up architectures

The African National Congress was behaving like most governments with a stranglehold on executive government in closing down genuine bottom-up power. Executive governments wanting to keep their hands on most levers of power are only one of the threats to growing transitional justice bottom up. Commodification and professionalisation of development assistance are others. Indeed, almost all the types of 'community empowerment' we see on the ground in rural areas of poor countries are enfeebled by the commodification of the aid business. Some of the commodification is driven from developed economies where volunteerism has been displaced by development professionalism and NGO advocacy professionals. We see it in Western universities where academics are pressed to capture some of their country's aid budget for the benefit of the university. Progressively in developed economies, we see more of the public's contributions to development being captured by development professionals working for NGOs, by universities, by businesses that specialise in aid, even by the Big Four global accounting firms.

At the receiving end, a commodification dynamic unfolds that mirrors the commodification dynamic of supply of transitional justice and other forms of development assistance from wealthy economies. 'Community empowerment' has become NGO-ised by local development professionals. I have lost count of how many of my friends in developing countries have told me they are going to start a business. Oh, what sort of business, I enquire? 'A human rights NGO', 'a transitional justice NGO', or some such, comes back as the answer. The aid business reinforces old inequalities in new ways, through what rural people in my recent Bangladesh fieldwork with Bina D'Costa referred to as the 'new NGO class'. In societies with caste systems we see this with the healthy push for gender empowerment – the women who get the NGO salaries so often are upper caste and live in cities in comfortable houses with servants. Lower caste women in remote villages are rarely to be found on foreign-funded NGO salaries. They do great work, but as volunteers. This widely dispersed rural volunteerism of the poor seems the right thing to support. How can that support be accomplished in the face of the long march to ever-growing power of justice and development commodification (and of executive governments in the capital)?

How do we encourage that volunteerism away from cities to the rural areas where the most neglected poor are found, where the truth commission does not hold hearings? One notable democratic institutional innovation is the Panchayat (assembly of elders) reforms for village self-government that Rajiv Gandhi pushed to become the 73rd Amendment to the Indian Constitution in 1993. These reforms bogged down after his death. Sonia Gandhi pushed to re-energise Panchayat reform in the twenty-first century. One westerner who has been focused on the importance of diagnosing the strengths and weaknesses of the Indian Panchayat reforms is UNDP Administrator and former New Zealand Prime Minister Helen Clark. UNDP interest arises because the attempt to shift Panchayat power from corrupt local government apparatchiks further down to very local village assemblies of the district–block–village hierarchy of Panchayats has been associated with village-level Panchayats taking control of the largest anti-poverty program the world has seen (operating in 778,000 villages). This is the Mahatma Gandhi National Rural Employment Guarantee Act. It is a 'right to work' reform that seeks to guarantee 100 days of publicly funded work every year, mostly on water conservation projects in rural areas, to the poorest people of India. As one would hope for an innovation of contestatory democracy (Pettit 1997), it has been exposed to critiques of its corruption by the Indian government's own Comptroller and Auditor General and media (Times of India 2013), social audits by Indian state governments, as well as critical analyses by Indian and foreign researchers (Shankar 2010; Nagaragan *et al.* 2013).

There is more hope for the village Panchayats than for the higher-level Panchayats that have also been riddled with corruption and maladministration in Nepal, Pakistan and Bangladesh. Hope for the village-level Panchayats persists, notwithstanding formidable problems revealed by audit contestation. The hope is that the checks and balances that the audit society can occasionally deliver can be complemented with taking India back to the checks that assembly democracy can offer in a village. Actually, the village Panchayats have the potential to become a rich hybrid of assembly democracy, representative democracy and monitory democracy (Keane 2009: xxx, 627–628). They are also a strategic site for reflecting on the meaning of community empowerment implied by the relational conception of justice articulated by Ami Harbin and Jennifer Llewellyn's chapter in this volume. The Indian Constitution requires one third of elected Panchayat voting members to be women and proportional representation of scheduled castes such as 'untouchables'. More than a million women have been elevated to become elected representatives for the first time. This probably has contributed to an outcome for the Mahatma Gandhi National Rural Employment Guarantee Act of 54 per cent of the days worked going to women and 39 per cent to scheduled (lowest) castes or *adavasi* ('tribal peoples') in 2013 (Mahatma Gandhi 2014). Fifty million households (a quarter of all rural Indian households) have been helped. While there clearly continues to be corruption in the program, it is hard to see it as captured by corrupt upper caste men to the degree that so much of Indian governance is corrupted. Elected village assemblies are not a remote form of representative democracy; Rupert Murdoch shows no interest in taking over the intermediation of Panchayat political communication; one chats with one's elected member on a daily basis in the village. In addition, those elected must deliberatively account to the whole village in a kind of assembly democracy. We can take some heart from an anti-poverty program that has helped more poor people than any before it and that is overwhelmingly going to extremely disadvantaged people. It involves a new hybrid of deliberative, electoral and contestatory democracy taking root in the world's largest democracy with the world's largest number of poor people.

As with the UNDP, I also have hopes for the Community Empowerment Programs initially trialled by the World Bank in Indonesia from 1998 and now rolling out to dozens of developing countries. These provide a village-level development budget to be spent by a village assembly, at least a third of which must be women in most programs, as a condition of getting the cash. In Poso, Indonesia (site of a Muslim–Christian war that killed thousands up to 2006, a training camp for the Bali bombers), I was inspired by the training in deliberative democracy offered to village assemblies as part of UNDP, World Bank and World Vision support for the Kecamatan (sub-district) Development Program. Villagers were invited in this training to vision alternative futures for how they might use their village development budget. 'If we used it to build a bridge across the river there, we could develop new fields on the other side; the bridge could open up some new markets for our agriculture' (Eastern Indonesian interview for the Peacebuilding Compared project).

The key feature is an empowerment role for village assemblies in deciding how to spend an annual village development budget. The village assembly aspect is perhaps the hope for a simple form of horizontal accountability to prevent corruption, waste and NGO-isation. Though development professionalism is of course needed up to a point to connect remote villages to suppliers of water pump technology if a water pump is what they prioritise, to build capacity in some basics of tendering, and to enforce rules on participation of women and lower-caste people in the decision making as a condition of funding.

If the village assembly votes for transitional justice or restorative justice as one of their budget priorities, then they may need support from some transitional justice or restorative justice professionalism. There is some appeal in the idea that transitional and restorative justice should only be allowed to flourish in village societies when village assemblies decide to allocate to it some of a village development budget that is under their control. This would be a good check against restorative justice going the way of 'rule of law programming' in UN and development budgets generally, where so much of the cash goes into the pockets of foreign lawyers who rarely venture out from secure compounds in capital cities. A transitional justice that failed to help transform the lives of victims and failed to rebuild justice in harmonious communities would stand little chance of winning village assembly votes against water pumps and bridges (see generally Bhandari 2014). An attractive feature of such Community Empowerment Programs in principle is that they are demand driven from the villages, not demand driven by NGOs in capital cities. More importantly, they are not supply driven by what donors, development professionals and transitional justice professionals in the west think it is important to supply.

Sadly, most of the 'community empowerment' work that we see on the ground that is funded by countries such as Australia is supply driven. This is as true of programs in remote Aboriginal communities in Australia as it is true in West Papua. It is great to support a program that supplies water pumps or solar power generators for remote villages. But it is better to supply them only when a village assembly ratifies a demand for them from a village development budget over which the village has ultimate control. The village might decide the water from our river is fine, but our priority is first to rebuild the trust in our community that was destroyed by the war. A reconciliation process for our village is the crucial thing for us because until we heal our wounds we will be incapable of working together for any kind of development and social justice. If we do prioritise reconciliation through transitional justice, we will discuss who is going to repair it, and how, if it falls apart in five years time, long after the western donors have lost interest. Likewise if we prioritise a water pump or a solar panel for our precious budget, we are going to discuss who is going to repair it when it breaks down.

As I travel from one conflict zone to another for my *Peacebuilding Compared* project, I see places where this kind of village empowerment with control over its own development budget has worked badly, such as Timor-Leste (Braithwaite *et al.* 2012: 119–127; 240–251), but other hopeful least likely cases (Eckstein 1975) for testing its implicit democratic theory such as Aceh in Indonesia during and after its civil war and tsunami (Braithwaite *et al.* 2010a: 380–425), Afghanistan, where 10.5 million people were reached with surprisingly low levels of corruption as a result of villages being required to put in some of their own money according to Princeton's Innovations for Successful Societies (Majeed 2013) program, and even some hope in the least likely place of all for a democracy innovation to work, the Democratic Republic of Congo. There may be less corruption in these programs than in corporatised programs that get 'sliced' in the cities, but there is still corruption, still capture by local 'big men'.

Part of Mahatma Gandhi's 'village republicanism' vision for Panchayats as a deliberative corrective to metropolitan representative democracy was that Panchayats would take on the functions of courts of law and state police in the villages. This happened with many village Panchayats, though only a small proportion of them. The contemporary research agenda of some of India's most distinguished criminologists, such as M. Z. Khan (Khan and Sharma 1982; Latha and Thilagaraj 2013), is to study how justice works in villages where Panchayats have seized justice back from the police and courts through village-level restorative justice. These Indian criminologists are interested in reviving ancient Indian *nyaya panchuyats* (village courts), hybridised with learnings from the global social movement for evidence-based restorative justice.

In Punjab province of Pakistan, there are also village *panchayats* that run a kind of restorative justice. Even more interesting have been *jirgas* in the Pakistan provinces bordering Afghanistan that compete not only with the law courts of the Pakistan state, but also with the Sharia courts offered by the Taliban. In spaces where ordinary people live in constant fear of violence, winning the competition for hearts and minds by offering them a form of justice that they feel protects them is politically crucial. One way the Pakistan Taliban seeks to compete is by sending suicide bombers to the deliberative justice meetings of the *jirgas*. Assassination campaigns have eliminated 700 traditional *maliks* responsible for convening *jirgas*. A response by the Pakistan police has been to establish hybrid state–traditional restorative justice *Muslahathi* (reconciliation) Committees inside the heavily fortified walls of police stations. After observing more than 100 of these deliberatively democratic institutions of criminal justice, Braithwaite and Gohar (2014) concluded that they are succeeding in interrupting many cycles of revenge killing, particularly through their handling of murder cases.

The last section of this chapter was about all societies pondering the insight that they are overly ossified into a top-down Westphalian tripartite separation of powers. Therefore they might consider the 'new governance' vision of Sun Yat Sen's more complex separation of powers. And they might consider locating truth and reconciliation commissions within a fourth branch of governance. Because that is just another top-down solution driven from the metropole, this section has sought to complement that idea with a new governance vision demand driven from villages rather than supply driven from governance templates supplied from metropoles.

Scaling up restorative justice

Does the path of a permanent reconciliation architecture with guaranteed independence within the separation of powers have a solution to the challenge of 90+ per cent of victims of atrocity not testifying before transitional justice hearings? Could it enable transformation of structural injustices that induced conflict and suffering? There is room for great strides in answer to these questions, because such small strides have been taken. One diagnosis of why they have been so small is that modern management techniques have never been applied to transitional justice. This was also the point about long-term commitment to iterated cycles of fail fast, learn fast, adapt fast. The computer industry had many decades of producing dud computers, or computers that were of little use to us ordinary citizens, before the contemporary era where most of us carry a computer in our purse or pocket most of the time.

A permanent commission could be mandated to achieve long-run continuous improvement in access to transitional justice. This would mean consultations with transitional justice stakeholders to set performance indicators. The commission could be required by law to maintain records on how many victims had received different kinds of justice, how satisfied they were with the justice they received, with the quality of listening to their grievances, with whether they had an opportunity to say all the things they wanted to say and ask for all the things they wanted to request, whether their rights were respected in the process, whether they were treated with dignity, whether post-traumatic stress disorder services and other forms of counselling were provided as needed, and so on.

Such data should be independently collected because CEOs of Permanent Truth and Reconciliation Commissions should be evaluated partly according to how successful the society is in improving justice indicators during their watch. Many other indicators could be identified by stakeholders as measurements the commission must collect, such as refugees and IDPs resettled, mines cleared, schools rebuilt, child soldiers completing their education and getting jobs, ethnic and religious discrimination surveys, equality measures of various kinds, restorative justice circles completed and followed up to the satisfaction of participants, criminal prosecutions completed, named victims memorialised through ceremonies to unveil memorials, peer review evaluations from transitional justice practitioners from elsewhere on the strategic and reconciliatory qualities of the prosecutions, restorative justice circles, reparations, and other initiatives. Put another way, this is a proposal to scale up restorative justice and other forms of transitional justice, both in terms of the proportion of survivors benefitting from it and in terms of quality, by mandating a permanent truth and reconciliation commission (or a permanent peace committee architecture) to invest in management and cultural change to continuously improve transitional justice. Critically, the last section argued that a good test of continuous improvement is how transitional justice is evaluated by hybrid village democracy. In village societies, if villages are empowered with budgets to choose transitional justice and none of them do, then transitional justice has failed to scale up. The question must then be asked if it deserved to fail.

In the first few years of operation, one could expect a permanent commission to fail slowly, learn slowly and adapt slowly. This is just to say that it would need to learn how to manage itself, how to open itself to feedback from stakeholders and peer reviewers. Such a reasonable expectation about how a management system might mature gradually to cultivate learning through monitoring (Dorf and Sabel 1998) goes to why it seems so naïve to believe that a transitional justice institution that wraps up in three years could achieve great things. Hope for transformation in three years is worse than a triumph of hope over experience (managerial experience). It is ritualism of victim rights (Charlesworth and Larking 2014). It is about the politics of being seen to be 'doing something' about victim rights, without a sustained strategy for succeeding at justice that matters with all or most victims, over time.

Notes

1 It also suffered from the usual allegations that some working for it may have been former rights abusers themselves (see Stanley 2009).
2 In my *Peacebuilding Compared* fieldwork in Nepal, one prominent advocate for victims of war crimes felt so honoured that a new tap in his village had been named in honour of his disappeared father.

References

Bhandari, R. (2014) 'Class and Justice', *Kathmandu Post*, 30 July, 2014. www.ekantipur.com/the-kathmandu-post/2014/07/29/oped/class-and-justice/265548.html.

Braithwaite, J. (2014) 'Traditional justice', in J. Llewellyn and D. Philpott (eds) *Restorative Justice, Reconciliation and Peacebuilding*, New York: Oxford University Press.

Braithwaite, J. and Gohar, A. (2014) 'Restorative Justice, Policing and Insurgency: Learning from Pakistan', *Law & Society Review*, 48(3): 531–561.

Braithwaite, J., Charlesworth, H. and Soares, A. (2012) *Networked Governance of Freedom and Tyranny: Peace in Timor-Leste*, Canberra: ANU Press.

Braithwaite, J., Cookson, M., Braithwaite, V. and Dunn, L. (2010a) *Anomie and Violence: Non-truth and reconciliation in Indonesian peacebuilding*, Canberra: ANU Press.

Braithwaite, J., Dinnen, S., Allen, M., Braithwaite, V. and Charlesworth, H. (2010b) *Pillars and Shadows: Statebuilding as peacebuilding in Solomon Islands*, Canberra: ANU Press.

Causevic, S. and Lynch, P. (2011) 'Phoenix Tourism: Post-conflict tourism role', *Annals of Tourism Research*, 38(3): 780–800.

Charlesworth, H. and Larking, E. (2014) *Human Rights and the Universal Periodic Review: Rituals and ritualism*, Cambridge: Cambridge University Press.

Clamp, K. (2014) *Restorative Justice in Transition*, London: Routledge.

Collier, P. (2009) *Wars, Guns and Votes: Democracy in dangerous places*, New York: Harper.

Dorf, M. and Sabel, C. (1998) 'A Constitution of Democratic Experimentalism', *Columbia Law Review*, 98: 267–473.

Eckstein, H. (1975) 'Case Study and Theory in Political Science', in F. Greenstein and N. Polsby (eds) *Handbook of Political Science*, Volume 7, Reading, MA: Addison-Wesley..

Majeed, R. (2013) *Building Trust in Government: Afghanistan's National Solidarity Program, 2002–2013*, Princeton, NJ: Princeton University.

Keane, J. (2009) *The Life and Death of Democracy*, New York: Simon and Schuster.

Kent, L. (2004) *Unfulfilled Expectations: Community views on CAVR's Community Reconciliation Process*, Dili: Judicial System Monitoring Program.

Khan, M. Z. and Sharma, K. (1982) *Profile of a Nyana Panchayat*, Delhi: National.

Latha, S. and Thilagaraj, R. (2013) 'Restorative Justice in India', *Asian Journal of Criminology*, 8: 309–19.

Lennon, J. T. and Foley, M. (2002) *Dark Tourism: The attraction of death and disaster*, London: Continuum.

Mahatma Gandhi National Rural Employment Guarantee Act (2005) 2014 Report to the People. http://nrega.nic.in/netnrega/writereaddata/Circulars/Report_People_Eng_jan_2014.pdf.

Montesquieu, Baron Charles de Secondat (1977) *The Spirit of the Laws*, D. W. Carrithers (abr. and ed.), Berkeley, CA: University of California Press.

Nagarajan, H., Raghbendra, J. and Pradhan, K. (2013) *The Role of Bribes in Rural Governance: The case of India*, ASARC Working Paper 2013/03, Canberra: Crawford School, Australian National University.

Nickson, R. (2013) *Great Expectations: Managing realities of transitional justice*. Ph.D. thesis, The Australian National University.

Nickson, R. and Braithwaite, J. (2013) 'Deeper, Broader, Longer Transitional Justice', *European Journal of Criminology*, 11(4), 445–463.

Parker, C. (2002) *The Open Corporation*, Cambridge: Cambridge University Press.

Pettit, P. (1997) *Republicanism*, Oxford: Oxford University Press.

Sapsomboon, S. and Khundee, S. (2007) 'Referendum law or penalty law?', *The Nation* (Thailand), July 7, 2007.

Shankar, S. (2010) *Can Social Audits Count?* ASARC Working Paper 2010/09. Canberra: Crawford School, Australian National University.

Shearing, C. and Froestad, J. (2007) 'Beyond restorative justice – Zwelethemba, a future-focused model using local capacity conflict resolution', in R. Mackay, M. Bosnjak, J. Deklerck, C. Pelikan, B. Van Stokkom and M. Wright (eds) *Images of Restorative Justice Theory*, Frankfurt: Verlag fur Polizeiwissenschaft.

Sorensen, E. (2006) 'Metagovernance: The changing role of politicians in processes of democratic governance', *American Review of Public Administration*, 36(1): 98–114.

Stanley, E. (2009) *Torture, Truth and Justice: The case of Timor-Leste*, London: Routledge.

The Times of India (2013) 'CAG finds holes in enforcing MNREGA'. *The Times of India*. http://timesofindia.indiatimes.com/city/bengaluru/CAG-finds-holes-in-enforcing-MNREGA/articleshow/21498524.cms.

11 When does transitional justice begin and end?

Colonised peoples, liberal democracies and restorative justice

Chris Cunneen

Introduction

There are overlaps between restorative and transitional justice with their empha-sis on inclusion, non-adversarial approaches, and values such as 'truth, account-ability, reparation, reconciliation and participation' (Clamp and Doak 2012: 341, also Cunneen 2006). This chapter explores the relationship between these justice paradigms specifically in the context of Indigenous peoples in the settler colonial states of Canada, the US, Australia and New Zealand. While these states may, to varying degrees, be associated with restorative justice, they are not normally considered within a transitional justice framework. This chapter argues there is some value in challenging this assumption, and that indeed settler colonial states might be seen as 'transitional societies' in their need to confront and remedy past injustices arising from their own colonial histories (Balint *et al.* 2014; Cunneen 2008).

When Ruti Teitel's (2000) important book *Transitional Justice* was pub-lished, I was struck at the time by some of the unarticulated assumptions that underpinned the ideas behind transitional justice, in particular that transitional processes involved a movement to a Western liberal-democratic ideal. In 'estab-lished democracies', adherence to the rule of law was taken as given. The need for transitional justice was something that was required 'out there' in the wider world of genocidal conflicts, faltering military dictatorships, post-communist and post-fascist regimes and failed states. The subliminal message was clear: liberal democracies represented the ideal of justice, the place to which Others would be *transitioned*, perhaps through a concentrated period of tutelage. There was an assumption that democratic societies had either resolved the conflicts and injustices of their own past, or that these past injustices were inconsequential enough to be safely ignored and buried.

The 1990s and early 2000s was also a period of growing demand within the settler colonial states of the US, Canada, Australia and New Zealand for various forms of reparations, restitution, recognition and compensation. These demands, by both Indigenous peoples and, in the case of the US, African Americans, were for a variety of historical events, policies and practices from lynching to mass murder and genocide, from broken treaties to stolen and abused children, and from fraudulently used trust funds to slavery, forced labour and systematic racial discrimination. They had common elements: the various injustices had their genesis in the experience of being colonised; the colonial states that had profited from various forms of exploitation were today well-established liberal democracies; and, further, the contemporary social, economic and political marginalisation, particularly of Indigenous peoples, was argued to have its derivation in colonial oppression. These arguments for reparations, compensation and the recognition of Indigenous peoples' inherent sovereignty, and the political and legal strategies that were developed to progress these claims, can be seen to largely parallel Teitel's (2000) identification of the elements of transitional justice, that is, criminal, administrative and historical investigations of past wrongdoing, processes for reparations (including acknowledgement and compensation) and transitional constitutionalism.

The same period also saw the inexorable rise of restorative justice. By 2002 restorative justice was established on the United Nations agenda when the Economic and Social Council adopted the *Basic Principles on the Use of Restorative Justice Programs in Criminal Matters*. Restorative justice increasingly appeared to offer a plausible strategy to a range of crime control problems, from local domestic issues like juvenile offending to international crimes and human rights abuses in transitional societies (Cunneen and Hoyle 2010). The South African Truth and Reconciliation Commission (TRC), for example, was identified not as an instrument within a political settlement, but rather as an example of traditional African restorative justice in action. In the West, the TRC was seen as providing reparative and restorative justice for post-apartheid South Africa, but reparative and restorative approaches for Indigenous peoples and formerly enslaved peoples at home was met politically with far more limited acceptance, if any. While the language of restorative justice was not ruled out completely in relation to some historical injustices, for the most part restorative justice was understood in the settler colonial states as a domestic and localised crime control strategy, particularly for juvenile offenders. Further, the idea that there could be a legitimate need for transitional justice processes in the settler colonial states appeared almost perverse. Settler state governments frequently and firmly argued that their existing laws and legal processes were adequate to respond to the claims for the redress of past wrongs, such as the forced removal of Indigenous children and subsequent residential school abuses. One result of this was that Indigenous peoples were forced into decades of slow, expensive and often futile litigation.

In this chapter I propose to argue four general points. First, settler colonialism involved substantial and systematic violence against Indigenous peoples. Second, the various forms of systematic racial discrimination were both historical injustices in their own right, and have led to the profound immiseration of Indigenous peoples within contemporary settler societies. Third, where states have been moved to consider a reparative approach to these injustices, these responses have been limited, begrudging, and only developed after years of adversarial litigation by Indigenous peoples. Finally, past historical injustices have a direct link to perhaps the most pressing human rights issues facing contemporary Indigenous peoples: that is, their contemporary over-representation in settler state criminal justice systems. The final section of this chapter opens up a new way of considering the link between restorative and transitional justice, and their connection to Indigenous concepts of justice, particularly through healing. Indigenous healing approaches have application to both criminal justice, and to broader problems of changing and challenging the effects of colonialism. Indigenous justice, through the concept of healing, has potential to challenge the contemporary problem of high levels of criminalisation *and* provide an important part of the reparative process for historical injustice. Indigenous justice is thus necessarily a decolonising strategy, bridging notions of both restorative and transitional justice.

Liberal democracies and the return of the colonised

In 1955 Aime Cesaire wrote the *Discourse on Colonialism* where he articulated the decivilising effect that colonialism has on the coloniser: 'We must study how colonisation works to *decivilise* the coloniser, to *brutalise* him in the true sense of the word, to degrade him, to awaken him to buried instincts, to covetousness, violence, race hatred, and moral relativism...' (Cesaire 2000: 35). For Cesaire, the rise of fascism in Europe during the course of the twentieth century was not an aberration, but the application to Europe of 'colonialist procedures' that had hitherto only been applied against the colonised (Cesaire 2000: 36). While Cesaire was not specifically concerned with Indigenous peoples in Anglo-settler societies, his argument on the decivilising effects of colonialism nevertheless holds true. There is indeed a blindness to and silencing of the Indigenous past. There is a disavowal of both the ongoing effects of colonisation found in the contemporary marginalisation of colonised peoples, and Indigenous demands for a response to historical injustices. Martin writes that, by neglecting colonialism, 'Anglo-white society [can] re-write history as if these events had never occurred ... what emerges is a sense of triumphalism among the dominant population which is so seamless, pervasive, and pronounced' (Martin 2014: 238).

Settler colonialism requires violence, or its threat, to achieve its outcomes. 'People do not hand over their land, resources, children, and futures without a fight.... In employing the force necessary to accomplish its expansionist goals, a colonising regime institutionalises violence' (Dunbar-Ortiz 2014: 8). Settler colonialism was a process of invasion, settlement and nation-building which fundamentally altered the lives of those original peoples and tribal nations living in the occupied territories. It was a particular type of colonialism where the primary economic objective was securing the land and where sovereignty was asserted usually on the basis of 'discovery'. As Wolfe (2006) has argued, settler colonialism was a form of the colonial experience whereby Indigenous peoples had to be either eliminated, or contained and controlled in order to make land available as private property for the settlers who had come to stay. The substantial loss of land for Indigenous peoples in Australia, New Zealand, Canada and the US contributed directly to the contemporary material conditions of socio-economic disadvantage. Further, many argue that settler colonialism was fundamentally genocidal, either directly through extermination in the violence of the initial colonial onslaught, or later through processes of forced assimilation designed to bring about the destruction of Indigenous societies and cultures (Dunbar-Ortiz 2014; Stannard 1992). By their very presence, Indigenous people threaten assertions of colonial sovereignty and rights to land. As Bignall and Svirksy (2012: 8) argue, colonial sovereignty functions

> as a part of a fundamentally circular and self-validating performance that grounds the legitimacy of settler-state rule on nothing more than the axiomatic negation of Native peoples' authority to determine ... for themselves the normative principles by which they will be governed.

Or, in the words of Watson (2009: 45), the claim of colonial sovereignty is the 'originary violence' at the foundation of settler states that today 'retain a vested interest in maintaining the founding order of things'.

The imposition of colonial systems of law (including criminal, civil, property and constitutional law) was core to the assertion of sovereignty. Colonial law was a tool *both* for legitimising the use of force *and* in imposing a range of cultural, social and institutional values and processes. Importantly, colonial law imposed criminal and penological concepts that were foreign to Indigenous peoples. As Quince (2007: 341) notes in relation to New Zealand, there were fundamental differences between colonial and Indigenous concepts of law: individual responsibility compared to collective responsibility for wrong-doing; the removal of the victim from the judicial process; the concept of the state as the injured party rather than the collective group; the separation of the criminal process from the community; the distinction between civil and criminal law; and differences in the justifications for, and types of, punishment (for example, imprisonment compared to restitution and reparation). Although Indigenous nations differed between themselves in cultural values and law, in general they were often in opposition to the values represented by colonial criminal law.

The justificatory logic of the coloniser's 'civilising mission' rested on foundational beliefs of racial superiority, and provided an overarching basis to governmental law and policy towards Indigenous people in settler states throughout the eighteenth, nineteenth and twentieth centuries. Racism was a precondition for the colonial genocides and the systematic abuse of human rights. The suspension of the rule of law and the use of violence against Indigenous people was contextualised and legitimated within racialised constructions of Indigenous people as inferior human beings. Racialised and gendered constructions of Indigenous people also facilitated legalised and institutionalised discrimination, irrespective of whether they were designed to eradicate, protect or assimilate the 'Native'. Furthermore, legal protections could be suspended and otherwise unlawful behaviour by the colonialists could be ignored in the higher interest of the betterment, protection or control of colonised peoples.

Indigenous law was viewed disparagingly by British colonialists: it became defined as 'customary' law and was regarded as distinctly inferior to colonial law. The delegitimisation of Indigenous law was part of the 'civilising' process designed to bring the superior political and legal institutions of the West to the native, and the imposition of colonial systems of law was integral to the civilising process. The colonising impact of settler law had a number of consequences. First, it meant the continued subjection of Indigenous peoples to legal processes that were systemically racist, built on the denial of the legitimacy of Indigenous law. Second, it led to equating *justice* with the law of the colonising power. Settler colonial states continue to choose whether and which Indigenous laws can be recognised. Yet it is clear that many Indigenous peoples see state criminal justice systems as oppressive, and insist on Indigenous law as a rightful alternative to an imposed system of law (for example, Black 2010; Jackson 1994).

The laws of the coloniser were also always applied ambiguously, anomalously, strategically (Shenhav 2012). Colonised peoples were 'both within the reach of the law and yet outside its protection' (Anghie 1999: 103). Criminal law and penality reflected different cultural understandings of Indigenous people compared to non-Indigenous people. For example, ideas of modernity and the development of modes of punishment that disavowed corporal punishment and public execution were seen as inapplicable to Indigenous people because of their perceived racial and cultural characteristics, and were utilised on Indigenous people long after their demise for non-Indigenous offenders. Thus a genealogy of crime and punishment in settler societies must consider the symbiotic links between punishment and race, or what has been referred to elsewhere as a penal/colonial complex (Cunneen *et al.* 2013).

In summary then, the 'return of the colonised' exposes fundamental questions about the claims of sovereign power, and about the foundations, nature and legitimacy of law in settler societies. While governments and courts can proclaim unitary and indivisible visions of sovereign power in settler societies, Indigenous peoples have long challenged the validity of these claims, and laid bare the foundational violence upon which these claims to sovereignty rest. Such questions go to the heart of transitional justice, particularly in relation to the need for inclusive national-building and constitutional change which respects principles of non-discrimination and self-determination.

Historical injustices and reparations

There were specific historical injustices against Indigenous people that require appropriate state responses in the context of both restorative and transitional justice. I explore two examples in more detail below. However at the outset it is important to note that claims concerning historical injustices and human rights abuses against Indigenous peoples are multi-layered. At the highest level is the claim that particular colonial practices against Indigenous people constituted genocide. Below genocide are claims of mass murder, racism, ethnocide (or cultural genocide), slavery, forced labour, forced removals and relocations, the denial of property rights, and the denial of civil and political rights. The claims of genocide against Indigenous people in the settler colonies of North America and Australia have been controversial (Alvarez 2014; Van Krieken 2004). However there seems little doubt that genocide is the appropriate description for specific colonial laws and practices at particular times and places and targeted at specific tribal nations (Dunbar-Ortiz 2014; Moses 2000). More broadly, the concept of ethnocide or cultural genocide captures the aggressive attempt to 'civilise' Indigenous peoples through a range of state-endorsed laws, policies and practices.

For the purposes of this chapter, I want to concentrate on two specific and long-term historical injustices: first, the forced removal of Indigenous children from their families and communities, and their placement in institutions and residential schools, and, second, government fraud and corruption in relation to the management of Indigenous peoples' finances and property. As I argue further below, in line with transitional justice, both have been the subject of demands for apologies, compensation and reparations by Indigenous people. Both arose directly from government *policies* aimed at regulation and assimilation of Indigenous peoples and also bear a direct responsibility in bringing about the contemporary immiseration of Indigenous people. Further, and this is particularly important to the relationship between restorative justice and criminal justice, both can be seen to directly contribute to crime and victimisation. In other words, they demonstrate the contemporary *criminogenic* effects of colonial policies.

Residential schools and the stolen generations

One process for 'civilising' Indigenous people was through the focus on children: their removal and placement in institutions, their instruction in English and prohibitions on Indigenous languages and cultures. Various policies designed to implement these outcomes were introduced in Australia, Canada and the US. The Canadian residential school system lasted for more than a century from the 1870s to the 1980s. The policy was 'violent in its intention to "kill the Indian" in the child.... The system was, even as a concept, abusive' (Milloy 1999: xv). The policy relied on a church–state partnership, with the Department of Indian Affairs providing the funding, setting the standards and exercising legal control over the children who were wards, and various Christian churches operating a nationwide network of schools (Milloy 1999). Authorities would frequently take children to schools far from their home communities as part of a strategy to alienate them from their families and tribal culture. In 1920, under the *Indian Act*, it became mandatory for every Indian child to attend a residential school and illegal for them to attend any other educational institution. More than 150,000 First Nations, Métis and Inuit children were placed in these schools. There are an estimated 80,000 former students still living (TRCC 2012a: 2).

In the US the main period of the Indian residential school movement was from the 1860s to the 1980s. The number of American Indian children in the boarding schools reached a peak in the 1970s. As in Canada, Indian children were removed from their culture, language and identity. More than 100,000 Native American children were forced to attend these residential schools (Smith 2004: 89). Conditions in the schools were harsh and abusive. Investigations revealed many cases of sexual, physical and mental abuse occurring in these schools, with documented cases of sexual abuse at reservation schools continuing until the end of the 1980s (Smith 2004, 2007).

By the late nineteenth and early twentieth centuries, most states of Australia developed a systematic policy of Aboriginal child removal utilising both church and state-run institutions (NISATSIC 1997: 25–149). Removal policies rested on specific assumptions about race, 'blood' and racial hygiene. Law was fundamental to the categorisation and separation of individuals within racialised boundaries. According to social Darwinist ideas, 'full blood' Aboriginal people were bound to die out because of their inferiority. However, the concern for the state was the apparently rapidly growing population of 'mixed blood' children. It was these children that became the target of intervention. By permanently removing them from their families and communities it was believed that this group of children would, over generations, eventually be biologically absorbed into the non-Indigenous population. Their Aboriginality would be 'bred' out. Eugenicist arguments required a proactive state to manage, cleanse and maintain the 'white' population. It was estimated that about one in ten Indigenous children were removed from their families (NISATSIC 1997).

Long-term outcomes of indigenous child removal

In Canada, the US and Australia, authorities saw the removal process as essential to eradicating Indigenous cultures. The system in all three countries was characterised by 'denial of identity through attacks on language and spiritual beliefs, frequent lack of basic care, the failure to ensure safety of children from physical and sexual abuse, [and] the failure to ensure education' (RCAP 1996: 187). It is important to recognise the contemporary multiple effects of policies of child removal. These have been well documented in various inquiries and reports. In Australia, a 1997 federal inquiry found that basic legal safeguards that protected non-Indigenous families were cast aside when it came to the removal of Indigenous children (NISATSIC 1997). Unlawful practices under the Aboriginal child removal policies included deprivation of liberty, deprivation of parental rights, abuses of power, and breach of guardianship duties. In relation to international human rights, the main obligations imposed on Australia and breached by a policy of forced removals, particularly after 1948, were the prohibitions on racial discrimination and genocide (NISATSIC 1997).

In Australia, twice as many Indigenous people who were removed as children have reported being arrested; and those who were removed have reported significantly poorer health (NISATSIC 1997: 15). Almost one in ten boys and more than one in ten girls reported that they were sexually abused in children's institutions; and three in ten girls reported sexual abuse in foster placements (NISATSIC 1997:

163). There has also been a range of complex trauma-related psychological and psychiatric effects that have been intergenerational. These relate to issues such as poorer educational and employment outcomes, loss of parenting skills, unresolved grief and trauma, violence, depression, mental illness, and other behavioural problems including alcohol and other substance abuse. A large-scale survey in Western Australia of Aboriginal people who had been forcibly removed found that one-third had also had their children removed (NISATSIC 1997: 226). The links between early childhood removal and later juvenile and adult criminalisation were clearly articulated in the reports of the Royal Commission into Aboriginal Deaths in Custody (see, for example, Wootten 1989).

The Manitoba Justice Inquiry found that, in Canada, residential schools laid the foundation for the prevalence of domestic abuse and violence against Aboriginal women and children. Generations of children grew up without a nurturing family life (Hamilton and Sinclair 1991). The Canadian Truth and Reconciliation Commission noted that, 'while some former students had positive experiences at residential schools, many suffered emotional, physical and sexual abuse, and others died while attending these schools. The unresolved trauma suffered by former students has been passed on from generation to generation' (TRCC 2012a: 2). A sense of worthlessness was instilled in many students, which resulted in low self-esteem and self-abuse through high rates of alcoholism, substance abuse, and suicide (TRCC 2012b: 5–8).

In the US, inquiries dating back to 1920s considered the effects of the Indian Residential Schools. In 1928 a Brookings Institution report found the schools were a 'menace to both health and education'. Malnutrition, grossly inadequate care, and routine institutionalisation were all documented (Meriam 1928). The report found that the work by children in the boarding schools would violate child labour laws in most states (Meriam 1928). Forty years later the Kennedy Report (Committee on Labour and Public Welfare 1969) reiterated serious deficiencies: the school environment was 'sterile, impersonal and rigid' with an emphasis on discipline and punishment, teachers and administrators still saw their role as 'civilising the native', and Indian boarding schools were 'emotionally and culturally destructive' (Committee on Labour and Public Welfare 1969: 100–103). The Boarding School Healing Project (BSHP 2008: 3–7) noted both the human rights abuses in these schools and the continuing effects which include increased physical, sexual and emotional violence in Indigenous communities; increased rates of suicide and substance abuse; loss of language and cultural traditions; increased depression and post-traumatic stress disorder; and increased child abuse.

Seemingly indicative of a restorative justice approach, the long-term harm caused by the forced removal of Indigenous children and their treatment in institutions has been recognised through formal apologies in Canada and Australia (for more on formal apologies, see Doak, this volume). However, it is important to recognise that it was only after years of litigation by Indigenous peoples that these settler states were forced into recognition of the harms caused by removals. It was after class actions, and to avoid ongoing litigation, that the Canadian government agreed to the Indian Residential Schools Settlement Agreement[1] in 2006, with the federal government and the churches involved agreeing to pay individual and collective compensation to residential school survivors. A Truth and Reconciliation Commission was also established.

In both the US and Australia, lawsuits filed by Indigenous people for abuse which occurred in institutions have met with only limited success, and there have been no federal reparation packages in either country. In Australia the federal government refused to consider monetary compensation even before the Australian Human Rights Commission inquiry into the 'stolen generations' was completed (NISATSIC 1997). The recommended Reparations Tribunal was never established, and it was to take another ten years, and a change in federal government, before an apology was issued. In the US, Congress apologised to Native Americans for the 'official depredations, ill-conceived policies ... [and] for the many instances of violence, maltreatment and neglect' (Public Law 111–118, sec 8113). However, Congress did not refer explicitly to Indian residential schools, and the apology itself was 'buried in the billions of dollars of spending on new weapons and other items' in the Defense Appropriations Act 2010 (McKinnon 2009). Further, the apology explicitly noted that it was not intended to support any lawsuit claims against the US government.

Government fraud, indigenous trust funds and forced labour

Settler colonial states were involved in vast frauds against Indigenous people who were under their care and protection. These included such matters as missing trust monies, stolen wages, widespread corruption, mismanagement and bribery. The precondition for this fraudulent activity was the extensive state control over Indigenous people that was instituted as part of colonial policies of protection and wardship in the periods after open warfare. State agents clearly engaged in activities which were defined *at the time* as unlawful (such as breaches of fiduciary or guardianship duties), and in many cases were clearly criminal (acts of fraud).

In the US, fraud, corruption, and bribery were endemic to the Bureau of Indian Affairs (BIA). Local BIA officials had discretionary control over money, goods, trading licences, and supplies provided by the Bureau. 'Substantial portions of the supplies and annuity payments owed to the tribes were routinely siphoned off by traders, in cooperation with corrupt federal Indian agents' (Piecuch and Lutz 2011: 384) and by the 1860s the BIA 'was rife with corruption' (Pierpaoli 2011: 101). Such corruption was publicly acknowledged at the time, the *New York Times* describing, in an editorial on 12 December 1868, 'the dishonesty which pervades the whole Bureau'. A decade later systematic corruption by the BIA was again noted. In commenting on an official investigation of the Bureau, the *New York Times* described it as a 'Disgrace to the Nation' with 'frauds in goods and supplies, frauds in receipts and accounts, frauds in the management of Indian trust funds' (8 January 1878). Over the next century, various US House of Representatives and Congressional reports identified the defrauding and gross mismanagement of Indian trust funds arising from the Dawes Act 1887. In the end it was not a commitment to reparations or restorative justice that drove government policy but adversarial litigation on the part of Indigenous people. In 2009 after a protracted 13-year lawsuit involving some 11 separate appellate court decisions, there was a $3.4 billion settlement to a class action relating to the mismanagement of hundreds of thousands of American Indian trust accounts (Riccardi 2009; also Kidd 2006: 28–35). According to President Obama, the settlement cleared 'the way for reconciliation' (CNN Wire Staff 2012). However, the settlement was tempered by the fact that it was far short of the estimated $46 billion that was owed. Elouise Corbell from the Blackfeet Nation who led the class action noted in relation to the settlement, 'time takes a toll, especially on elders living in abject poverty. Many of them died as we continued our struggle to settle this suit. Many more would not survive long to see a financial gain, if we had not settled now' (quoted in Riccardi 2009). The settlement provided for a $1,000 payment to individual trust account holders, plus allocations for land purchases for tribes and educational scholarships.

In Australia, governments put in place legislative and administrative controls over the employment, working conditions and wages of Indigenous workers. These controls allowed for the non-payment of wages to some Aboriginal workers, the underpayment of wages to others, and the diversion of wages into trust and savings accounts. Legislation set minimum wages. For example, in Queensland the Indigenous wage was less than one-eighth the 'white wage'. The regulation of Aboriginal labour amounted to forced labour in some states. Many Aboriginal workers in Western Australia were not paid wages and were remunerated through rations such as flour, tea, tobacco and clothing until as late as the 1960s (Toussaint 1995: 259). The exploitation of Aboriginal workers in the pastoral industry was often considered as 'unpaid slavery' at the time (Haebich 1992: 150). Australia was clearly in contravention of various International Labour Organisation conventions to which it was a party. In 1930 Australia had signed the Forced Labour Convention that generally prohibited forced labour and working for rations, although the practice of working for rations was to last for decades later.

In addition there were negligent, corrupt and dishonest practices that led to the withholding of moneys from Aboriginal wages that had been paid into savings accounts and trust funds. The defrauding of trust funds and savings accounts was widespread. In 2006 the Australian Senate Standing Committee on Legal and Constitutional Affairs [the Standing Committee] released the report of its inquiry into what had become known as Indigenous 'Stolen Wages'. The inquiry itself was the outcome of many years of Indigenous political agitation around the issue (Kidd 2006). The inquiry defined 'wages' broadly to include wages, savings, entitlements, and other monies due to Indigenous people. The Standing Committee found

compelling evidence that governments systematically withheld and mismanaged Indigenous wages and entitlements over decades ... there is evidence of Indigenous people being underpaid or not paid at all for their work. These practices were implemented from the late 19th century onwards and, in some cases, were still in place in the 1980s.

(Standing Committee 2006: 4)

The inquiry found that Indigenous people had been 'seriously disadvantaged by these practices across generations' (Standing Committee 2006: 4), and subsequently this created a cycle of poverty.

Given the depth of contemporary Indigenous detriment across all social, educational, health and economic indicators (SCRGSP 2014), and the active role played by the state in controlling Aboriginal access to wages and entitlements, the outcome of this colonial process was one of *immiseration:* the forcible imposition and maintenance of structural conditions of extreme poverty. Some of the long-term impacts are captured below:

Aboriginal people were subject to a disabling system that denied them proper wages, protection from exploitation and abuse, proper living conditions, and adequate education and training. So while other Australians were able to build financial security and an economic future for their families, Aboriginal workers were hindered by these controls. Aboriginal poverty ... today is a direct consequence of this discriminatory treatment.

(Standing Committee 2006: 68)

The elephant in the room

The above discussion on residential schools and various forms of fraud and misappropriation of Indigenous finances raises several issues. First, it is important note that where there have been moves towards a more restorative and reparative approach, such as in Canada, this has only occurred after a sustained period of adversarial litigation. Second, where there have been federal inquiries which have recommended a reparations approach to historical injustices such as the 'Stolen Generations' inquiry in Australia (NISATSIC 1997), these have been ignored by government particularly in relation to compensation (Cunneen 2006: 363–365). Third, when governments have moved to provide some monetary compensation, these have often been seen to be woefully inadequate, either because of restricted eligibility criteria, small compensation sums compared to the harms suffered, or because of a 'lottery effect' depending on which state or territory the effected person resided. For example, in Australia compensation schemes for stolen wages and trust funds varied from $2,000, to $4,000 and $25,000 depending on eligibility criteria and whether the person fell within state-based schemes in Western Australia, Queensland or New South Wales. In addition, Indigenous people living outside of those state jurisdictions received no compensation at all (Behrendt *et al.* 2009: 59–64). Despite Indigenous demands, these responses have fallen far short of what might be expected in any comprehensive restorative justice approach.

It is important to note that in specific contexts Indigenous people may be reluctant to have their claims for compensation framed within a restricted restorative justice paradigm. Understanding the reasons for this reluctance sheds light on the reason why Indigenous people show some scepticism towards narrowly defined approaches to restorative justice.

For example, in the US the BSHP (2008), while certainly not discounting a reparations approach, has noted potential limitations to such a strategy in relation to the survivors of American Indian boarding schools. The limitations include the commodification of harm that essentially relegates colonialism to a problem of the past. Compensation forces a monetary value on past harms, which by its nature implies that the harms are only a matter of the past. Thus colonialism becomes a process relegated to 'history', rather than an ongoing structural relationship existing through a range of manifestations (for example, through high levels of criminalisation and contemporary child welfare removals). Related to the above point is that a reparations process may fail to address structural oppression (see also Balint *et al.* 2014). The BSHP notes that

> It may be possible that a reparations struggle can be a strategy for bringing attention to the underlying structures and ideologies that give rise to specific human rights violations, but they can also normalize these structures and ideologies by positioning specific atrocities as an exception to the system rather than as an integral part of systemic oppression.
>
> (BSHP 2008: 12)

These structural conditions may include capitalist processes that entrench Indigenous poverty and disadvantage. If structural problems are not addressed, Indigenous people receiving reparations may not have the means to change their impoverished conditions: 'cash payments do not generally result in poor people becoming less poor' (BSHP 2008: 12).

More fundamentally, reparations do not challenge the colonial relationship between settler states and Indigenous people: settler state sovereignty can remain unaffected by a reparations process because the broader issue of Indigenous sovereignty is left unaddressed. The inviolability of settler state sovereignty is maintained and, as a result, the colonial relationship between Indigenous people and settler states is further solidified (BSHP 2008: 11 see also Balint *et al.* 2014: 201). According to Corntassel and Holder (2008), reconciliation and truth commission mechanisms have failed Indigenous people because states have separated these processes from considerations of Indigenous sovereignty and self-determination. They note that, 'If apologies and truth commissions cannot effectively address historic and ongoing injustices committed against Indigenous peoples, then they are fundamentally flawed mechanisms for transforming intergroup relations' (Corntassel and Holder 2008: 466). This linking of the contemporary oppression of Indigenous peoples with the colonial past is a fundamental part of Corntassel and Holder's argument, with Indigenous people 'disproportionately the target of state violence as well as neoliberal reforms'

(2008: 466). The indivisibility between the colonial past and the colonial present is also a core argument of this chapter. The problem is that restorative approaches to historical injustices can often fail to recognise this indivisibility between past and present. Colonialism can remain the 'elephant in the room': its contemporary manifestations remain unseen, unacknowledged and unaddressed.

Rethinking the relationship between restorative justice and indigenous justice

I have argued in this chapter that the historical injustices of settler colonialism are usually not considered within the framework of transitional justice and, more specifically, that restorative and reparative justice has had a very mixed history in relation to responding to the multiple harms of colonialism. Another way of thinking about restorative justice, however, is in the context of contemporary settler society criminal justice systems. In a nutshell, the argument I propose is that the contemporary over-representation of Indigenous people in criminal justice systems is itself a product of the effects of colonialism, and that restorative justice conceptualised within a context of Indigenous self-determination may offer a pathway out of the mass criminalisation and incarceration of Indigenous peoples in settler societies (see, for example, Cunneen 2014a). Restorative justice, conceived as *Indigenous justice*, may be both a response to historical injustices by recognising the criminogenic effects of colonialism, as well as a more effective way of responding to contemporary criminal justice problems. I return to how we might conceptualise restorative justice as Indigenous justice in more detail below. First though it is important to acknowledge the contemporary criminogenic effects of colonialism, and the current limitations of restorative justice in settler societies in responding to the problem of criminalisation.

Colonialism and criminalisation

The loss of an economic foundation to land and resources created the social and economic disadvantage among the colonised that we see today. At a general level, settler colonialism is criminogenic to the extent that it actively produces dispossession, marginalisation and cultural dislocation. However, this marginalisation has been exacerbated by specific colonial policies and practices including, among others, the forced removal of Indigenous children from their families and communities, and government controls over Indigenous resources and finances. Over-crowded housing, low incomes, chronic health issues, substance abuse, lower life expectancies, poor educational outcomes, child protection concerns, the psychological and social effects of racism and discrimination – precisely the factors known to be associated with higher levels of violence and offending – can be related in various degrees to the policies of settler colonialism.

As I have argued in this chapter, the relationship between Indigenous people and the colonial settler states exhibits the features of a transitional setting where basic questions of justice, participation, legitimacy and human rights need to be addressed. And these basic questions of justice are particularly revealed in the way criminal justice systems operate in relation to Indigenous people. When the Canadian Royal Commission On Aboriginal Peoples reported in 1996 on criminal justice issues, they introduced their findings by making two core points. First, what Aboriginal people experience is not justice but the injustice of a system that is alien and oppressive. Second, Aboriginal people think of justice differently, reflecting

> distinctive Aboriginal world views and in particular a holistic understanding of peoples' relationships and responsibilities to each other and to their material and spiritual world.... Aboriginal conceptions of justice must be understood as part of the fabric of social and political life rather than as a distinct, formal legal process.
>
> (RCAP 1996: 3)

These two points capture succinctly Indigenous demands for the recognition of their distinct Indigenous status with all that entails: political rights to self-determination and inherent sovereignty, and cultural and social rights to practise and maintain their distinct cultures free from discrimination.

The limitations of existing restorative justice approaches in settler societies

The question arises then as to whether we can think of restorative justice, conceived as Indigenous justice, as offering a pathway forward. I argue that we can, but with a number of important caveats. In the first instance, we need a far more radical approach than currently found in state-sponsored restorative justice schemes. As I have argued elsewhere (Cunneen 2012), the limitation for Indigenous people of current restorative justice practice arises in part because of the broader political conditions under which it emerged. Restorative justice developed in settler states at a time of mass imprisonment – when imprisonment rates were progressively reaching historic highs. The rise of restorative justice also occurred concurrent with research identifying that higher imprisonment rates are associated with societies that have higher levels of inequality (Wilkinson and Pickett 2009) and a lesser commitment to social democratic and inclusionary values (Lacey 2008). Among Western democracies, it is those who have most strongly adopted neoliberalism that have the highest imprisonment rates and these include the settler states of the US, Canada, Australia and New Zealand.

Relatedly, *some* of the values associated with restorative justice can be consonant with more punitive law-and-order politics, such as free will, individual responsibility, accountability and a narrowly defined, individualised sense of civic obligation. The promotion of a free-market individualism can downplay the need for social and structural responses to crime, such as reducing unemployment rates, improving educational outcomes, increasing wages, ensuring proper welfare support, and improving housing and urban conditions (Brown 2009). In this context it is perhaps not surprising that state-sponsored restorative justice approaches have not had a great benefit for Indigenous people, despite the claim often made that they are based on Indigenous approaches to justice (Cunneen and Hoyle 2010). Indeed, in the area of juvenile justice, Indigenous over-representation has deepened since the introduction restorative justice approaches (Cunneen 2014b: 13).

As McCaslin and Breton (2008) articulate it, the fundamental problem with restorative justice from an Indigenous perspective is that colonialism remains as an invisible backdrop to the harms which restorative justice seeks to remedy. While there might be some temporary fixes to problems, there is no broader or deeper decolonising vision that would tackle the structures that lead to social harms in the first place. For McCaslin and Breton (2008: 518), 'decolonization is the only hope, but as yet, it is not on the restorative justice radar'.

An alternative vision

It is possible however to see an alternative vision of restorative justice that can resonate with Indigenous justice. Clamp (2014) identifies four core values necessary for restorative justice in transitional settings: engagement, empowerment, reintegration and transformation. The Indigenous approach to *healing* is aligned with these values and is an integral part of Indigenous justice. As a political process of individual and collective change, it is somewhat akin to the Friereian notion of *conscientisation*. It involves shifting the epistemological priority given to Western understandings of crime and control. It begins from a disbelief in the functionality and the legitimacy of state-centred institutional responses: criminalisation and incarceration are seen as destructive of family, community and culture; cause further social disintegration; and do not change the behaviour of offenders. A focus on healing relies on inter-relationality rather than individualism, and the importance of identity and culture in the process of decolonisation. As Archibald notes:

> The experience of being colonised involves loss – of culture, language, land, resources, political autonomy, religious freedom, and, often, personal autonomy. These losses may have a direct relationship to poor health, social and economic status of Indigenous people. Understanding the need for personal and collective healing from this perspective points to a way of healing, one that combines the socio-political work involved in decolonization with the more personal therapeutic healing journey.
>
> (Archibald 2006: 49)

Indigenous healing approaches start with the collective experience, with the collective harms and outcomes of colonisation, and draw strength from Indigenous culture. Inevitably, that involves an understanding of the collective harms and outcomes of colonisation, the loss of lands, the disruptions of culture, the changing of traditional roles of men and women, the collective loss and sorrow of the removal of children and relocation of communities. Wanganeen (2008) discusses seven phases to cultural healing which include acknowledgement of ancestral losses, contemporary grief and loss (such as child removal) and future strength through a contemporised traditional culture.

Indigenous healing processes have developed in many of the settler states and focus on a number of different areas. These include residential school survivors, members of the Stolen Generations, people involved in family violence, child protection, alcohol and other drug addictions, and those in various stages of the criminal justice system (for a variety of specific examples, see Archibald 2006: 39–48; ATSISJC 2008: 167–176). At a broader level, these approaches cover three pillars: reclaiming history, cultural interventions and therapeutic healing (ATSISJC 2008: 167). Reclaiming history allows an understanding of the past and present impacts of colonialism. 'Healing from historic trauma brings history and culture together with personal healing on a journey that is both individual and collective in nature' (Archibald 2006: 26). Cultural interventions are focused on recovering and reconnecting with language, culture and ceremony. However,

> culture isn't limited to traditions and the past, it is a living breathing thing. These programs foster identity and pride, dispelling the negative stereotypes that many hold about Indigenous peoples. [By providing] a different way of understanding … they are actively creating a new culture of pride and possibilities.
>
> (ATSISJC 2008: 174)

The third pillar is therapeutic healing. These might include individual counselling, men's and women's groups, healing circles and traditional ceremonies. They may involve traditional Indigenous counsellors, healers and medicine people, as well as modified or adapted western approaches (see for example, Archibald 2006: 29–30 on developments in postcolonial psychology).

Healing is not simply about addressing individualised offending behaviour. It is fundamentally about addressing trauma. Three types of trauma have been identified: situational trauma caused by discrete events (for example, the contemporary child welfare removal of children); cumulative trauma caused by pervasive distress over time (for example, the long term effects of racism); and inter-generational trauma which is passed down from one generation to another (for example, the forced relocation of communities, the denigration of Indigenous cultures) (ASTISJC 2008: 153–154). The process of healing is inextricably linked to Indigenous spirituality and culture and to repairing the effects of trauma in its various manifestations (ASTISJC 2008: 152).

The importance of a healing approach is that individual harms and wrongs are placed within a collective context. On the one hand, offenders are dealt with as individuals responsible for their own actions; their pain and the forces that propel them to harmful behaviour towards themselves and others are confronted. However, they are *understood* within a collective context of the experience of

Indigenous peoples in a non-indigenous society. What this means in a practical context is that there is a focus on factors such as grief, depression, spiritual healing, loss of culture and educational deficits and a recognition that these needs must be addressed because they are directly related to criminal offending (Gilbert and Wilson 2009: 4). For example, grief and loss, which is experienced by Indigenous people in settler societies at a much higher frequency and much younger age than non-Indigenous people, have been identified as a core issue that healing programs can and need to address (Gilbert and Wilson 2009: 4). Overall the explanatory context for individual behaviour is within the collective experiences of the Indigenous peoples. In this sense Indigenous healing approaches are unique because they seek individual change within a collective context.

Indigenous healing approaches are also Indigenous controlled and are consistent with the principle of Indigenous self-determination. One of the consequences of this is the tension that is created between Indigenous approaches and state-controlled interventions. In the current period we see an institutional emphasis on various behavioural modification programmes put in place as a result of the identification of narrowly defined individualised 'deficits'. Reviewing the international literature on the Indigenous healing movement, Lane *et al.* (2002: 23) highlight the ways in which the many inter-connected outcomes of Indigenous healing have led to increased emphasis upon the need for a transformation of existing mainstream approaches. As McCaslin and Breton (2008: 518) explain, 'coloniser programming' in the criminal justice system is permeated by a view of Indigenous peoples as the problem and the colonisers as the solution. Unless colonialism is brought 'front and centre and named as the root cause' of Indigenous overrepresentation in the criminal justice system, Indigenous peoples will continue to be oppressed through processes of state criminalisation. Governments favour those approaches that it can closely administer, control and monitor – and these tend to be programmes reliant on expert interventions that further privilege dominant definitions of crime and disavow the voices of Indigenous peoples. They also tend to be programmes that are 'off-the-shelf' and are not programmes that are organic to Indigenous people and their communities, or their needs and experiences. While Indigenous people are most likely to be the subjects of these programmes as offenders, they are far less likely to be in control of defining or delivering these professionalised interventions (Cunneen 2014a: 399–401).

In summary, the concept of healing is a fundamental part of Indigenous concepts of justice. Indigenous healing processes have been developed in many of the settler states and they cover a range issues as outlined above. Healing is focused on addressing trauma, for both individual and collective harms. They are based on principles of Indigenous control and self-determination.

Conclusion

As argued throughout this chapter, there are parallels between transitional justice and Indigenous demands for reparations and compensation for past wrongs, and for constitutional developments that are inclusive of contemporary Indigenous claims for recognition of their rights as peoples. In this sense, settler states can be seen as societies in need of some form of transitional and restorative justice. However, it has been also argued that state-defined restorative justice has failed Indigenous people both as a reparative process for past wrongs, and as a process within criminal justice systems responding to contemporary harms. A key reason for both failures has been the inability to confront the structural conditions of colonialism. However, I do not believe this has to be the case. Restorative justice has a role to play where it is conceived as Indigenous justice, where Indigenous law, culture and politics define the values, processes and practices of restorative justice.

Restorative justice thus conceived can play a fundamental part in the broader struggle of decolonisation, that is, the process towards remedying both past and contemporary injustices. Settler states might then begin the transitional process of resolving their own conflicts and injustices. I do not suggest that this is necessarily an easy task. As McCaslin and Breton (2008: 511) state, 'Healing our communities from the onslaught of imperialism and colonisation in every form – economic, political, social, educational, emotional, religious, cultural, cognitive – is a complex, sometimes confusing, and often over-whelming process'. However, opening up a process of *transitional decolonisation* built on an Indigenous-defined restorative justice would be a welcome start.

Note

1 A $2 billion settlement to redress a reported $11 billion in lawsuits (BSHP 2008: 31).

References

Alvarez, A. (2014) *Native America and the Question of Genocide*, Lanham, MD: Rowman and Littlefield.

Anghie, A. (1999) 'Francisco de Vittoria and the colonial origins of international law', in P. Fitzpatrick and E. Darian-Smith (eds) *Laws of the Postcolonial*, Ann Arbor, MI: University of Michigan Press.

Archibald, L. (2006) *Decolonization and Healing: Indigenous Experiences in the United States, New Zealand, Australia and Greenland*, Ottawa: Aboriginal Healing Foundation.

ATSISJC (Aboriginal and Torres Strait Islander Social Justice Commissioner) (2008) *Social Justice Report 2008*, Sydney: Australian Human Rights Commission.

Balint, J., Evans, J. and McMillan, N. (2014) 'Rethinking Transitional Justice, Redressing Indigenous Harm: A new conceptual approach', *The International Journal of Transitional Justice*, 8: 194–216.

Behrendt, L., Cunneen, C. and Libesman, T. (2009) *Indigenous Legal Relations in Australia*, Melbourne: Oxford University Press.

Bignall, S. and Svirksy, M. (2012) 'Introduction: Agamben and colonialism' in M. Svirksy and S. Bignall (eds) *Agamben and Colonialism*, Edinburgh: Edinburgh University Press.

Black, C. (2010) *The Land is the Source of the Law: A dialogic encounter with an Indigenous jurisprudence*, London: Routledge-Cavendish.

Brown, D. (2009) 'Searching for a Social Democratic Narrative in Criminal Justice', *Current Issues in Criminal Justice*, 20(3): 453–6.

BSHP (Boarding School Healing Project) (2008) *Reparations and American Indian Boarding Schools: A critical appraisal*, www.boardingschoolhealingproject.org/files/A_Critical_Appraisal_of_Reparations_final.pdf.

Cesaire, A. (2000) [1955] *Discourse on Colonialism*, New York: Monthly Review Press.

Clamp, K. (2014) *Restorative Justice in Transition*, Milton Park: Routledge.

Clamp, K. and Doak, J. (2012) 'More than Words: Restorative justice concepts in transitional settings', *International Criminal Law Review*, 12: 339–360.

CNN Wire Staff (2012) 'US Finalizes $3.4 billion settlement with American Indians', CNN, http://edition.cnn.com/2012/11/26/politics/american-indian-settlment/.

Committee on Labour and Public Welfare, United States Senate (1969) *Indian Education: A national tragedy – a national challenge*, Washington, DC: US Government Printing Office.

Corntassel, J. and Holder, C. (2008) 'Who's Sorry Now? Government Apologies, Truth Commissions, and Indigenous Self-Determination in Australia, Canada, Guatemala and Peru', *Human Rights Review*, 9: 465–489.

Cunneen, C. (2006) 'Exploring the relationship between reparations, the gross violations of human rights, and restorative justice' in D. Sullivan and L. Tift (eds) *The Handbook of Restorative Justice. Global Perspectives*, New York: Routledge.

Cunneen, C. (2008) 'State crime, the colonial question and Indigenous peoples' in A. Smuelers and R. Haveman (eds) (2008) *Supranational Criminology: Towards a criminology of international crimes*, Antwerp: Intersentia Press.

Cunneen, C. (2012) 'Restorative justice, globalization and the logic of empire', in J. McCulloch, and S. Pickering (eds) *Borders and Transnational Crime: Pre-crime, mobility and serious harm in an age of globalization*, London: Palgrave Macmillan.

Cunneen, C. (2014a) 'Colonial processes, Indigenous peoples, and criminal justice systems', in T. Bucerius and M. Tonry (eds) *The Oxford Handbook of Ethnicity, Crime, and Immigration*, Oxford: Oxford University Press.

Cunneen, C. (2014b) 'Youth justice in Australia', in M. Tonry (ed.) *Criminology and Criminal Justice, Oxford Handbooks Online*, Oxford University Press, New York. http://dx.doi.org/10.1093/oxfordhb/9780199935383.013.62.

Cunneen, C. and Hoyle, C. (2010) *Debating Restorative Justice*, Hart Publishing: Oxford.

Cunneen, C., Baldry, E., Brown, D., Brown, M., Schwartz, M. and Steel, A. (2013) *Penal Culture and Hyperincarceration*, Farnham, UK: Ashgate.

Dunbar-Ortiz, R. (2014) *An Indigenous Peoples' History of the United States*, Boston: Beacon Press.

Gilbert, R. and Wilson, A. (2009) *Staying Strong on the Outside: Improving the post release experience of Indigenous young adults*, Brief No 4, Indigenous Justice Clearinghouse. www.indigenousjustice.gov.au/briefs/brief004.pdf.

Haebich, A. (1992) *For Their Own Good: Aborigines and Government in the South West of Western Australia 1900–1940*, Perth: University of Western Australia Press.

Hamilton, A. and Sinclair, M. (1991) *Report of the Aboriginal Justice Inquiry of Manitoba: The justice system and Aboriginal people*, Vol 1. www.ajic.mb.ca/volumeI/toc.html.

Jackson, M. (1994) 'Changing Realities: Unchanging truths'. *Australian Journal of Law and Society*, 115(10): 115–129.

Kidd, R. (2006) *Trustees on Trial: Recovering the stolen wages*, Canberra: Aboriginal Studies Press.

Lacey, N. (2008) *The Prisoners' Dilemma: Political economy and punishment in contemporary democracies – the Hamlyn lectures*, Cambridge: Cambridge University Press.

Lane, P. Jr, Bopp, M., Bopp, J. and Norris, J. (2002) *Mapping the Healing Journey: Final report of a First Nation research project on healing in Canadian Aboriginal communities*, Ontario: Aboriginal Corrections Policy Unit.

Martin, F. A. (2014) 'The Coverage of American Indians and Alaskan Natives in Criminal Justice and Criminology Introductory Textbooks', *Critical Criminology*, 22: 237–256.

McCaslin, W. D. and Breton, D. C. (2008) 'Justice as healing: going outside the colonisers' cage', in N. Denzin, Y. Lincoln and L. T. Smith (eds) *Handbook of Critical and Indigenous Methodologies*, London: Sage Publications.

McKinnon, A. D. (2009) 'U.S. Offers an Apology to Native Americans', *The Wall Street Journal*, 22 December 2009. http://blogs.wsj.com/washwire/2009/12/22/us-offers-an-official-apology-to-native-americans/.

Meriam, L. (1928) *The Problem of Indian Administration*, Baltimore: The Johns Hopkins Press. Extracts available: www.npr.org/templates/story/story.php?storyId=16516865.

Milloy, J. (1999) *A National Crime. The Canadian Government and the Residential School System 1879 to 1986*. Winnipeg: The University of Manitoba Press.

Moses, D. (2000) 'An Antipodean Genocide? The Origins of the Genocidal Moment in the Colonisation of Australia', *Journal of Genocide Research*, 2(1): 89–106.

NISATSIC (National Inquiry into the Separation of Aboriginal and Torres Strait Islander Children from Their Families) (1997) *Bringing Them Home*, Sydney: Human Rights and Equal Opportunity Commission.

Piecuch, J. and Lutz, J. (2011) 'Indian ring scandal', in S. C. Tucker (ed.) *The Encyclopaedia of North American Indian Wars, 1607–1890. A Political, Social and Military History*, Santa Barbara, CA: ABC-CLIO.

Pierpaoli, P. G. (2011) 'Bureau of Indian Affairs', in S. C. Tucker (ed.) *The Encyclopaedia of North American Indian Wars, 1607–1890. A Political, Social and Military History*, Santa Barbara, CA: ABC-CLIO.

Quince, K. (2007) 'Maori and the criminal justice system in New Zealand', in J. Tolmie and W. Brookbanks (eds) *The New Zealand Criminal Justice System*, Auckland: Lexis Nexis.

RCAP (Royal Commission On Aboriginal Peoples) (1996) *Bridging the Cultural Divide: A report on Aboriginal people and criminal justice in Canada*, Ottawa: Canada Communications Group.

Riccardi, L. (2009) 'U.S. Settles Indian Trust Account Lawsuit', *Los Angeles Times*, 9 December 2009. http://articles.latimes.com/2009/dec/09/nation/la-na-indian-settlement9-2009dec09.

SCRGSP (Steering Committee for the Review of Government Service Provision) (2014) *Overcoming Indigenous Disadvantage: Key Indicators 2014*, Canberra: Productivity Commission.

Senate Standing Committee on Legal and Constitutional Affairs (2006) *Unfinished Business: Indigenous stolen Wages*, Canberra: Commonwealth of Australia.

Shenhav, Y. (2012) 'Imperialism, exceptionalism and the contemporary world', in M. Svirsky and S. Bignall (eds) *Agamben and Colonialism*, Edinburgh: Edinburgh University Press.

Smith, A. (2004) 'Boarding School Abuses, Human Rights, and Reparations', *Social Justice*, 31(4): 89–102.

Smith, A. (2007) *Soul Wound: The legacy of Native American schools*, Amnesty International, www.amnestyusa.org/node/87342.

Stannard, D. (1992) *American Holocaust*, New York: Oxford University Press.

Teitel, R. (2000) *Transitional Justice*, New York: Oxford University Press.

Toussaint, S. (1995) 'Western Australia', in A. McGrath (ed.), *Contested Ground*, St Leonards: Allen and Unwin.

TRCC (Truth and Reconciliation Commission of Canada) (2012a) *Backgrounder*, Winnipeg: Truth and Reconciliation Commission of Canada.

TRCC (Truth and Reconciliation Commission of Canada) (2012b) *Interim Report*, Winnipeg: Truth and Reconciliation Commission of Canada.

Van Krieken, R. (2004) 'Rethinking Cultural Genocide: Aboriginal child removal and settler–colonial state formation', *Oceania*, 75(2): 125–151.

Wanganeen, R. (2008) 'A loss and grief model in practice', in A. Day, M. Nakata and K. Howells (eds) *Anger and Indigenous Men*, Leichhardt, Australia: Federation Press.

Watson, I. (2009) 'In the Northern Territory Intervention: What is saved or rescued and at what cost?', *Cultural Studies Review*, 15(2): 45–60.

Wilkinson, R. and Pickett, K. (2009) *The Spirit Level*, New York: Bloomsbury Press.

Wolfe, P. (2006) 'Settler Colonialism and the Elimination of the Native', *Journal of Genocide Research*, 8(4): 387–409.

Wootten, H. (1989) *Report of the Inquiry into the Death of Malcolm Charles Smith*, Royal Commission into Aboriginal Deaths in Custody, Canberra: Australian Government.

12 Towards a transformative vision of restorative justice as a response to mass victimisation

Some concluding thoughts

Kerry Clamp

Introduction

A plurality of justice approaches for dealing with international crimes or mass victimisation is evident within the transitional justice landscape. The importance of this is explained by Roht-Arriaza (2006: 8) as 'only by interweaving, sequencing and accommodating multiple pathways to justice could some kind of larger justice in fact emerge'. The complex milieu in which mass victimisation occurs means that creative responses need to be devised. Even though current practice is perhaps not as progressive as some would hope, the rich diversity of institutions and mechanisms has to be acknowledged. Indeed, while the contributors within this collection might call for a quite radical reframing of our justice responses to human rights abuses carried out during periods of undemocratic rule, there is an acknowledgement that complementary justice practices are needed to respond to the complex and varied needs of those most affected by the conflict.

This collection has focused on one element of this diverse justice landscape, namely on the contribution of restorative justice in responding to mass victimisation/collective violence. While there is a burgeoning literature on restorative justice theory and praxis in democratic settings, restorative scholars have been slow to comment on the integration of restorative justice into the transitional justice discourse. As such, this collection sought to pull together a number of contributors who are intimately familiar with the restorative justice literature to shine a light on the understandings and application of restorative justice within transitional settings and how this may or may not align with restorative justice theory. Authors have explored restorative justice as a *form* of truth-telling (Braithwaite, this volume, Chapter 10), accountability (Bueno *et al.* this volume, Chapter 3), apology and reparation (Doak, this volume, Chapter 5), and reconciliation (Lambourne, this volume, Chapter 4); and as a *mechanism* through which to devolve power down to communities (Chapman and Campbell, this volume, Chapter 7) to increase the participation of victims (Nickson, this volume, Chapter 6), to transform long-standing colonial abuses (Cunneen, this volume, Chapter 11) to produce meaningful outcomes for victims and communities (Findlay, this volume, Chapter 9), and to achieve collective responsibility (Harbin and Llewllyn, this volume, Chapter 8).

What emerges is further insight into the conceptual, theoretical and practical applications of restorative justice in transitional settings and the key themes that emerge when restorative justice and transitional justice interact.

In particular, contributors have demonstrated how current conceptions of restorative justice within the transitional justice landscape are under-developed and have thus resulted in limited outcomes for victims, offenders and/or communities that perhaps do not align with what restorative justice scholars would expect. Contributors have also demonstrated how transformative restorative justice can be if we embrace broader conceptions of restorative justice and think more creatively about the manner in which we design and deliver justice. Proposals have included: harnessing local institutions to allow stakeholders – victims, offenders and communities – to feed into macro-level processes (Clamp, Chapter 2 and Nickson, Chapter 6); paying attention to notions of restorative accountability which prioritise the restoration of the victim and reintegration of offenders (Bueno *et al.* Chapter 3); reconceiving restorative justice as Indigenous justice (Cunneen, Chapter 11 and Lambourne, Chapter 4); expanding notions of stakeholders to include the state and to further plot what role the state may play in restorative justice processes (Doak, Chapter 5); devolving power down to communities (Chapman and Campbell, Chapter 7); calling for an increased focus on collective responsibility as opposed to individual responsibility (Findlay, Chapter 9 and Harbin and Llewellyn, Chapter 8); and finally, increasing the time and space for victims to share their experiences through living memorials (Braithwaite, Chapter 10).

In this final chapter, the key arguments of each of the contributors will not be repeated at length. Rather, space will be devoted to discussing, in more detail, some of the overarching themes that are present within the collection. In drawing these themes together, a call is made for 'lengthening' the restorative justice lens to move beyond the confines of current praxis. It is important not only to respond to the past and what individuals have done, but also to create tangible opportunities to break down barriers between former adversaries and to create a peaceful future.

Lengthening the restorative justice lens

Given that a key consequence of protracted periods of conflict is the destruction of social capital, it is important that strategies are devised to respond to this deficit. Putnam defines social capital as the 'features of social organisation, such as trust, norms, and networks that can improve the efficiency of society by facilitating coordinated actions' (1993: 167). The important role that restorative justice can play in harnessing social capital can be illustrated in drawing on his conceptions of 'bonding social capital' (the building of bonds and networks *within* groups) and 'bridging social capital' (the building of bonds and networks *across* groups). Northern Ireland provides a good example whereby bonding social capital is strong and bridging social capital is weak. During the conflict, fighting between republicans and loyalists resulted in a withdrawal from public spaces and reduced contact between individuals from those communities (Steenkamp 2009). Given that the police were regarded with suspicion and actively targeted, this left a policing vacuum resulting in the use of paramilitaries to deal with anti-social and criminal behaviour impacting on community life and to serve as protectors against attack from the other community (see further Chapman and Campbell, this volume, Chapter 7; Clamp 2010). As such, bonding social capital can be viewed as a political strategy in this context to respond to inequality by situating the community in opposition to the state and/or another community (Leonard 2004; Steenkamp 2009).

Although there have been significant strides in reducing conflict post-transition, ten-metre high peace walls continue to separate communities and sectarian violence still occurs. What is missing is the development of bridging social capital, a crucial requirement for community development and the improvement of inter-ethnic relations post-transition (Steenkamp 2009). Initiatives have been developed to deal with conflict *within* those communities, but there has been a lack of engagement *between* those communities resulting in ongoing suspicion and hatred (also see Manktelow 2007). As Putnam (2000: 23) states, while bonding social capital is important for reinforcing a particular self-image and for 'getting by', bridging social capital is essential for establishing 'broader identities and reciprocity' thus breaking down barriers and allowing people to move forward together despite differences. A lack of bridging capital within transitional settings thus results in a 'negative peace' (i.e. the absence of violence) with a continued threat that violence could reignite at any moment.

At the heart of restorative justice is the opportunity that it provides for those directly affected, and those with the greatest stake in the outcome, to engage with one another, thus increasing opportunities to address the lack of bridging capital outlined above. Within a criminal justice setting, this might entail the victim receiving some sort of recompense for any harm suffered and devising strategies to address the underlying causes of behaviour. The time given to the discussion of thoughts, experience and feelings about the incident during this process may lead to an increased understanding of each stakeholder's circumstance and a breaking down of stereotypes (see, for example, Shapland *et al.* 2011). Within transitional settings, if we abide by the spirit of restorative justice, a process *should* involve an opportunity for adversaries (this can be between communities or between communities and state agencies, such as the police) to engage with each other on points of difference in a non-violent way. As Doak (this volume, Chapter 5) highlights, 'increased opportunities for encounter may assist the transition process in the longer term by humanising the "other", and thus challenge the pre-existing prejudices and collective stereotyping'.

However, restorative justice in transitional settings is often reduced to a process that includes 'victims' and 'offenders' or to a particular outcome such as 'reparation' or 'an apology', thus losing its problem-solving quality that is so necessary for breaking down stereotypes. In many respects, the use of labels and processes to generate 'solutions' appeals to our human nature, our desire for accomplishment, so that we can see that something has been done. However, as Christie warns us:

> it is important not to presuppose that conflict ought to *be solved.* The quest for solution is a puritan, ethnocentric conception.... Conflicts might be solved, but they might also be lived with.... Maybe participation is more important than solutions.
>
> (1982: 92–93, italics original)

While Christie was not commenting on transitional settings, learning to live with and accept difference is perhaps even more pressing where communities have regarded each other with suspicion for significant periods of time and committed atrocities against one another (Clamp 2014). Adopting such a stance would result in a 'lengthening' of the restorative justice lens whereby one incident and one meeting is traded for discussions of broader experiences over a significantly longer period of time, contributing to the rebuilding of trust between communities by creating the space where empathy may develop (Fletcher and Weinstein 2002). As Braithwaite (this volume, Chapter 10) notes: 'Lengthening justice means making transitional justice permanent!' In pursuing such an agenda, a case has been made within the collection for restorative justice to be characterised by three elements: first, restorative justice should be inclusive; second, restorative justice should be culturally appropriate; and finally, restorative justice should be forward looking.

Restorative justice should be inclusive

A common theme within the chapters in this collection is the charge that transitional justice is driven by elites (see Clamp, this volume, Chapter 2; Doak, this volume, Chapter 5; Nickson, this volume, Chapter 6; Braithwaite, this volume, Chapter 10). Those who are familiar with the restorative justice literature will be aware that part of the reason for looking for alternatives to criminal justice was a desire to return conflict back to its rightful owners by *de*professionalising justice. While there have been attempts by transitional justice architects to allow this to happen, they have fallen short of the type of engagement envisioned by a restorative justice framework and led to disappointment among victims. For example, Nickson (this volume, Chapter 6), argues that, despite the International Criminal Court being touted as 'restorative' because of increased opportunities for victim to participate, elites: (1) determine the nature and scope of victim involvement; (2) evaluate and determine who may access participation and the spaces where participation is performed; and (3) mediate and control the participation of victims, thus elevating the requirements of legal justice above those of the interests of victims. This leads him to argue that, rather than creating an opportunity for victims to participate in international criminal justice, this approach actually serves to disempower them and therefore cannot be considered 'restorative'.

A number of contributors have called for an increased opportunity for stakeholders to become more involved in the design and implementation of institutions to respond to the past and address the underlying causes for conflict (see Clamp, this volume, Chapter 2; Cunneen, this volume, Chapter 11; Nickson, this volume, Chapter 6). These suggestions go beyond the cursory community engagement exercises carried out by governments more generally (see Lundy and McGovern 2008) to engagement that allows a form of 'process control' (see Nickson, this volume, Chapter 6) resulting in input into the design of the process, the nature and the scope of institutions used to tackle the past and to develop a peaceful future (see Clamp, this volume, Chapter 2). It is this problem-solving aspect of restorative justice that needs to be emphasised to a much greater extent in societies that have experienced protracted periods of conflict and oppression. In this manner, we can harness local knowledge and facilitate local actors to develop, engage with and pursue outcomes that are both relevant and sustainable, thus securing what Pranis (2001) refers to as 'grassroots democracy at work'.

In seeking to be truly inclusive, it is important that all stakeholders are given an opportunity to shape the post-transition milieu. There is a tendency for the literature to skew attention in favour of so-called victims. This is not to deny that there are victims who have not contributed in any way to the harms that they have endured, but it is important to acknowledge that often the lines between 'victims' and 'offenders' are blurred and when we speak of these categories from the 'outside-in' we may oversimplify the relationship between different groups and/or elevate one group above that of another thus resulting in further oppression (also see McEvoy and McConnachie 2012). In the pursuit of a sustainable peace, it is important that all factions play an active role in dealing with the past and creating the future (Clamp 2014). As Bueno *et al.* (this volume, Chapter 3), Clamp (this volume, Chapter 2) and Chapman and Campbell (this volume, Chapter 7) note, this entails a concern for the harm suffered by 'offenders' and the community as well. Viewed in this way, therein lies the possibility of devising institutions, mechanisms or responses that will more fully pay attention to the underlying causes of the conflict and create opportunities for future proofing by identifying potential triggers for further conflict.

Restorative justice should be culturally relevant

There have been a number of criticisms of transitional justice for being dominated by legalism (McEvoy 2008; Weinstein 2014); for being predominantly 'Western' in its orientation (Millar 2011); and for failing to create enduring peace (Lundy and McGovern 2008). Hinton (2011) highlights that global standards, expectations and mechanisms will often clash with local realities, needs and cultures, and Sikainga and Alidou (2006) suggest that the reason for this is the manner in which transitional justice is approached and conceptually framed by the international community. Experience shows that the standard templates of transitional justice – criminal trials and truth commissions – will often take precedence over local justice institutions. Even in the case of more 'restorative' approaches such as truth and reconciliation commissions, Lambourne (this volume, Chapter 4) notes that these have only been devised 'when trials are seen as inadequate or not politically feasible'. Throughout this collection, contributors have stressed the importance of local ownership of and empowerment during restorative justice processes to avoid these pitfalls. Braithwaite (this volume, Chapter 10), for example, argues that justice approaches should be rooted in local understandings of justice and he warns against the marginalisation of victims by the international community in a bid to be seen to be 'doing something' about the harm that has been caused.

Not only might Western approaches to dealing with conflict be 'foreign' to some local actors, but others may actually hold quite a negative perception of it on the basis of personal experience. As Cunneen (this volume, Chapter 11) highlights, Indigenous people have become over-represented in criminal justice systems around the world and, despite the claim that restorative justice approaches are based on Indigenous justice practices, often they have not been to the benefit of Indigenous people. Braithwaite (this volume, Chapter 10) thus calls for us to deal with local justice mechanisms in their own spirit rather than labelling them 'restorative justice' mechanisms and holding them to the standards of Western conceptions of the process. In seeking to highlight the distinctive approach of Indigenous justice mechanisms, Lambourne (this volume, Chapter 4) draws attention to the fact that Indigenous cultures often *combine* restorative and retributive practices in their response to crime, rather than the tendency in the Western literature to seek to uncouple each approach.

Restorative justice needs to be forward looking

Finally, contributors have called for restorative justice conceptions to become much more future oriented. On the one hand, this is due to the gap within current praxis in transitional settings in addressing the underlying causes of the conflict and therefore creating the conditions for sustainable peace. On the other, it is about a lack of attention being paid to the ongoing social, cultural, and political consequences of the previous regime, which may perpetuate victimisation in the new democratic order. Daly (2008: 9) suggests that there are two types of inequality to consider in the pursuit of justice. The first relates to the inequality caused as a direct result of a criminal act whereby the offender is elevated to a position of superiority over the victim. Justice, in responding to this inequality, restores the moral imbalance of the criminal act. The second is a macro perspective of inequality as it relates to the structural environment in which offending takes place. This collection has demonstrated that more attention has been paid in responding to the former than the latter.

However, support may be found for the 'lengthening' of our conceptions of restorative justice in reviewing the empirical research findings on the views of victims, witnesses and survivors of undemocratic regimes. These studies increasingly demonstrate that more importance is attached to creating a sustainable future than to focusing on what has happened in the past, and that neither retributive justice, nor truth-telling on their own are perceived as 'justice' (Millar 2011; Weinstein 2014). Those surveyed report prioritising improvements to their quality of life (peace, sufficient housing, improved infrastructure, social services, food, water and education) over retribution or truth-telling (see Millar 2011; Pells 2009; Robins 2010; Vinck and Pham 2008; Vinck *et al.* 2007). Vinck and Pham (2008: 404) suggest that, until basic needs are met and safety is guaranteed, social reconstruction programs, including transitional justice mechanisms, will not be prioritised nor will they be supported by victims. As Pham *et al.* demonstrate in their survey of victim needs in Cambodia:

> most respondents said it was more important for the country to focus on problems Cambodians face in their daily lives than the crimes committed by the Khymer Rouge. This suggests that the ECCC [The Extraordinary Chambers in the Courts of Cambodia] must find ways to ground its activities in the current concerns and needs of the population.
>
> (2009: 5)

Furthermore, reflecting on his empirical findings on the perceptions of the truth commission in Makeni, Sierra Leone, Millar (2011) states that demands for social goods and reconstruction were high upon the agenda of local residents, rather than learning about who had done what during the conflict. As such, he critiques both retributive and restorative conceptions of transitional justice, given that, in their current manifestations, they are primarily backward looking (i.e. focused on events that have already occurred) rather than forward looking (i.e. focused on how the lived realities of residents might be improved). For Millar, any response to dealing with the past has to place basic human needs at the heart of conceptions of justice: 'just as the outbreak of war is related to impoverishment, unemployment, and de-development, so post-war justice must account for those violations' (2011: 529).

But, if we viewed conflict resolution from a restorative justice paradigm, both the causes and the consequences should be dealt with simultaneously. In practice, however, there is a tendency to reduce the conflict to individual acts and thus the pursuit of individual accountability post-transition which leaves the broader structural factors that underpin conflict and/or oppression in transitional settings intact (see Chapman and Campbell, this volume, Chapter 7; Cunneen, this volume, Chapter 11; Findlay, this volume, Chapter 9; Harbin and Llewellyn, this volume, Chapter 8). Millar (2011: 530) argues that, if we can accept that groups are also capable of being victimised and perpetrators, it is important that we 'expand the definition of infringement to include collective infringements on rights to social and collective needs, and, by extension, to see society itself as an actor, both a victim and a perpetrator'. Addressing this means that our starting point should not be seeking accountability, but rather *addressing needs* within transitional justice settings.

There is no reason why addressing immediate needs cannot become the first step in our justice response. By harnessing community-based mechanisms such as those outlined by Clamp (this volume, Chapter 2), Doak (this volume, Chapter 5) and Nickson (this volume, Chapter 6), government relief and local strategies to build networks and services could be devised. Once immediate needs had been responded to, it could then be possible for the past to be addressed at the local level and for the key themes and findings that emerge to be fed into macro-level processes. In an acknowledgement that the needs of individuals living in societies emerging from conflict evolve over time (Braithwaite, this volume, Chapter 10), restorative justice mechanisms at the local level could continue to exist and respond to the changing needs of the community by drawing attention to new priorities and providing a forum through which resources can be harnessed to address those priorities. Such an approach would allow what Bueno *et al.* (this volume, Chapter 3) refer to as 'restorative accountability' to emerge and for legitimate avenues for ex-combatants to contribute positively to the new democratic order (Clamp, this volume, Chapter 2).

Final thoughts

It has been stated throughout this collection that restorative justice, in its traditional form, has been applied to interpersonal conflict where there is a known victim who has been harmed and a known offender who accepts responsibility for the harm caused. This is problematic in transitional settings because the actions of an individual cannot be removed from the broader political climate in which that act took place and because the lines between victims and offenders are often blurred. As such, there is growing currency in the perception that both restorative justice and transitional justice are too limited to deal with the complex and historical causes of protracted periods of violence (Arthur 2009; Mani 2014; Millar 2011). For the most part, this is based on allegations that these approaches are too focused on the past on the one hand, and that they are too transient on the other. However, Johnstone argues that:

> Those who debate the virtues and vices of restorative justice need to be aware of the full range of transformations which the restorative justice movement seeks to bring about … in discussing a particular agenda, they are not discussing restorative justice per se, but only one dimension of it.
>
> (2008: 76)

This collection provides strong support for the view that, if restorative justice is conceived in a much more expansive way than it currently is, it can have a much more significant impact in the lives of those affected by conflict. If restorative justice is about increasing contact between individuals and providing a safe space through which to increase dialogue, then there is no reason why restorative justice cannot be harnessed as a mechanism through which to create institutions and to set the agendas of those institutions so that they are responsive to the needs of *all* stakeholders. Conflict occurs as a result of *inequality* (perceived or otherwise) and it is this injustice that needs to be addressed if further conflict is to be avoided. Restorative justice can play an important role in allowing perceived and actual injustices to come to the fore and for strategies to respond to those injustices to be challenged. This collection has begun to plot how this might be realised.

References

Arthur, P. (2009) 'How "Transitions" Reshaped Human Rights: A conceptual history of transitional justice', *Human Rights Quarterly*, 31(2): 321–367.

Christie, N. (1982) *Limits to Pain*, Oxford: Martin Robertson.

Clamp, K. (2010) 'The receptiveness of countries in transition to restorative justice: A comparative analysis of the role of restorative justice in transitional processes and criminal justice reform', unpublished thesis, University of Leeds.

Clamp, K. (2014) *Restorative Justice in Transition*, London: Routledge.

Daly, K. (2008) 'Seeking justice in the 21st century: towards an intersectional politics of justice', in H. Millar (ed.) *Restorative Justice: From theory to practice*, Bingley, UK: Emerald Group.

Fletcher, L. and Weinstein, H. (2002) 'Violence and Social Repair: Rethinking the contribution of justice to reconciliation', *Human Rights Quarterly*, 24: 573–639.

Hinton, A. (2011) *Transitional Justice: Global mechanisms and local realities after genocide and mass violence*, Piscataway: Rutgers University Press.

Johnstone, G. (2008) 'The agendas of the restorative justice movement', in H. Millar (ed.) *Restorative Justice: From theory to practice*, Bingley, UK: Emerald Group.

Leonard, M. (2004) 'Bonding and Bridging Social Capital: Reflections from Belfast', *Sociology*, 38(5): 927–944.

Lundy, P. and McGovern, M. (2008) 'Whose Justice? Rethinking transitional justice from the bottom up', *Journal of Law and Society*, 35(2): 265–292.

McEvoy, K. (2008) 'Letting go of legalism: developing a "thicker" version of transitional justice', in K. McEvoy and L. McGregor (eds) *Transitional Justice From Below: Grassroots activism and the struggle for change*, Oxford: Hart Publishing.

McEvoy, K. and McConnachie, K. (2012) 'Victimology in Transitional Justice: Victimhood, innocence and hierarchy', *European Journal of Criminology*, 9(5): 527–538.

Mani, R. (2014) 'Integral justice for victims', in I. Vanfraechem, A. Pemberton and F. Ndahinda (eds) *Justice for Victims: Perspectives on rights, transition and reconciliation*, London: Routledge.

Manktelow, R. (2007) 'The Needs of Victims of the Troubles in Northern Ireland: The social work contribution', *Journal of Social Work*, 7(1): 31–50.

Millar, G. (2011) 'Local Evaluations of Justice through Truth Telling in Sierra Leone: Postwar needs and transitional justice', *Human Rights Review*, 12(4): 515–535.

Pells, K. (2009) 'We've got Used to the Genocide; it's Daily Life that's the Problem', *Peace Review: A Journal of Social Justice*, 21(3): 339–346.

Pham, P., Vinck, P., Balthazard, M., Hean, S. and Stover, E. (2009) *So We Will Never Forget: A population-based survey on attitudes about social reconstruction and the extraordinary chambers in the courts of Cambodia*, Berkley, CA: Human Rights Centre, University of California. [Online]. Available from: www.law.berkeley.edu/files/HRC/Publications_So-We-Will-Never-Forget_01-2009.pdf.

Pranis, K. (2001) 'Restorative justice, social justice, and the empowerment of marginalised populations', in G. Bazemore and M. Schiff (eds) *Restorative Community Justice:*

Repairing harm and transforming communities, Cincinnati, OH: Anderson Publications.

Putnam, R. (1993) *Making Democracy Work: Civic traditions in modern Italy*, Princeton, NJ: Princeton University Press.

Putnam, R. (2000) *Bowling Alone: The collapse and revival of American community*, New York: Simon & Schuster.

Robins, S. (2011) 'Towards Victim-centred Transitional Justice: Understanding the needs of families of the disappeared in postconflict Nepal', *International Journal of Transitional Justice*, 5(1): 75–98.

Roht-Arriaza, N. (2006) 'The new landscape of transitional justice', in N. Roht-Arriaza and J. Mariezcurrena (eds) *Transitional Justice in the Twenty-First Century*, Cambridge: Cambridge University Press.

Shapland, J., Sorsby, A. and Robinson, G. (2011) *Restorative Justice in Practice: Evaluating what works for victims and offenders*, Milton Park and New York: Routledge.

Sikainga, A. and Alidou, O. (2006) 'Introduction', in A. Sikainga and O. Alidou (eds) *Postconflict Reconstruction in Africa*, Trenton, NJ: Africa World Press.

Steenkamp, C. (2009) *Violence and Post-war Reconstruction: Managing insecurity in the aftermath of peace accords*, London: Palgrave Macmillan.

Vinck, P. and Pham, P. (2008) 'Ownership and Participation in Transitional Justice Mechanisms: A sustainable human development perspective from Eastern DRC', *International Journal of Transitional Justice*, 2(3): 398–411.

Vinck, P., Pham, P., Stover, E. and Weinstein, H. (2007) 'Exposure to War Crimes and Implications for Peace Building in Northern Uganda', *Journal of the American Medical Association*, 298(5): 543–554.

Weinstein, H. (2014) 'Victims, transitional justice and reconstruction: who is setting the agenda?', in I. Vanfraechem, A. Pemberton and F. Ndahinda (eds) *Justice for Victims: Perspectives on rights, transition and reconciliation*, London: Routledge.

Index

CPSIA information can be obtained
at www.ICGtesting.com
Printed in the USA
LVOW03*0838190316

479877LV00001B/5/P